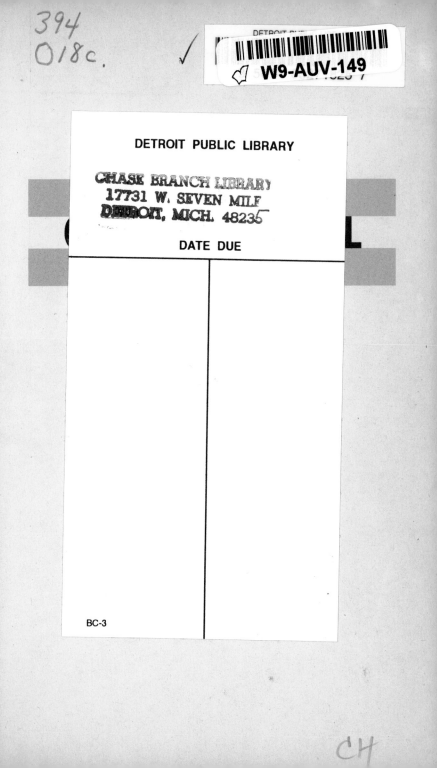

CUSS CONTROL

THE COMPLETE BOOK ON
HOW TO CURB YOUR CURSING

James V. O'Connor

Three Rivers Press
New York

Published by Three Rivers Press, 201 East 50th Street, New York, New York 10022. Member of the Crown Publishing Group.

Random House, Inc. New York, Toronto, London, Sydney, Auckland

www.randomhouse.com

THREE RIVERS PRESS is a registered trademark of Random House, Inc.

Printed in the United States of America

Designed by Susan Maksuta

Library of Congress Cataloging-in-Publication Data

O'Connor, James V.

  Cuss control ; the complete book on how to curb your cursing / James V. O'Connor
    p. cm.

  1. Swearing. I. Title

BJ1535.S9 O25 2000

179'5—dc21   99-050274

ISBN 0-609-80546-0

10 9 8 7 6 5 4 3 2

THIS BOOK IS DEDICATED TO MY FATHER, RICHARD T. O'CONNOR, WHO SAID, WHEN I TOLD HIM THAT I WANTED TO BE A WRITER, THAT AN ABILITY TO WRITE WOULD BE A GOOD BACKUP SKILL FOR A REAL JOB. IF HE WERE HERE, HE WOULD BE PROUD OF ME, BECAUSE HE ALWAYS WAS.

CONTENTS

ACKNOWLEDGMENTS

I will be forever grateful to Lynda, my dedicated and loving wife, business partner, and friend, whose boundless energy and enthusiasm, relentless drive, and valuable contacts made everything happen and happen fast. She found the best agent, and most of the people interviewed in chapter 6.

Special thanks go to my sister Jean, who conducted all but one of the interviews found between chapters and several of the other interviews in this book, and who provided more information than I could fit into the last chapter. It was fun working with her after so many years apart.

My colleagues John Steele, Janna Kimel, and Bill Wilson contributed research, contacts, wit, anecdotes, insights, and encouragement. I am grateful for their support and patience.

The humor in this book is a product of the years I spent with my parents and seven brothers and sisters and with the Byrne family, all of whom know how to have a good time.

Credit and love go to my children, Anne and John, now young adults, who rarely gave me any reasons to swear.

Finally, a huge thanks goes to my agent, Ellen Geiger, and to my editor, Shaye Areheart, who made getting this book published seem easy.

INTRODUCTION

I don't know why I started swearing. I was just a kid at the time. I could blame my three older brothers, but I'm not certain it was their fault. Who can remember, when it was almost fifty years ago? I came from a good Catholic family, a happy family, with far more laughter than fights and arguments. I never heard a swear word from my father, a wonderful man. I remember my mother saying "damn" occasionally, but as the mother of eight children, she was entitled to a few frustrating moments.

Neither I nor any of my siblings dared to swear in front of my mother. She had rules, and she had a temper. One day when she was doing the laundry, she found a list of words in my brother Alan's pants. He was in the fifth grade at the time, a naturally curious age. He had looked up sex-related words in the dictionary, words like *fornication* and *genitals*. They were not what we would call dirty words, but forbidden nevertheless. She confronted me, thinking it was mine. "Is this yours?" she screamed, towering over me. I quickly denied ownership before she could explode. "Go find your brother," she demanded. I did, and with fear on his face, he went home. I stayed outside, not wanting to witness the tongue-lashing and his banishment to the room we shared.

Despite the potential penalty, I know I swore as a child because I remember my first confession, way back in 1952. I was 8 years old, too young to have any serious sins to tell the priest in the dark and eerie confessional but convinced that swearing was a serious and evil violation. The procedure was to say how many times you had committed each sin you were confessing. I hadn't exactly been keeping count in anticipation of this day, and I wasn't certain what the penalty was going to be, but my objective was to give a realistic number and get out of there as fast as possible.

"Bless me, Father, for I have sinned," I said, as the nun had instructed. "I disobeyed my parents five times, and swore ninety-nine times." I was afraid if I went over a hundred, the priest would send me to hell. My strategy worked, and I was sent on my way with instructions to say three Hail Marys and three Our Fathers, and to "Go in peace and sin no more."

Despite the order, I kept on swearing and became very good at it, learning new words as I got older. I also learned new sins of a much higher caliber and stopped confessing the cussing by the time I was in sixth or seventh grade. Other than blasphemy, which is taking the Lord's name in vain, bad language didn't seem to be forbidden by any of the Ten Commandments.

The best I can recall, all my friends used bad language—in high school, in college, in the army, and as adults. I never thought much about it, until the early 1990s. By then it seemed to me that the F word was used too freely in movies, on cable TV, and by the teenagers in the malls. Why did it bother me? I used that word all the time. But then it occurred to me. I had always been discreet. I only swore with people I assumed didn't mind. Never in public, in front of strangers, especially women and children. It was rude, inconsiderate, and uncivilized. I no longer liked the sound of it, especially coming from me. I didn't want to contribute to the decline of civility and the rise of bad manners, so I decided to stop.

But lifelong habits are hard to break. The self-help section at the bookstore had a solution for every problem imaginable, except how to stop swearing. So I developed my own techniques.

Other people who swear, including men and women who get immense joy from it, know it is not proper and refrain from cursing in front of certain people and in certain places. Assuming they recognized it was a bad habit that they were not particularly proud of, I decided to help them. I created the Cuss Control Academy as a division of my public relations firm in August of 1998. It seemed like a natural extension of the PR business, which strives to create a positive image and favorable reputation for companies and their products. People need to project a favorable image as well.

In my first official act as president of the Cuss Control Academy, I issued a press release predicting that certain swear words, once whispered in private, were about to become commonplace as the result of Bill Clinton's activities with Monica and the introduction of Viagra. It would be liberating and fun and sexy but would contribute to the deterioration of the English language and the growing crassness of society.

Apparently, lots of people agreed. I was interviewed by newspapers and appeared on TV stations. By December I was getting four to six calls a day from radio stations. In January of 1999, Oprah Winfrey had me on her show and was telling her audience how much she wished she could stop swearing. I decided the world needed a book.

Whether you purchased this book to cure yourself of the cussing habit or received it as a not-too-subtle message from someone close to you (within earshot), I believe you will enjoy it as well as benefit from it. It was not inspired by religious beliefs, but by a desire to help people improve their image and their relationships and, in the process, restore a degree of civility.

Do I still swear? Yes. Like someone on a diet, I cheat now and then, and often regret it afterward. But it is okay for me, and it is okay for others, depending on the circumstances. It is one of the ways we communicate, a form of expression. As a political and social liberal, I am a firm believer in freedom of speech and just about anything that makes life easier and less restricted for individuals without disrupting social order. The problem with foul language is that we use it too often, failing to communicate clearly, ignoring the sensitivities of others, and damaging the positive perception we want people to have of us. It certainly isn't the worst thing we can do, but making an effort to speak in a more civil manner is one small thing each of us can do to make the world a little nicer.

If this book helps you stop swearing altogether, good for you. The purpose of this book, however, is not to eliminate the use of bad language in our culture, but to help people control when and where they swear. As you will discover, the best way to clean up your language is to change your attitude, to accept life's aggravations, to find the humor in many of our daily annoyances, and to cope and not cuss. The side benefit is greater peace of mind.

Yes, it can feel good to swear, but it feels much better not being in the state of mind that makes you want to swear. Your goal should not be to become a person who doesn't swear, but a person who simply doesn't need to swear.

James V. O'Connor

ONE

Do We Really Swear Too Much?

"YOU USE THAT LANGUAGE around this house one more time, young man, and I'll wash your mouth out with soap!"

Decades have passed since dirty-mouthed little boys heard this threat from their mothers. In fact, what many kids hear from their moms today are the dirty words that got previous generations of youngsters in trouble. In some homes, cursing is more common than cookies and milk. Tongue-scrubbings have disappeared along with terms such as "barnyard epithets" and "locker-room language" that implied swearing was restricted to areas inhabited by animals, whether the four-legged or two-legged variety.

During the last few decades, swearing gradually rose from the gutters and drifted into offices, and shifted from street corners into the schools. Words that are still considered taboo are nevertheless pervasive in the movies, fearlessly flaunted by shock jocks on radio, easily found on cable TV, creeping into network television, printed in magazines, freely shared on Internet chat lines, emblazoned on T-shirts and hats, shouted out at ball games, overheard in shopping malls, and mimicked by the mouths of babes.

How did this happen? And, with so many other things to worry about, does it matter? Offensive language is arguably the least of our social ills, and the increased frequency of its use could be considered a natural evolution of our language. Words considered vulgar and raunchy can be traced back more than a thousand years, but probably have been with us forever. It's likely that Adam cussed out Eve for forcing their eviction from God's version of the Magic Kingdom, and Eve had plenty to swear about trying to raise a cave full of howling babies and bickering teenagers. Foul language intensified throughout history, soaring to successive record heights as diseases wiped out villages, men engaged in battle, storms sank ships, and Henry Ford unwittingly paved the way for road rage.

The true history of swearing is somewhat obscure. Generations of civilized people did not permit it in writing, so its evolution and the etymology of many words have been poorly documented. In the 1300s, Chaucer added spice to his *Canterbury Tales* by freely using the Old English versions of the same bawdy words that we are using seven centuries later. Censorship existed by the time Shakespeare was writing plays in the late 1500s, but part of his genius was finding ways to sneak titillating terms into his prose.

What constitutes nasty language has varied through the ages and from culture to culture. Early on, the most offensive language was related to religion, such as blasphemy, which is irreverence for sacred deities. Cursing, which currently is barely distinguished from cussing and swearing, once meant calling upon supernatural powers to strike a blow or send grave misfortune to an enemy. Even today, in some strongly religious countries, men and women will seek shelter when cursed by someone powerful, fearing an immediate whack from the heavens.

Profanity, obscenity, vulgarity, and epithets are all categories of swearing. There is a distinction as well as some overlap, but definitions aren't essential since all of them refer to negative remarks that are unpleasant to hear. The meaning of menacing words and their degree of harm depends on who says them, why, to whom, and under what circumstances. To complicate matters, the rules regarding cussing have changed over the years, ranging from absurd to realistic to outrageously permissive.

A CENTURY OF PROGRESSIVE PROFANITY

The most dramatic changes took place in the last half of the twentieth century. Most of the young people today are unaware of how hard previous generations fought in the courts and in the streets so that their children and grandchildren could be free to gross out their parents, speak rudely in public places, and use the same two or three words to describe everything they don't like.

The puritanic policies of the first half of the century were bound to be challenged. Any word that was in any way sexually suggestive or associated with private body parts was taboo. A man could not say *leg* when referring to a woman's lower limbs. Women went to the *powder room* and men to the *lavatory* to avoid saying the word *bathroom,* itself a euphemism for a room that, more often than not, didn't include a bath. Even the word *pregnant* was once considered perilously related to matters of sex, so it was more proper to say a woman was "in a family way."

These ridiculous rules of verbal etiquette were often violated in conversations, but laws were enforced when the virtue of the masses was threatened by exposure to evil language. The truly nasty slang words and curses were banned from books, newspapers, movies, and even dictionaries. Prior to 1950, authors writing about their personal accounts in the battlefields of World War II were not permitted to use swear words in their books. Norman Mailer's book *The Naked and the Dead* introduced a strange new word—fug—that the soldiers allegedly used in various forms to express their pain and anguish and what they would rather be doing.

The censors loosened up a bit in 1951 for the publication of *From Here to Eternity* by James Jones, deleting only 208 uses of the real F word from the 258 in his original manuscript. However, they were all deleted from the paperback version since it was more affordable than the hardcover book and likely to be read by a larger portion of the general public.

The bad-word battles began in earnest about the time television came into the living rooms in the 1950s. When Lucille Ball became pregnant in 1952, CBS and Philip Morris, the sponsor of the show *I Love Lucy,* wanted to hide her condition behind tables and sofas. Lucy and Desi Arnaz demanded realism and got their way. However, the scripts called her an "expectant mother," never using the word *pregnant.* All scripts were reviewed by a priest, a rabbi, and a minister to make certain they were in good taste.

Lucy was the first pregnant woman ever to appear on TV, and no one objected. In fact, when the episode about the day her son was born was aired, nearly 70 percent of the TV sets in the country were tuned in. Americans seemed ready to accept public discussion of such controversies as birth.

Having a baby, yes, but going to the bathroom, no. In 1962, the host of a late night talk show, Jack Parr, told a joke on the air that involved a *water closet,* a European term for bathroom that was unknown to many American viewers. Nevertheless, the censors bleeped out the expression. Parr was furious when he found out. The next night, in his opening monologue, he complained about the censorship and, on live TV, resigned and walked off the set. The network refused to settle the dispute and replaced him with a young comedian named Johnny Carson.

Dos and Don'ts were established for the movie industry beginning with the first sound picture in 1927. The most notable challenge to the language guidelines came with the 1939 classic, *Gone with the Wind.* Near the end of the film, when an exasperated Rhett Butler decides to leave Scarlett, she asks him what will become of her. He delivers one of the most powerful lines in cinema history: "Frankly, my dear, I don't give a damn."

Tame by contemporary standards, the timing was perfect, and the line became legendary. But director David Selznick, who fought to change the line from a simple "I don't care," was fined $5,000 by the Production Code Administration for using a forbidden word.

By the 1960s, Hollywood was getting bolder and saltier, partly to offer an alluring option to the wholesome programming on TV that was threatening to thin out the movie crowds. In 1966, for example, Elizabeth Taylor and Richard Burton appeared in *Who's Afraid of Virginia Woolf?* Explicit language was permitted because the film was based on a play that was considered a major work of art. Far more offensive than the language were the sloppy, drunken, raging, depressing, and pathetic roles played by Taylor and Burton who, at the time, were leading lives that were sloppy, drunken, raging, depressing, and pathetic.

According to a study conducted by Timothy Jay, author of *Cursing in America,* the movie had 46 words that were considered vulgar or offensive. A few years later, a movie that was not only critically acclaimed and wildly popular, *Midnight Cowboy,* contained 107 nasty words by Jay's count. To put the period in perspective, it was 1969, the same year that half a million rebellious, liberated, disenchanted, and fun-loving youths migrated to Woodstock to hear, in addition to the best rock and roll of the era, Country Joe lead them in a cheer spelling out F-U-C-K. That three-day event of music, mud, and drugs later became an award-winning documentary of the times.

Documentaries record reality, but do other films? Movies have been blamed for promoting and encouraging bad language, sex, and violence, but Hollywood claims movies portray contemporary behavior rather than influence it. Movies about Vietnam were certainly more realistic than previous war movies in which soldiers didn't swear or bleed much, but most Hollywood productions are about as real as a silicone breast, unless you happen to live in a city where high-speed car chases are everyday occurrences, you get sex after saying hello, computer-generated animals talk to you, detectives swear at each other more than at the bad guys, and even motor scooters dramatically explode in fiery crashes when run off the road.

The ultimate reality regarding swearing didn't reach us through the movies, but from the least likely of places. Genteel America was appalled by the blatant and defiant language of the Woodstock generation, but a few years later heard it from the solemn corridors of decorum, the White House. When the Watergate incident forced Richard Nixon to reveal the content of his tapes from the Oval Office, he spent hours blackening out the bad language on the transcripts or inserting "expletive deleted." He feared his choice of words was more embarrassing and unacceptable than evidence of break-ins, illegal wiretaps, cover-ups, and obstruction of justice. He had to maintain his dignity, you see.

He was the wrong guy at the wrong time. Nixon and the conservative forces were struggling to contain the boisterous demands for free speech, equality, and self-expression that were all part of the sexual revolution, the women's liberation movement, civil rights, gay rights, protest against the Vietnam War, and a host of other causes that were, in fact, worthy and righteous.

Unfortunately, everyone began demanding entitlements. We were spared the battle for Stupid Jerk Rights only because it lacked leadership, organization, and brain cells. Nevertheless, the right to be crude and rude rather than considerate and courteous is now just as important to the man in the street and the kid in school as life, liberty, and the pursuit of a big screen TV.

As evidence, we have the 1999 full-length feature cartoon *South Park: Bigger, Longer & Uncut,* which has a record 399 words that are crude, obscene, or sexually suggestive, according to a count by Movie Index of Colorado Springs. Most of the words come from the mouths of animated children. The movie is a satire on the censorship of language, which barely seems to exist.

> *I think swearing in the movies has reached a saturation point. Back in the fifties, people got upset with the word* virgin *in Otto Preminger's movie* The Moon Is Blue. *The floodgates of change began in the sixties, and by the eighties, it was almost a joke. I think it was very important in the early days, bringing a new realism, and it was very liberating for a while, but then it became like a nervous tic that was more inexpressive than expressive. Swearing became sort of a crutch, especially for young filmmakers.*
>
> *I certainly hear from audience members who are sick of it. I get comments from journalists I work with at* Newsweek. *I definitely see a backlash. It is hard to make generalizations, and context is important, but I don't see why more movies can't be made without swearing. It isn't always necessary. If it's used sparingly, it has more of a charge.*
>
> —David Ansen, *Newsweek* movie critic, in an interview for this book

SWEARING IS CHILDISH BEHAVIOR

If modern movies truly reflect contemporary language and our nation's leaders can swear, why do some people still make a fuss when others cuss? Why do rating systems exist that include "L" to caution viewers of the rough language? Why don't you see swear words in daily newspapers? Why don't sportscasters use them? Why can't you find them on your computer's spell checker or thesaurus? Why do most schools and some companies have written policies forbidding the use of bad language?

Obviously, some sense of propriety still exists in our civilized nation, even though the days are gone when gentlemen didn't curse in front of women and nice girls never swore. The public policy on profanity focuses on keeping it away from children. A noble idea, but kids old enough to tell potty jokes love to giggle at dirty words, and probably no demographic group swears more than children just under the age of 17.

Discouraging curious young minds from learning and using words that amuse them seems a bit unfair. Is swearing a privilege of adulthood? Something is wrong here. Adults should have the maturity, emotional control, and expanded vocabulary to avoid using the trashy language they used when they were teenagers. Yet, in a national poll conducted in May 1999 for an ABC News feature on bad manners, 48 percent of the adult men said they had cussed in public recently, and so had 37 percent of the women.

Swearing was long considered a trait of poorly educated, lower-class people, but the upper echelons of society always had greater access to it. Students in ghettos never spent much time studying Chaucer. The first books with obscene language that were allowed to be printed in the United States, James Joyce's *Ulysses* and D. H. Lawrence's *Lady Chatterley's Lover,* were considered literary classics that were much more difficult to read than *Hollywood Confidential* or the *National Enquirer.* Nightclub comedy acts, particularly after Lenny Bruce broke all the barriers to bad taste in the early 1960s, only admit people old enough to drink enough to laugh at anything. Broadway productions have always been regarded as entertainment primarily for sophisticated audiences, but the raw language of some plays is more common among segments of society who could never afford a ticket. "Artistic expression" has been the excuse for breaking the rules ever since the great sculptors and painters cleverly convinced society that bare bodies had more to do with beauty and nature than with sex.

We can express our disgust with the openly foul mouths of kids today, but it's not their fault. They are growing up in a cursing culture. They are exposed to rough language everywhere and take it in stride. Baby boomers are more likely to swear in front of their children than their own parents did. *Damn* and *hell* are considered harmless gnats. Even words like *ass* and *bastard* rarely offend anyone. Just about anyone other than an 80-year-old nun could utter a timely and appropriate profanity and get away with it. For that matter, a cuss word from the mouth of an 80-year-old nun would probably get a good laugh.

IDENTIFYING FORBIDDEN WORDS

So what words are we talking about? In 1973, comedian George Carlin said on New York radio station WBAI that there are seven words you can't say on the air: *shit, piss, fuck, cunt, cocksucker, motherfucker,* and *tits.* Said in this order, they sounded like someone falling down the stairs, and while Carlin got battered for violating the rules, he made his mark in broadcast history and his career soared rather than tumbled. Years later, after other comedians exploited and eventually exhausted the shock effect of vulgar humor, Carlin ended a performance at Carnegie Hall by reading his expanded list of forbidden words and phrases. They numbered well over a hundred.

Obviously, there are too many to mention, and some people will argue that any type of name-calling, from ethnic slurs to *fatso* and *pinhead,* are dirty words. Others would add words like *crap, crotch, suck, booger,* and *screw* to the heap. Despite the disputes, most of us know which words not to use in front of Grandma or the kids.

Ironically, most of the taboo words describe some of our favorite body parts and the way we use them to engage in some very pleasant activities. As the old saying goes, life isn't fair. Alexander Woollcott spoke for everyone decades ago when he said, "Everything I like to do is either illegal, immoral, or fattening."

Most of Carlin's original seven words still cannot be spoken on the radio or network TV, but time has decriminalized at least one of them: *piss.* The expression "pissed off" has become so universal that many young people don't know why it would be outlawed. The F word has found many fans, male and female, but its use can still get you thrown out of fine restaurants and even a few bars.

Hovering near the top of the danger list is the four-lettered C word, which generates outrage among women when men use it. As a classic example of reverse discrimination, women seem entitled to call men *dicks,* and don't get penalized for referring to some jerk by the closely related and rhyming P word. Oddly enough, Carlin didn't include any words describing a man's privates among his seven.

The air is filled with foul language, but we do have many clear days. In fact, most people living or working in a relatively tame environment can make it through an entire day without hearing anyone utter an ugly word. Newspapers avoid using the nastier words, even when quoting abusers. As for our own choice of words, we still have to watch our language when talking to new acquaintances, particularly of the opposite gender. And we have to be careful what we say at work, primarily to avoid charges of sexual harassment or creating a "hostile environment."

Despite the restrictions, we still have plenty of opportunities to be lax with our language, even if we are just muttering to ourselves about our idiot boss, clothes that we claim shrank, or arrogant drivers who cut in front of us. We feel entitled to vent a little frustration when we are having a bad day. If someone hears us—well, no big deal. We know they've heard it before.

So What's the Problem?

Mark Twain represented all defenders of offensive language, especially those who use it sparingly, when he noted, "In certain trying circumstances, urgent circumstances, desperate circumstances, profanity furnishes a relief denied even in prayer." There are those trying moments of anguish when an immediate burst of profanity seems to clear the head, expelling the frenzy of emotion that otherwise blocks our ability to find rational solutions to whatever is tormenting us.

The frequency of modern-day cussing, however, suggests that our lives are truly miserable and frustrating. Either that or a large portion of the population has been afflicted with Tourette's syndrome, a severe neurological disorder characterized by compulsive and continuous streams of obscenities.

Emotional release is a worthy argument supporting salty language, but it doesn't explain why some of us choose to pepper every other sentence with spicy words. Maybe swearing does make us feel good once in a while, but it doesn't earn us respect and admiration, enhance our reputation, exhibit our intelligence and maturity, display even a fraction of our acceptable vocabulary, reflect strong character, get us romantically connected, help us solve disagreements, set a positive example, or help us get hired or promoted.

Since we feel free to do it, swearing becomes a habit. The classic cuss words start to sound right for certain occasions. As a consequence, we use certain curses all the time, neglecting other fine words that would serve just as well, even better, to make our point.

The number one offender, you can easily guess, is *shit*. It packs more punch than *stuff* or *shoot* but isn't as abrasive as some of the other four-letter words. It floated to the top of the cesspool of unacceptable slang to become the most widely used obscenity in the country. Just about anyone can use it and get away with it.

The word has taken on more meaning than the disgusting substance it actually is, but the imagery is still there. The word in its true definition only has a joyful ring to it among people who are constipated.

Shit is the all-purpose word, eliminating the need for us to choose from hundreds of other words to express ourselves. We use it to describe everything. It does little to convey our real message, or the fact that our education continued beyond fifth grade. It is grossly overused. That's why it provides convincing evidence that, yes, we do swear too much.

To prove the point, this list contains seventy common uses of the word:

>Who the shit knows?
>Who the shit cares?
>You're shit out of luck.
>Don't give me that shit.

Cut the shit.

What the shit's wrong?

She thinks she's hot shit.

He's really shit on wheels.

He had a shit fit.

She went ape shit.

You're up shit's creek without a paddle.

It's a shithole.

It's a piece of shit.

I don't give a shit.

She doesn't know shit.

I have a shitload of stuff.

No shit.

We were shooting the shit.

He scared the shit out of me.

I was scared shitless.

He's a dipshit.

I'm in deep shit.

Shit happens.

He's full of shit.

He's a bullshitter.

Bullshit.

That's horseshit.

What a lucky shit.

Holy shit.

I took a lot of shit from him.

Oh, what the shit.

He's a shithead.

I'm really getting my shit together.

He drank until he was shitfaced.

Don't be a chickenshit.

That's really bad shit.

I'm on his shitlist.

I wore my shitkickers.

He's got that shit-eating grin.

She sticks to him like shit on a shovel.

They're as happy as pigs in shit.

It's not worth jack-shit.

I feel like shit.

You look like shit.

He can't hear shit.

The food here tastes like shit.

This place smells like shit.

This is the best shit I ever had.

Is this your shit?

What's this pile of shit doing here?

That's my good shit.

I have to take a shit.

He really knows his shit.

I got stuck with the shit work.

He beat the shit out of him.

That movie was funnier than shit.

Today's lunch is shit on a shingle.

I nearly shit in my pants.

The shit hit the fan.

The guy's a shitbag.

He has shit for brains.

He doesn't know shit from Shinola.

I've got the shits.

Shit or get off the pot.

She was built like a brick shithouse.

He thinks his shit doesn't stink.

>Everything I touch turns to shit.
>
>I was knee-deep in shit.
>
>Eat shit.
>
>He's a fat shit.

Have you had enough of this shit? This word really stinks, and we should consider flushing it out of our vocabulary.

Robert Thompson of Syracuse University, who accepts the reality of swearing but chooses not to engage in it himself, is not alone in his argument for reducing its use. By practicing self-restraint, you preserve the power of profanity for when you need it.

"All the cuss words are very old, and no one has been able to introduce any significant new ones for at least several decades," he points out. "They are a precious natural resource that we are using up, sapping them of their energy. We need to practice curse-word ecology so that current and future generations can continue to call upon them when and where their impact is required."

Guy Martin, writing in *Men's Health,* says cursing can be effective, but only when it is imbued with meaning.

"Swearing all the time renders foul language impotent. We become as inured to it as we are to the violence on the nightly news. We ought to set a moratorium on it—like the one placed on the Atlantic striped bass for a few years—to give the words a chance to build back some muscle."

At the rate we are going, swearing will be so common that it will be about as much fun as a nudist camp. There will be no mystery, and most people won't be very attractive. A wiser choice is to learn how to speak politely by tapping into our own vast resource of simple but descriptive words.

Points to Ponder

- Swearing is not the worst thing you can do, but you must be careful about when and where you swear to avoid offending others and appearing ignorant.

- The increased use of bad language could be considered part of the natural evolution of the English language, but the trend does not make it acceptable. Cursing is still considered improper in most public places, in newspapers and broadcast news, and in front of children.
- Adults should have the maturity, vocabulary, and emotional control to avoid using profanity. They have a responsibility to show younger people how to communicate in a civilized manner.
- Cursing can provide power and force when it is needed, but not if we wear it out.

JEFF ZIMMER, 40, LEGAL CASE CLERK

I grew up in Lincoln, Nebraska. Went to high school and community college there. Do I swear? Fuck, yeah! Several fucking times a day. The only swear words I don't use are Jesus Christ *and* God damn, *because of my religion. I was brought up that you respect women, so I try not to swear around them. But most of my friends swear. Isn't that fucking wonderful?*

I first started using fuck you *and* asshole *when I was a senior in high school, 1977, just because I was a senior so I thought I could do anything. In junior high I didn't even know what those words meant. I lived a sheltered life, what can I say?*

When I was younger, once you said a bad word around my mother, it was the biggest mistake of your life. Either she'd pop you one, or she'd grab you by the collar and get you upstairs to wash your mouth out with soap. I mean literally. When you swore, it was good-bye. And we're not talking about a small bar. It was the whole damn bar. She'd just take that soap and shove it in. And the more you struggled, the worse it was. You're already crying, so the saliva is going and that made it worse. Soap got stuck to your teeth. You know that song, "Tiny Bubbles"? That was it: Tiiiiiiiiny bubbles, iiiiiiiinn your mouth, makes me feel like puking. No, my parents made no bones about punishing us when they felt we needed it. It was all part of growing up. My mother is Italian, and Catholic, and you just don't swear around her, that's it. She would keep washing out your mouth till she was ready to stop. And you know what, I respect her for it. I respect both my parents. Their respect for the language had to do with their respect for themselves. Yeah, I love my mother. Oh, and if she couldn't get you upstairs to the bathroom, she'd use the liquid soap in the kitchen.

I think that all broke down and I started to really swear when I was about 17 or 18. My parents got divorced, and my mom moved to a town you couldn't make a movie about, it was so small: Milford. Just a gas station, a post office, and a general store. Drive down the dirt road till you get to the windmill. Turn right, drive to the five mailboxes and turn left, you'd be at my mom's house. We're talking Petticoat Junction here. The bend in the road where my swearing took off, you could say. But still not in front of her!

Everyone I know swears. It's just a habit. Even my neighbor, he swears in Mexican. But I offended some lady at the bankruptcy court the other day. I was talking to one of the case clerks there. He asked me what I'd be doing for Easter. I said, "Monkey-fucking around in Santa Cruz," and this lady, about 50, making copies, she went pale. She stopped what she was doing. She wouldn't even look at me. I said, "Oh, please forgive me, I'm so sorry," and I meant it. So some people are still offended, even though swearing is everywhere. I do try to curb my language. It just comes out when I'm around other people who also swear. And I don't know anyone personally who doesn't.

Except my mother, who won't say anything worse than "the world today is going to hell in a handbasket." Nobody swore in the fifties and sixties. Those words weren't even invented back then! Jesus Christ, hell, *and* damnation: *you could say those words in church on Sunday. Everybody got to swear on Sunday, but on the other six days, no one swore. Nowadays, the only time I don't swear—and mean it—is in church, and I only go to church three times a year.*

I think language went into the shitter with Nixon. He was the first public figure who got caught. All the institutions as we knew them got shaky all at once. But you don't really notice social changes happening until it's really in your face. Remember, before that, it was LBJ and Vietnam: "One, two, three, four, we don't want your stinking war." When did it become the fucking war?

Even both my grandmothers swore by the time they got older. When she was up there in age, one of them bought a hat. It was her "go to hell" hat. She would put that hat on, she would look at you and say, "Go to hell." But if I'm back home and I go out to the lake and the nieces and nephews are there, we try not to use those words. When I'm really angry, too, it doesn't necessarily lead to swearing. What is that going to prove? It sometimes makes a fight worse and that's not a good thing.

TWO
Yes, Cussing Can Be Fun

THE PRACTICE OF PSYCHOANALYSIS believes that a first step in overcoming our habits is to understand why we have them. The same principle applies to swearing. If you analyze why you swear, you can decide if your vocal behavior is justified. Most of the time, it won't be. Sometimes it will be, but not everyone whose ears are burned by your fiery words will agree.

You don't have to delve too deeply into your murky memory to determine if childhood traumas, an evil uncle, or the naughty neighbor boy were responsible for your shameless mouth. Most of us picked up the habit for the same reasons, and they weren't sinister. As young children, we were amused by pee-pee and poo-poo jokes. We advanced to words identifying the gender-specific parts that we were learning to hide from the public, reflecting our innate defiance of rules and the pleasure of talking about taboo topics. Eventually we heard about sex in its various forms and gleefully graduated to the rough language supposedly reserved for people old enough to perform it.

There are two major categories of swearing: casual and causal. We know that *casual* swearing is wrong, but we do it for the fun of it, sort of like casual sex. *Causal* swearing, on the other hand, is brought about or *caused* by an emotion, such as anger or frustration, like when we fail in our attempts to have casual sex.

Most of the time you can hide the fact that you use bad language, but it's difficult to mind your tongue when something upsets you. If bad words are stored anywhere in your vocabulary bank, nothing will keep you from blurting out obscenities when you are truly livid, unless you are engaged in the most solemn of ceremonies, in the presence of priests, or visiting a museum with your grandmother.

It can be argued that swearing is a healthy way to vent anger. A stubbed toe, a car that won't start, a dog that eats the groceries—some things warrant a good curse. Or do they? And what about the impact of your words and your temperament on the people around you? More on that later.

Dealing with anger and other strong emotions is complex, so let's start by examining casual swearing. It's much easier to control, and thus a good starting point. It's almost completely voluntary. Nothing serious prompts it.

So why do we do it? What is the point behind what could be called recreational swearing?

SWEARING IS LAZY LANGUAGE

As previously noted, the S word and several other obscenities have many applications. When we get mentally and verbally lazy, these words are always on call, sparing us the task of scanning our brain and downloading even the most simple noun or adjective. There seems to be no need to make the effort when talking intelligently is rarely a social requirement, and curse words are as common as bad grammar.

It's rare to hear anyone described as *eloquent,* a word reserved for the great orators of the past. Even speech writers for the president keep the lingo simple. The trend is to speak the language of the common man, the average woman, so we can all relate to one another. To speak poetically might be perceived as pompous and arrogant. Even words like *shall* have faded away like old soldiers, such as General MacArthur's dramatic declaration, "I shall return," and the civil rights cry, "We shall overcome." Winston Churchill frequently used *shalls* in bunches, ending one famous sixty-eight-word sentence with ". . . we shall fight on the beaches, we shall fight on the landing grounds, we shall fight in the fields and in the streets, we shall fight in the hills, we shall never surrender."

One wonders if he could have inspired the free world and given hope to his compatriots the way many modern military leaders and coaches have done dozens of times by shouting, "Let's get out there and kick some ass!"

Then again, maybe Churchill had the right idea. How about, "We shall get out there, and we shall kick some ass!"

To be fair, we average Joes and Janes can't be making pronouncements on world conditions, formulating theories behind the evolution of the universe, or even discussing the merits of different laundry detergents without getting a little sleepy. It's easier to end a conversation with "what the hell"—or some variation of that sign of mental exhaustion—than it is to say the topic warrants further consideration after more probing analysis.

Swearing Can Be Funny

Any word or phrase that generates a good laugh could be considered a worthy remark. Every day brings difficulties of varying degrees, beginning with getting up. Humor is a wonderful antidote for daily annoyances, and a crude remark gets a good laugh if it is timely, unexpected, and . . . well . . . crude!

The 72-year-old mother of a doctor in Georgia had a serious operation, and two days later her son visited her and said, "Mom, you look terrific!" She responded, "Thanks, but I know I look like a bag of shit." Her son bellowed with laughter for several reasons:

1. *He didn't expect his mother to use the word* shit.
2. *Referring to herself as a "bag" of shit was more descriptive than unpackaged shit.*
3. *He knew she was half joking rather than expressing self-pity.*
4. *Her humor was a sign of recovery and a welcome relief.*
5. *They both knew that she really looked closer to terrible than to terrific, but she made light of his polite pretense.*
6. *He said what he was supposed to say as a son as well as a doctor, so she caught him on his pretense at two levels.*

Suppose she had kept it clean and said, "Thanks, but I know I look dreadful." Instead of humor and relief, she creates discomfort, concern, and tension.

If you rank the reasons why we swear by degree of offensiveness, swearing to amuse others is on the bottom of the list. The only risk is that it *has* to be funny, and humor is subjective. It helps to know your audience.

We Know We Can Get Away with It

Even if we don't intend to swear, we assume no one will be offended if we say we laughed our ass off at a movie, finally cleaned all the shit out of the garage, or were so scared we nearly peed in our pants. Most of us know which swear words are tame or acceptable. We know that no one is likely to be appalled if we slip and say a Big One. Even monks sequestered in the Himalaya Mountains have heard it all by now. If we jolt someone with a crude word, a quick apology is often all that is needed to redeem our dignity and demonstrate respect for whomever we might have miffed.

Oprah Winfrey admitted on her show that, in her private life, she uses bad language. "I swear, and it's the one thing I don't like about myself," she said. She wouldn't make this open confession if she thought it would be humiliating or scandalous. She revealed her flaw because she knew that a large percentage of her viewing audience also swears and would take comfort in knowing that a top celebrity engages in the same breach of discretion and shares the same modest level of guilt.

Our Peers Do It

We all have a need to belong, and we choose to behave much like the others in our social group or workplace. If they swear, we swear. If our speech is too purified, we fear that our friends or coworkers will suspect we disapprove of them or are judging them. Pressure to conform with the crowd is particularly demanding during our teen years, a period when crass words are imbedded in our heads and become difficult to pry out years later.

There's no need to pick on teenagers, however, and don't think swearing is used only by sailors, gangsters, prisoners, lumberjacks, sports jocks, shock jocks, and trailer trash. Some of the most vile language bounces off the walls in the newsrooms occupied by college-educated journalists who, ironically, are masters of the English language and skilled communicators. Swearing is common in any profession that deals with deadlines, high stakes, a fast pace, unreasonable bosses, lazy workers, and demanding customers. That covers just about everything except sheepherding.

Jeff, a successful real estate developer, says crude language is almost a requirement in his field. "A guy came to my office one day and said, 'Jeff, you stupid bastard, I can't believe you aren't bidding on the State Street project, you dumb fuck. What are you fucking thinking?' And this guy likes me! Imagine how my adversaries talk to me!"

Even though Jeff and many of his competitors are multimillionaires, money doesn't buy good manners.

MEN SWEAR BECAUSE THEY ARE NATURALLY AGGRESSIVE

It's no big surprise to find rough language in real estate development and construction, since the business is still dominated by Real Guys. Men swear more than women. They always have, and probably always will. Throughout history, men have been expected to take care of the rough stuff, like moving boulders, building shelters, making fires, killing animals, and slaughtering each other. It was difficult to engage in physical labor and violent acts with only words like "Ouch!" to shout when the cabin roof collapsed or you were pierced by a sword. Rugged words had to be invented for moments when no other words, groans, or actions would cure the problem.

Modern life has made us more civilized and has modified the role of the man. We now have prefab homes, Duraflame logs, and frozen veggieburger patties to make life easier, and atomic weapons to end life faster. Nevertheless, men still need strong words to vocalize frustration from broken lawnmowers, aggressive drivers, and bad calls by blind referees.

Boys will be boys, and men must be macho. Assertive behavior is still needed for survival, even if the battle is for a good job or a promotion. Swearing never helped advance anyone's career except the likes of George Carlin and Chris Rock, but choice words come in handy when a less competent person gets the job, or you are among many good workers downsized and banished from the corporate kingdom.

So what does this have to do with *casual* swearing? The struggle to survive and get ahead introduced a bundle of words that oddly became as applicable for fun as they were for frustration. Men get weary of working, thinking, and being polite most of the day. Coloring their conversations with a few crudities is relaxing. It allows them to drop the formalities for a moment and be regular guys. And when they are together with their friends watching a game or joking around, the language is, shall we say, spirited.

WOMEN USE CUSS WORDS AS EQUALIZERS

Back in the 1970s, conservatives warned that the women's liberation movement combined with the sexual revolution would do women more harm than good. Nevertheless, you can't stop progress, and social progress usually means a relaxation of social conventions.

It was once very unbecoming for women to swear. It wasn't "lady-like." Besides, they were home with the children, joyfully baking cookies and biscuits, and seemingly had very little to swear about. If you ever spent more than two hours with a 2-year-old, you might think differently.

It could be that women now have more reasons to swear than men do. The majority of mothers are now employed and under many of the same pressures as men, yet caring for the kids and the drudgery of housework is still primarily their responsibility. Keeping both the house and their mouth clean is a serious challenge. And if their working environment is male dominated and swearing is tolerated, women can succumb to the habit. Just as with men, stressful situations provoke casual swearing among women, and they get comfortable using the same words casually.

But what about the casual swearing by women who aren't part of the working mom demographics? In their struggle for equality a few decades ago, women not only had to prove that they could do what men do but were *entitled* to do what men do. Like swear! Why should vulgarity be a male privilege? The double standard on swearing was just as unfair as the one that tolerated young men having premarital sex but scorned women who did (which raised the question of whom all those men had sex with).

Quite possibly, women chose to emulate one of the least pleasing qualities of the male species because it was the easiest one to adopt. The more admirable qualities expected of a true gentleman—strength, maturity, courage, character, a sense of duty and responsibility—are just as difficult for most men to live up to. And long before women abandoned the rule that nice girls don't swear, men were ignoring the rule that boys don't swear in front of girls.

The conclusion many women have drawn is that, to make it in a man's world, you have to act like a man—by today's definition. In the 1997 movie *G.I. Jane*, Demi Moore undergoes the rigors of military training to prove she is as good as any man but doesn't firmly convince everyone until she spits out a vulgarity. In the scene near the end of the movie, she is physically brutalized by an instructor who has continually taunted her to prevent her from succeeding as the first woman to make it through training as a Navy SEAL. Just when her fellow trainees—and the audience—think she is beaten, she struggles to her feet and screams at her tormentor, "Suck my dick!"

What a crowd pleaser! Her outburst was by no means casual cursing but made audiences howl and applaud. She not only survived, challenged authority, and risked further punishment, but got a laugh by using an expression reserved for men by the nature of their anatomy. She fought for survival and demonstrated her ability to be as aggressive and as crude as a macho man at war.

SWEARING CAN BE SEXY

In the right situation, a woman can use a body-part word or sex term and the guys love it. The *G.I. Jane* example also applies here. Demi

Moore has more sex appeal than most women in the military, and any reference to a fellatious act conjures up fantasies in the minds of hopeful men.

Talking dirty can be a form of flirtation. Sly women know that their casual use of sexy words is often a turn-on for men, as is telling dirty jokes or talking frankly about sex. When a man says the F word or makes references to sex organs in front of a woman and she doesn't flinch, it is a form of flirting and wishful thinking.

> *I am occasionally shocked at the various conversations I've had with the fictional women friends of mine on* Sex and the City. *It's not about, "I am pure and good and they are bad." It's just the way I choose to communicate with my friends. I think my costars have a certain comfort level with language and they do it beautifully. I couldn't pull it off, frankly.*
>
> —Actress Sarah Jessica Parker, interviewed by the *Sun Sentinel* in Florida, which reported that she is so uncomfortable with some of the expletives in her TV series that she whispers them during the rehearsals

SWEARING IS LIBERATING AND CANDID

When men and women—and boys and girls—talk dirty, it is gratifying defiance of the rules. We are all shackled by rules and policies on behavior, and the burden constantly tempts us to break them. We often have to be polite when we don't want to be. We sometimes feel like hypocrites when we must behave in polite company but act like barbarians when the social pressure is off. We view swearing as a harmless deviation from social propriety, a rule we can break without committing a crime.

Many people find themselves in business and social situations that they perceive as unnecessarily formal. By candidly including a mild cuss word in their conversation, they let their hair down and signal to others that it is okay to do so. If everyone is at ease, the tone changes and so does the content of the conversation.

MANY OF OUR ROLE MODELS SWEAR

Who are the role models of today? Our earliest and most important role models remain the same from generation to generation—parents. The difference is that the modern mom and dad—if both of them happen to be around—have a much shorter time to establish standards for their children. Their influence begins to wane about the time a child learns how to manipulate the remote control for the TV. Adding to the problem is that most parents today are either Baby Boomers, the generation that defied the conventions against swearing, or Generation Xers, who brought the art of swearing to a new level—the lower level.

Nevertheless, parents and everyone else in a position of authority and responsibility should consider themselves role models, and not just for children. The behavior of teachers, police officers, supervisors, labor leaders, and politicians influences others. Husbands influence wives, and wives influence husbands. At least they try to.

Most of these holders of traditional leadership positions are now overshadowed by hyped-up celebrities—primarily movie and TV actors, athletes, and rock stars. When they swear, they signal to others that swearing is okay, even cool. They authorize and validate the freedom to be foul.

> *Teenagers have sharp eyes and ears for hypocrisy. They see adults, their role models, often filled with rage and rudeness. Most men— 55 percent—think freedom of expression is more important than enforcing good manners. Women aren't so sure, with 46 percent agreeing. And more men have sworn in public lately—48 percent— while 37 percent of women have cussed.*
>
> —ABC News, in a special report, May 17, 1999

WE WANT TO EMPHASIZE A POINT

When relating an incident or describing an experience, we think a robust cuss word punctuates a point in our story. We don't have to be talking about an unpleasant or disturbing experience—it could be something as innocent as a weird dream. If we are amused by our own tale, laughing as we speak, we know we are not using swear words to attack anyone or to express anger, so we assume no one is offended.

For some people, it seems to be customary or even obligatory to inject the adjective *fucking* before every noun. This tendency is not strictly an American characteristic, by the way. The working classes from Australia to Scotland are fond of sticking it into each sentence as often as possible, and some of the upper crust are just as low.

The 1995 movie *Get Shorty,* starring John Travolta, may have broken all records for the number of times the F word was used. The comedy-drama was based on a book by Elmore Leonard, who intended to spoof the idiocy and limited vocabulary of gangsters and Hollywood types. Most audiences, apparently accustomed to hearing the word with rapid-fire frequency in their own social circles, failed to realize that the excessive use of the word was meant to be humorous. Movie reviewers commented on the "low-life dialogue," but they were referring to the inane sentences more than to the movie's only but often repeated adjective.

WE ARE UNHAPPY

Think about it. In our casual conversations, how often are we making a negative comment or observation? We might not be angry. We might even be addressing an issue in a good-natured or lighthearted way, with no malice intended. But the fact is, something is bothering us. Maybe it is jealousy, cynicism, skepticism, or disapproval of someone or something they did. Or maybe we just didn't get enough sleep, have a headache, are overworked, or are troubled about something completely unrelated. We can't be cheerful all the time.

Do you know anyone who always seems to be in a great mood, always friendly and jovial? Aren't there times when such people drive you nuts? It's one of the horrors of human nature that another person's happiness sometimes makes us very unhappy, and for some sick reason we feel a little better if we can tell them to shut up.

It's a Habit

This reason for swearing is saved for last because all the other reasons contribute to it. At some point in your life you started swearing, and various events through the years and days have provoked it on a regular basis. It is a habit, just like smoking, biting your nails, or craving desserts after dinner. And like any habit, it is difficult to break. It takes time and effort. Like shedding a couple of pounds a week, you might discover that the best you can do is to drop a couple of cuss words every few days, gradually reaching your desired state.

Points to Ponder

- All swearing can be classified in either of two categories: casual and causal. Casual swearing is bad language we use for the fun of it, because we are too lazy to use other words, and we can usually get away with it. Causal swearing is provoked by pain or an emotion, such as anger, frustration, or surprise.
- Casual swearing is often harmless, but you never know how listeners are reacting or judging you. We can usually control it when we have to, which makes it less excusable than swearing prompted by emotions.
- Casual swearing should be easier to eliminate than causal swearing, but like any habit, it takes time and effort.

KATE DOYLE BROWN, 49, SINGER

Oh yes, I do swear, and oh so often. On a regular basis. I try to stop but I can't. How terrible. If only I could be helped. I think it's so unladylike. I use all the words, except God damn it *and* Jesus Christ. *I always thought* God damn it *meant, "God, go to hell!" I don't know why I thought that, but it stuck in my mind that way, so I never wanted to say* God damn it. *That is angry swearing and I tend to swear casually, as a part of everyday conversation. But I have to be careful. The husband of one of my clients doesn't* like it when I swear. I overheard him saying to his 17-year-old daughter, "You don't have to use those words to express yourself." So I don't swear around him. He gets offended.

My husband says he doesn't want to stop swearing. I'm not sure why. But he says you shouldn't swear at inanimate objects, because they can't defend themselves. I think I started swearing just to be cool. Now I don't think it's attractive at all. But I can't control it. It's second nature to me. Maybe I should get a penny jar and put in a dollar every time I swear. I know a family that tried that. But I think they got bored and stopped.

People swear when they're angry, bored, frustrated, depressed, whenever. It's immature. We need new words to express ourselves. I made up my own language one time, I even had a dictionary for it, but that was another time and place and I don't remember the words now. But it can be done.

I'm sick of it in the movies. We've gone too far. Maybe we need some mild censoring. Swearing in movies has really gotten dumb, and so unnecessary. I mean a little bit is okay—a smattering, a smidgeon, a soupçon—I'm not like this prude. In earlier days you didn't find swearing in the movies. Those people had class. Why do they need it now? I don't know how it got to this point. I guess the pendulum is swinging. We can bring it back.

Fortunately no one ever swore at me during a performance, even when people got a little drunk and out of control. And I never let any of those words slip out during one of my shows.

When I hear people swearing I think, why do you have to talk that way? But it's stupid of me, because I talk the same way! It's such an unconscious part of my daily life. I recall getting into trouble once for saying a bad word. I was over at a friend's house and we both got caught swearing and her parents washed her mouth out with soap. I think they tried that on me. "Here, kid, take a bite of this soap." Right. No way! I would have kicked 'em in the shins.

Everything's gotten so complicated now. You've got these trenchcoat teenagers in Colorado who don't give a shit—see, there I go again—and you wonder, What next? I hate to say it but when you ask me to end this sentence, "The world is _____," I'd fill in the blank with fucked up*!*

THREE

Casual Cussing: The Negatives Outweigh the Positives

THE REASONS FOR CASUAL cursing seem justifiable, but if you consider them honestly, they begin to sound like excuses for slovenly behavior. Our peers and role models do it, we point out, so what's the big deal? No one seems to object, so it must be okay. We are being candid and genuine, rather than uptight and pretentious. We are proving our manhood, or we are women who are just as tough and streetwise as men. Strong expletives add force to our very important opinions and profound statements, and emphasis is essential in our emotionally charged, multimedia world where barking out profanities is a good way to be heard.

We can justify and we can rationalize, but if we must provide one summarizing reason for swearing, it would be this: we want the freedom to say whatever we want to say.

Yes, freedom of speech is one of our beloved entitlements as U.S. citizens. We should defend to the bitter end our right to speak out, to voice our opinions, to demand that wrongs be corrected. And we should be able to do so with language that . . . that . . . what? Reveals our wisdom and maturity? Demonstrates our wit, our mastery of the English language, our ability to dazzle others with the clever twist of a phrase? Helps us win arguments with confidence, composure, and convincing logic? Earns us praise and admiration? Builds warm relationships with our family, friends, coworkers, and new acquaintances?

About the best we can achieve with a liberated tongue and repertoire of profanity is an invitation to be a guest on the *Jerry Springer Show*. Our modern-day interpretation of freedom of speech isn't exactly what our founding fathers had in mind. The First Amendment to the U.S. Constitution intended freedom of speech to mean that citizens have the right to disagree with the policies of the government, to air grievances and expect a fair hearing, with the objective of ensuring a responsible, just, and democratic government.

In other words, the writers of the Constitution and the Bill of Rights were concerned about the common good, the general welfare of the citizens of the United States. Today, we seem to think that the rights of the individual take precedent over the comfort of the majority. The motto is not "We the people," but "Me, screw the people." We feel we have the right to use bad language, even if we offend everyone around us.

Nevertheless, in cities such as Raritan, New Jersey, and Fostoria, Ohio, there are ordinances against the use of profanity in public places. In businesses, swearing can be declared a form of sexual harassment and lead to lawsuits. Restaurants and retail establishments can ask customers to leave if they are using language that other patrons find offensive.

Constitutional lawyers believe that local laws prohibiting public swearing are likely to be successfully contested in court. We have the liberty to choose our words here in the land of the free and the home of the knaves, where we take pride in the red, white, and blue, and have the freedom to cuss a blue streak when we see red. But others have the right not to have to hear it. We can declare our constitutional right to be rude, crude, abrasive, and tasteless, but claiming our entitlements often overlooks basic good manners and a sense of community. At times, we would be wiser to bypass the First Amendment and practice the Fifth Amendment, which gives us the right to remain silent.

The legal ramifications surfaced as recently as 1999 during court hearings for Timothy Boomer, whose oral indiscretion made a big splash in the national news. While canoeing with his fiancée and four other couples in Arenac County, Michigan, Boomer fell in the water and began screaming the F word and various derivatives, allegedly for almost three minutes. Somewhere within earshot was a lady with her children, and around the bend was a sheriff's deputy who slapped Boomer with a ticket for violating a local law prohibiting cussing in front of women and children. When his lawyer declared freedom of speech, Arenac prosecutors said his words didn't classify as speech because they weren't "an expression of an idea or thought."

Boomer claims it was all in fun, that he was only pretending to be upset because it made his friends laugh. The courts don't make a distinction between casual and causal cursing, but Boomer's prolonged and exaggerated outburst fits the category of casual cussing since it was not an uncontrollable emotional reaction. His lawyer could argue that anyone would swear after taking a fully clothed spill into a chilly river, but since Boomer wasn't as upset as his canoe, the argument wouldn't hold any water. Regardless of how ridiculous the ordeal seemed to be, Boomer was found guilty.

> *The Constitution gives us the freedom to own a gun, but why do we need an AK-47? The Constitution gives us the freedom to swear, but why do we have to talk like Andrew Dice Clay? I grew up in New York in a neighborhood of Irish, Jews, Italians, everything. We swore, we called each other names, and we fought, but we used our fists. Today, somebody will come by and shoot your mother.*
>
> —Julian Barry, author of a book and a play about comedian
> Lenny Bruce, in an interview for this book

Claiming our verbal privileges as American citizens is often nothing more than an excuse to be lazy about how we speak. It's another way to avoid selecting other words to use, even if they are more effective, meaningful, and appropriate. The embarrassing fact is, cursing requires such a microscopic amount of brainpower that a 10-year-old twit with no schooling can match the foul mouth of a seasoned sailor. Furthermore, the vocal energy needed to mumble single-syllable, four-letter words is equal to the energy needed to drool. Kind of makes you proud, doesn't it?

The English language has thousands of monosyllabic nouns and adjectives that are easy to say and widely understood, even for people who don't know how to read. We just don't use many of the options available to us very often. It's strange, odd, weird, queer, dull, and dumb that we limit ourselves. Repeatedly using the same cuss words is easier, of course, especially when the words have so many different meanings and applications. As a consequence, when we are stuck in the rut of uttering rude words, more suitable words simply don't come to us. Our vocabulary becomes lazy, lifeless, listless, languid, and lethargic.

BEING TOO CASUAL CREATES CASUALTIES

Casual swearing, which can be so routine we often don't realize we are doing it, fits right in with our casual lifestyle. Casual can mean relaxed, informal, comfortable, and candid—which is more fun than reserved, stiff, formal, and distant.

Society has become more casual about everything, and in many regards, a relaxation of the standards has been merciful. Consider casual clothing. It not only reduces wardrobe expenses but also permits more blood to reach the brains of men who don't wear ties, hopefully helping them to make wiser decisions. Pants and jeans free women from tight pantyhose and the fear of flashing too much thigh. Casual dress among office workers reduces the distinctions of rank. A manager in a Tommy Hilfiger shirt is less intimidating and more approachable than one in an Armani suit. People who dress as if they have the same budgets are going to communicate less formally than a king who is dressed in his regal splendor does with his servants.

Likewise, when people of different ages and socioeconomic levels call each other by their first names, the tone is friendlier and the dialogue tends to be straightforward. Casual entertaining at home means time isn't wasted polishing and handwashing the rarely used wedding trays and silverware. In the world of what was once called courting, formal introductions aren't necessary, girls can now telephone boys, sex is less mysterious and awkward, and young men don't have to ask fathers for their daughters' hand in marriage.

Casual, in other words, has come to mean not having to exert much effort. In a casual culture, we tend to avoid doing anything we don't want to do. The terms that best define casual these days—nonchalant, showing little interest or concern, being lenient, and permissive—are neither harmless nor admirable. Casual is almost synonymous with lazy.

There's a difference between relaxed and lax. Casual language, like casual clothing, is more acceptable to everyone if it is clean, reasonably appealing, and appropriate for the occasion. A casual attitude puts everyone at ease, unless it's clear that you couldn't care less about issues that others take seriously.

Judith Martin, who writes the *Miss Manners* syndicated newspaper column, says casual was supposed to mean easygoing, not hard on everyone else. A casual occasion should be spontaneous and low-key, she says, but not indifferent to the sensitivities of others.

"From the tone in which people talk of being casual, it is hard to avoid noticing that they are bragging," she wrote in one of her columns. "Miss Manners prefers to admire people for what they do, rather than for what they fail to do."

The problem with the easy-way attitude is that other people often end up offended, neglected, or inconvenienced. The rules of etiquette and the standards of good manners were not created by prissy snobs, but evolved over time for a purpose. As the world became more civilized, society in general benefited from a sense of order and decorum. The rules of etiquette might seem structured and rigid, but abandoning them makes it difficult for some people to know how to behave when they have dinner at their future in-laws' home, visit the rich uncle they want to please, go on job interviews, or have meetings with the boss.

Likewise, when chronic cursers are in similar situations, they fumble over their words or simply avoid talking. Also, when curse words come easy, they sometimes pop up when even the speaker doesn't expect it.

"My tennis club was holding a day of mixed doubles, and I was playing with a guy I didn't know very well," reports Debbie. "Twice when I was serving, I double-faulted. After the second time, my partner turned to me and said, half-jokingly and half-seriously, 'You double-fault one more time and I'm going to break your fucking kneecaps.' Later, I was up at the bar level of the club watching him play with a different partner. He double-faulted, an opportunity for me to get revenge. I leaned over the railing and intended to yell, 'Do you want me to break your kneecaps?' I was telling myself to be sure to leave out the word *fucking,* but I spoke too fast and ended up saying 'Do you want me to fuck . . . ?' The whole place went silent, and heads turned to look at me. I stammered something, but there was no way I could explain it. The guys down at the court started to laugh, saying yeah, come on down! I was so embarrassed."

We even need to be careful in some of our private conversations that aren't so private anymore. In areas where homes and apartment buildings are close together, the conversations and squabbles next door float through the windows on warm summer nights. Most public telephones in office buildings, in airports, and on the streets are no longer in booths. In the business world, companies are abandoning private offices and jamming all the worker bees into cubicles assembled like honeycombs. It is easy to be involved on the phone with a family member or friend and forget the world of ears that surrounds you.

The same happens with people on cell phones in restaurants, commuter trains, and on the street. In private conversations, people feel free to use profanity, but the ubiquitous cell phones have brought many private conversations into the public arena.

OFF-COLOR HUMOR CAN EASE TENSION, OR CAUSE IT

You might agree that swear words are the least offensive when they are used in humor, but you need to be alert to when this is true and when it isn't. Everyone needs a good laugh now and then, but whether or not something is funny depends on what is said, who says it, when and where they say it, and who hears it.

A comment can be humorous because it is unpredictable and shocking, or clever, witty, imaginative, incongruous, self-deprecating, an insult, an indignity, a pun, a metaphor, an exaggeration, an understatement, an oxymoron, repetitious, out of sequence, and dozens of other reasons. Words can be amusing simply because two of them together rhyme, like *slick chick, boy toy, large barge, hot pot,* and *classy lassy.*

Fortunately for us, just about everything can be funny, depending on who hears it and how it is presented, including such undesirable experiences as death, divorce, taxes, pain, stress, bratty kids, hard work, and sexual dysfunction. Situation comedies and hilarious movies are built around these themes. Finding the funny side of life's foibles and struggles softens their seriousness, and that's good.

Humor can be an extension of our preference to be casual, to overcome our discomfort when faced with important decisions or conflicts. When a discussion gets too serious or heated, a humorous remark is a

good technique for cooling things down. It works well in situation comedies, but it is difficult to apply in real life. Not all parties involved are in a
joking mood.

Words and phrases referring to private body parts and their functions
have been a source of humor for ages. They fit into all of the forms of
humor, and sometimes manage to be funny without much packaging.
Crude humor even merits its own descriptive words, such as *ribald,
raunchy, racy,* and *risqué.*

Unfortunately, what's funny to one person can be offensive to another,
and that's never more true than with humor that is ribald, raunchy, racy, or
risqué. When in doubt, just leave it out. Many of today's professional
comedians do just the opposite, knowing that a segment of every audience will laugh at anything that includes the F word or has to do with
penises. Almost anyone can stand in front of a crowd and go for the
cheap laugh by telling Viagra jokes, which no longer makes the comedy
professional. Jokes about the size and rise of the male organ are currently
in vogue, replacing the worn-out references to female breasts. Men are
having their turn as the butt of the wisecracks.

In October 1998, the 94-year-old New York Friars Club televised one
of its roasts for the first time, heralding a new low in crass comedy. The
program, broadcast on Comedy Central, was promoted in newspapers and on the radio as the "Night of a Thousand Bleeps." In other
words, the language rather than the comedy was used as the enticement
for viewers.

A parade of old-guard and cutting-edge clowns took turns insulting
comedian Drew Carey, each one more crude and less funny than the previous joker. The program should have been tagged the night of five hundred bleeps, because the censors chose not to cut words like *asshole* and
balls. Dom Irrera, acknowledging the presence of aging sex adviser Dr.
Ruth, said, "Boy, I'd like to fuck you. I bet you'd be a great fuck." The
remark was a compliment, but in addition to lacking wit or subtlety, it
was a repulsive thought. Several comedians made open references to
Drew Carey's penchant for prostitutes as if it were his golf game. Dave
Atell said, "Your favorite music is the sound of your balls slapping the
ass of a hooker."

The audience, disguised as mature and sophisticated adults dressed in tuxedos and gowns, set a fine example for the viewers by laughing approvingly at one tasteless and talentless buffoon after another. Some of the comics further demonstrated their shortage of professionalism by launching into their routines with little or no mention of Drew Carey. Self-absorbed and enjoying the limelight, they seemed to forget why they were there.

> *There are some comics who are so funny, but I hate the fact that they are limited. They think they have to be vulgar to be funny, but they are doing themselves a disservice. Being funny and being profane are two different things. These young comedians grew up in a time when everybody wanted to be like Richard Pryor, but without realizing that his genius had nothing to do with his profanity. He never used profanity as a punch line. If you bleeped all of the profanity out of Pryor's stuff, it's still hilarious.*
>
> —Veteran comedian Dick Gregory, in *Jet* magazine, January 19, 1998

The genuinely talented comedians and comedy writers don't have to use profanity to get laughs. Their skill and their success can be measured by their appeal to a wide range of audiences with no segment offended. Some of the most popular TV shows from the 1950s to the present have entertained people of all ages, both genders, rich and poor, educated and not educated, with clean comedy, including such diverse programs as *The Honeymooners, I Love Lucy, Laugh-In, M*A*S*H, All in the Family, Family Ties, Cheers, The Cosby Show, Mad About You, Home Improvement,* and *Frasier.*

More and more contemporary shows deal with sex, which offends some people, particularly parents. Jay Leno's opening monologues cross boundaries that Johnny Carson barely approached. But sexually suggestive scenes and lines are often funny precisely because they don't use crass language. The indirect reference, the clever phrasing, and the subtle delivery also make them more acceptable to the censors and the public. And, with some luck, the younger kids don't get the humor.

Censorship in the 1970s kept outright vulgarity out of *All in the Family,* but it wasn't needed. Archie Bunker and his family addressed serious issues about sex, abortion, marriage, fidelity, racism, and a host of other moral issues, exposing our sanitized perception of family life and revolutionizing television programming. The show's presentations were made palatable and effective through the use of humor that was so brilliant that Archie Bunker became a sympathetic character liked by both liberals and conservatives.

Over time, humor has to break new ground to prevent the same jokes from getting stale. Comedy material with vulgarity was funny at one time because it was bold, shocking, risky, and outrageous. That era should now end, and comedians should find a fresh approach or stick with the wit, imagination, and clever commentary on the human condition that manages to keep each new generation laughing.

> *I'm a First Amendment nut. In 1958, I began publishing* The Realist, *a magazine of social and political satire and commentary. It was probably the first publication to spell out taboo words instead of using asterisks or dashes. I edited* How to Talk Dirty and Influence People, *the autobiography of controversial comedian Lenny Bruce. Ironically, if Lenny were alive today, he would be offended by some of today's stand-up comics. He wanted to liberate taboos, whereas they exploit taboos.*
>
> —Paul Krassner, author of several books on the counterculture, in an interview for this book

BE YOURSELF IF IT MEANS BEING BETTER

We swear because people around us swear. When wicked words are flung about you like a Frisbee free-for-all, you're going to catch a few and fling them back. You join in, rather than just sit there. You might not want to, but when they are coming your way from every direction, you're almost forced into the game.

If you started swearing at a young age, you probably picked it up from other kids and, like them, considered it fun to talk dirty, to break the rules. Some of your friends might have resisted, sticking to their religious or personal convictions, but they were taking a risk that they would be considered nerds or sissies. Or maybe you succumbed to peer pressure in early adulthood, a time when you began to think that the rules against dirty language were intended for children.

"I didn't do anything considered bad until I was in college, where I did it all," admits Cheryl, who went away to college in 1990. "Everybody was doing everything and having fun, with no one telling us not to. Swearing became part of it for me. It felt so free to talk dirty and swear at everything. I considered it the one vice I could engage in every day without getting pregnant or hungover! I figured I would clean up my act and return to being a proper lady when I got in the adult world, and I have, except for some of the swearing. It's hard to stop, but it's a minor infraction compared with everything else I used to do."

Cheryl now works for a real estate firm in Los Angeles and is trying not to swear, especially on the job. "I work with some very intelligent people, but lots of swearing goes on. It sounds immature to me. We're not juveniles anymore. I would expect the older people to be more sophisticated, more articulate. The swearing is so crass at times, it inspires me not to sound like everyone else."

Sounding like everyone else is what young people—and many adults—want to do. Without question, there is comfort in conforming. But retaining some individuality has its own reward. Why not sound a bit more polished than everyone else? Will they hate you for it? Will they even notice? More than likely, they will simply consider you an articulate and well-mannered individual.

"I went to a big high school in the suburbs," says Bill, a salesman for a long-distance phone service. "I didn't give swearing much thought at the time, whether it was right or wrong or made a difference. I swore, lots of my friends swore, but some didn't. But now I think about the guys who didn't. In almost every respect, they were nice guys. They weren't complainers, or the ones who criticized everyone else. Some were student leaders. Others were quiet, but more in a calm way than a shy way. Today, they're the kind of guys I would respect and trust."

Karen, a reporter for a major city newspaper, says she hardly ever swore prior to working for the paper. "I never experienced the compulsion to swear in high school or college. I was very straight, followed all the rules, and was comfortable with my principles. Oddly enough, I've felt more pressure as an adult to fit into the fraternity of reporters. I didn't consciously start to swear, though. I just picked it up like a parrot. I now regret that I let it happen. I don't like hearing myself."

Keith, Karen's brother, became a carpenter after high school and works on new home sites. He doesn't use profanity, but doesn't object if other people do. At one site, another laborer would tease him about not swearing. Keith laughed it off, but one day the guy pushed too hard.

"He kept bugging me to say something, throwing out words, saying how about this, how about that," Keith recalled. "I should have given him a cuss word to shut him up, but other guys were there and I felt like sticking to my guns. Then he said, 'Maybe if I piss you off, you'll swear.' I was trying to work, and he started poking me, and I blew. I grabbed him by the shirt and shoved him against a plywood wall and screamed, 'That's enough!' He was bigger than me, but he had a look of total shock on his face. It was a dumb thing to fight over, but he never bothered me after that."

THE LACK OF OBJECTION DOESN'T MEAN APPROVAL

Swearing has become so commonplace that many people don't think once before they swear in front of other people they know, don't know, or just met. Teenagers roaming shopping malls swear openly, unaware of their vocal volume and oblivious to the presence of other forms of life around them. Adult men at ball games think it's part of the fun to scream obscenities at referees and the opposing team's players. At any social event, whether it's friends enjoying a private party or strangers mingling in a bar, an occasional cuss word will pop up in a conversation, or even be innocently shouted out in laughter. If individuals sense they have crossed the border of good taste, they might say, "Excuse me," or "Pardon my French." This permits them to continue talking as if nothing really happened.

Chronic cursers swear more than occasionally, and not always innocently. They are unable to relate an incident in their day without punctuating every noun with the F'ing word. It's like an endless echo. After a while, it's more like a woodpecker hammering away at your eardrum.

In all of these situations, rarely does anyone tell the offenders to stop. They get away with it, remaining ignorant of how ignorant they sound.

Occasional cussers, on the other hand, recognize the need to be discreet under certain circumstances. Those circumstances are gradually diminishing, yet even guys whose language could give fresh ideas to Eddie Murphy or Chris Rock have been in situations where even they were uncomfortable with someone else's foul mouth. Perhaps it was in a library or a school, at a funeral or business function, or on a family picnic with all the uncles, aunts, cousins, nephews and nieces, not to mention Grandma. Yet, for some reason, it is uncommon in our culture for anyone to say, "Hey, keep it down," or "Excuse me, but you shouldn't use that kind of language here," or "You impudent oaf! Your language is more disgusting than slime in the sewers of Calcutta. Bite your tongue, or I'll have Mike Tyson bite it for you."

Consequently, big-mouthed cursers don't realize some people find them repugnant. Maybe they think they are being cute. People laugh politely. "Hee-hee, that's a good one, Uncle Remus. My young daughter here is particularly fond of your references to anal intercourse."

So don't think you are getting away with it every time. The person you are talking to, or somebody who overhears you, might think less of you.

The owner of a small machining company is disturbed by the fact that his employees feel free to swear in front of him. "Sometimes one of my men will say damn or something worse when they are talking to me, or I'll be walking right past some workers who are talking about a football game or something and they are using very crude language, shouting over the noise of the grinders or cutters," he reports. "I'm a friendly guy and very open with my employees. They all know I worked my way up through a shop, doing what they're doing, but for them to use those words in front of me strikes me as disrespectful. I guess they don't realize that I don't swear. I don't make an issue of it, because I want them to be open and honest with me, but they shouldn't consider me one of their buddies. The guys who are really bad don't sit well with me."

Roger, a manager at a large public relations firm, found himself in an awkward situation with colleagues.

"We landed a new client in an industry we knew nothing about, so I wanted to enlist the help of a smaller agency that knew the industry well. I asked the president of the agency to have lunch with me and my account supervisor, Jane, who was in her early thirties. Before we ordered lunch, Jane asked him if he knew so-and-so, a woman Jane had worked with early in her career.

" 'God yes,' he replied, 'She's a real ball-busting c___.'

"Jane recoiled, shocked to hear the worst of all words from someone we were interviewing to be a subcontractor. He didn't even notice her reaction. She sat frozen throughout the lunch, although her eyes seemed to be searching for a blunt object to smack him senseless. Obviously, he already lacked sense. I regret to this day that I never told him why we didn't hire him. He would have learned something."

BEING ONE OF THE (BAD) BOYS

Jane—as well as most women—would have been less offended if he had said bitch, but probably would have considered him a fool for criticizing someone whom Jane might have liked or admired. His only excuse for using the word at the top of the taboo list was his apparent experience with other women who didn't consider it objectionable.

Such women do exist. One of them is Sarah Miller, who wrote an article in the November 1998 issue of *Cosmopolitan* about how she loves to swear. "I use the S word and the F word," she wrote. "I even use the two C words. In fact, I use them as often as I can."

Sarah says she swears when is mad, glad, sad, and just for the hell of it, as in, "Pass the ice $#@%in' cream."

Once her mother asked her what she thought of a coconut cake she had made. Afraid that the word *delicious* failed to fully convey how she felt, she responded to her mother, "It's the best $#@%ing cake you've ever $#@%ing baked!"

Most men, even psycho serial killers and macho misogynists, wouldn't use this approach to compliment their mothers, nor would they make light of it in a magazine read by several million women. *Cosmopolitan* is a woman's magazine with a man's mentality, evident in articles in that same issue that focused on how to have sex as often as possible, and how to ditch a guy the morning after. Ms. Miller has gone beyond trying to be like a man and is proud of it.

"Paint a sentence with a lot of profanity," she continues, "and I promise, no one within earshot will ever say, 'Gee, tell us how you really feel!'"

Whether you are a man or a woman, do you care how she really feels? Is this the kind of person you would like to spend a good percentage of your time with, or bring home to your own mother?

> *Women use swearing as an equalizer with men. However, it's akin to making all the trees in the forest equal by chopping them down. Back when women didn't swear, they were mysterious creatures. Today, they are too much like men. I don't want to be around men all the time.*
>
> —John Hood, president of the John Locke Foundation,
> in an interview for this book

It would be a mistake to restore the old double standard that men are entitled to swear and have all the fun while women must behave, but in matters of manners, the movement toward equality went in the wrong direction. Men who don't swear, or who remember being instructed not to swear, typically say the admonitions came from their mothers or grandmothers. That will change. Informal surveys among high schools students have found that girls swear as much as the boys, whether they are alone in the girls' locker room or cavorting with the guys. Casual cursing has come out of the closet, and it's bisexual.

Points to Ponder

- You have the right to use whatever language you choose but should respect the rights of others who don't want to hear it.
- A relaxation of the rules in our casual culture makes life easier, but we must be careful not to sacrifice civility and consideration for others.
- If you swear frequently out of habit, you are likely to cuss occasionally at the wrong time, or have trouble finding a better word when you need it.
- Humor is healthy, but crude comedy should be subtle and witty. It's too bad that most tasteless humor is just too bad.
- Since it is rare for anyone to tell another person his or her language is offensive, you can't claim you only swear when you know it's okay.

SHELLEY STEWARD, 43, PROFESSIONAL MAGICIAN, BEREAVEMENT COUNSELOR, AND SELLER OF ADULT BOOKS

I'm going to call myself a swearer because I've noticed a marked difference in my language during the last fifteen years. I didn't swear in the corporate world, where I once worked as a claims adjuster. Language is infectious. It really depends on your environment.

I probably swear several times a day. When I'm out with friends, I love to use the word fuck *to punctuate things. I don't use* Jesus Christ *or* God damn. *I use the words* shit *and* fuck, *but I never used to use those words. I'm also fond of calling people a big dirty whore. But I'm not Andrew Dice Clay, I don't swear that much. When I'm really angry, I'll scream. But I don't scream in public because I have this high-pitched feminine scream that alarms people. Unfortunately, I swear more than most of my friends do, and I swear in front of both men and women. I'm an equal-opportunity cusser.*

I swear at the adult bookstore where I work, but I avoid swear-ing when I'm on the phone with my dear sweet parents. They would be very offended. I don't swear with clients or with the doctors at the organization where I counsel AIDS patients.

I've never been afraid of death. I studied with Elisabeth Kübler-Ross at Marlborough in England, in the context of social work and hospice care. So it's weird because I can deal with death easily, but I can't stand a picture on the wall being crooked. I'll say "shit" over little things like that. I don't swear in restaurants or in public, or where people don't know me. I avoid it. It's jarring to hear it on buses and such places, where there are so many different kinds of people, older people, children. It takes on a completely different quality in certain contexts. Even I get offended. It's like seeing a sexually explicit photo when you don't expect it.

I didn't swear in high school. I was in the Philippines then. I was born in England, but my father was the diplomatic attaché to the Philippines so I was there for high school. You can't believe how much my classmates were hung up on American culture. Some of them swore quite a lot. They thought it was very American. That and blue jeans and smoking American cigarettes. I don't blame them for wanting some variety. I recall seeing a whole calendar based on the harvest of the yam. Or was it papayas?

My father was an English Jew. He married an Italian, Rita Mastroianni, second cousin to Marcello Mastroianni. That makes me a Jewsieppe. My mother was Catholic so she never swore. I only heard my father swear once. We were at Harrods and I caught my foot in the escalator. My father froze. He put his hand to his forehead and said, "Jesus Christ!" Fortunately my aunt was with us. She pulled and pulled on my sneaker and finally pried it loose.

When I first heard people swearing, I thought it was vile. I would wonder, "What family did they come from?" It was in my late twenties that I started to join them. I was coming into my sex-uality and became more relaxed about everything, including my language. It was just the people I was hanging with at the time, I suppose.

My swearing is a habit that I wish I could do something about, because every once in a while a fuck *will break out and it can be very inappropriate. It's an insidious thing. You find yourself in an environment you once frequented—a different, more formal environment—and you falter.*

I remember offending some woman at a spaghetti feed. I knew it right after I said it, so I really felt bad about it. We were in line to get our food. We had assigned seating. I was with some friends, and I looked over and saw someone had taken our seats. I said to my friend, "Oh, someone took our fucking seats!" I saw the shoulders rise up on the woman standing in front of me in line. You know, she flinched a little. The poor woman was expecting spaghetti and meatballs, not some guy behind her complaining about "those fucking seats!"

Neither of my grandmothers swore, of course. My Jewish grandmother really acted like what I thought a grandmother should be, telling me I was right whenever I was wrong. My Italian grandmother was very religious and made me eat my vegetables. It would have been a sin for her to swear. In their day I'm sure only lower-class women used bad language. Prostitutes and such. Uneducated people.

Language defines a person, more so than the way a person dresses. Anyone can go out and buy nice clothing, but people judge you by your language. I do, too. If it's coming from someone I perceive as being educated, I find it amusing. I don't agree with those people who say swearing is a sign a person doesn't have a good vocabulary. I know some very glib people who pepper their conversation with swear words. It's not because they don't have other things to say. But if it's someone who has only a high school education, I find it sad. If you know that's all they know, where can they go in life? And I hate to say this about movies and television, but if you are doing a scene in a ghetto or some other rough situation, and you don't hear those kids swearing, it just won't ring true.

It would be nice if people were more civil. This cussing thing has gone wild. Our language is who we are. A civilization falls by its language.

FOUR
Causal Cussing: It's Not the Words, It's the Attitude

"THEY'RE ONLY WORDS THAT are labeled as bad by Bible-toting purists," argue the defenders of swearing. "As long as they get the message across, what does it matter?"

It matters precisely because there is a message, and swearing conveys secondary messages that say much more about you as a person. When your swearing is the reaction to an emotion, does the cause of the emotion really warrant your outburst? A woman coming down the aisle of a commuter train bumping everyone in the head with shopping bags might do it. Standing in zero-degree weather waiting for someone who is an hour late picking you up deserves a few icy expletives. But put aside bangs to the back of your head and intense anger from being thoughtlessly neglected or mistreated, and think of all those times you were simply impatient or annoyed. Did you overreact? Did swearing in any way help the situation? Did your swearing upset other people who had nothing to do with your problem?

Even occasional mutterings don't do you much good, possibly harming your relationships with other people. For example, Eric called his friend Bill on Saturday afternoon and his girlfriend answered the phone. Eric asked if Bill was there. "No, he went to some goddam baseball game."

Eric doesn't have to be a mind reader to get the real message behind her response. What does she expect to gain by letting him know she doesn't think much of Bill's interest in sports, or that he chose to do a guy thing rather than be with her? Since Bill is his pal, and he likes sports, too, Eric is not likely to feel sorry for her. Instead, he feels sorry for Bill because she probably made him feel guilty, and he will have to deal with her crabby mood with he returns. So Eric gets three messages: Bill went out, it upset her, and she's a shrew.

That night, Bill returned Eric's call. He says he was at his younger brother's baseball game, and Eric asks him how it was.

"Shitty. His team lost, even though the other team really sucked. The umpire was a blind bastard, and made total bullshit calls."

Bill recounts some of the bad calls. Eric asks a few more questions. Was it a championship game? No, it was the fourth game of the season, and the team's first loss. Was it cold and rainy? No, a perfect day. Did your brother stay on the bench? No, he had two hits and made a great play at second. Was his team creamed? No, they only lost by one run in a high-scoring game, 8 to 7. Do you wish you had stayed home and spent the day with your girlfriend? Nah, she was in a pissy mood.

It all made sense to Eric, sort of. Bill was disappointed, but he'll get over it in no time. Eric was hoping to go out with him and his girlfriend that night, but he remembers Bill's last remark about the mood she is in, and her comment about the goddam game. Then it occurs to him that this routine has happened before, and unless the night turns out to be nothing short of magical, neither of them will perk up. Eric decides he will have more fun staying home and watching reruns on the Weather Channel.

The curse words Eric's two friends used didn't upset him, their attitudes did. All of us have "dis" days that affect our mood—disappointments, disagreements, discouragement, dissatisfaction, discord, distress, disasters. Some of our days are downright dismal. Hiding our dispirited feelings is not always easy, but if we grumble to our friends about our aggravations, we can drag them down with us. We need to be selective, saving the moans for tragic moments that really matter, sharing only the problems that others might be able to help us solve. Otherwise, our frequent complaining and cursing spoils the day for people whose friendship we value.

It's possible, of course, to grumble without swearing. Bill's girlfriend could have said that he went to some *stupid* game. Or she could have said he went to some *stupid fucking* game. All three messages (he's gone, she's mad, and there's conflict) would be the same, but the last two messages—the implied anger and conflict that don't interest Eric or brighten his day—take on greater significance as the strength of the adjective intensifies.

All she had to say was, "No, he went to a baseball game. I'll tell him you called." Her tone might sound cold and abrupt, but maybe for reasons that have nothing to do with Bill.

A better option would have been "Hey, how are you? Bill went to his younger brother's baseball game and should be back by six o'clock. Any message, or should I have him call you?" She can still be upset, but Eric doesn't need to know. She rises above her dejection to be friendly. The tone of her voice spares Eric from knowing she's mad at Bill. Had she done this, Eric probably would have told her he was hoping to go out with the two of them that night, and maybe that's just what they needed.

SWEARING AT THINGS AND OURSELVES

Undesirable situations cause us to swear, but we also swear at people, at things, and at ourselves. Swearing at another person is not only the most egregious verbal assault, it's also risky—it can lead to bruised egos and broken noses. The rule of thumb is to never swear at a person with the ability to break your thumb. It's also unwise to swear at your mother, your employer, the person you sleep with on a regular basis, and anyone who appears to be heavily armed.

Directing your most vile words at inanimate objects seems harmless, but it doesn't make motors start, jars open, or heavy furniture move. Sometimes other people have to endure your fury, including the person capable of solving your problem. Just ask Howard, whose profession is fixing computers.

"At times I have to hold the phone two feet from my ear," reports Howard. "The worst was a frequent customer who one time screamed so loud and for so long that I put the receiver on my desk until I heard his yelling turn to sobbing. I picked the phone up and asked if he was okay. 'Yes,' he moaned, 'but my computer isn't. This time my data is lost forever.' Did your hard drive crash? I asked. 'Yes, along with the rest of the computer. I threw the fucking thing out my third-floor window.'"

You might find that you have more occasions to swear at yourself than at objects or people. A good portion of our self-assaults could be eliminated if we didn't procrastinate, left on time, read the directions, made notes as reminders, didn't misplace our notes, and could read our own writing. Even being organized and practical doesn't always work, though, if you are a stickler for always doing what you are supposed to do. Perfectionists place such high demands on themselves that the smallest goof-up on their part can set off a cussing tizzy. The solution is to develop a mental state that lies between an "I-don't-care" attitude and an "I-must-be-the-best" attitude. You might call it an "I-tried-my-best" attitude.

Make an effort to keep your self-flagellation to yourself. If you whip yourself in front of others, don't expect them to sympathize. No one cared about John's problem the night he and his wife, Sylvia, were asked to fill in for a couple who was unable to attend their monthly bowling night. Andrew regrets that he ever asked John and Sylvia to play.

"My game is a little rusty," confessed John. No problem, Andrew assured him, it's just for fun.

John's game wasn't terrible, but his attitude was. He swore angrily at himself every time he missed a spare. At first he apologized, eager to let everyone know that he used to be an excellent bowler, but his frustration and swearing got worse after a few beers. While the others chatted, he sulked.

"I'll never invite him again," said Andrew. "This is a social group, and we like to joke around during the games, but he added tension that took the fun out of it for everyone. We swear, too, but not like he did. They all liked Sylvia, even though her game was worse than his. Everyone felt sorry for her, but not for him."

CUSSING ON THE JOB CAN BE COSTLY

Some people learn at an early age the consequences of losing control of their emotions and their mouth manners. Brigette, a 20-year-old girl working as a camp counselor, was ushering kids out of the bus when two of them started fighting. She ran over to them and shouted, "What the fuck do you think you are doing?" She was fired on the spot.

Earl, a senior in high school, didn't see any problem with swearing because everyone in his neighborhood swore—the kids, the parents, the store owners, the police officers, everyone. It was the way everybody talked. After graduation, he got a job in telemarketing. On the second day, frustrated by phones that weren't answered and prospects that hung up on him, he swore over the phone at someone. His employer sent him home.

Joshua relates his brief experience as Barney the dinosaur: "When I was 17, a company hired me to dress like Barney for a promotion in a shopping mall. The costume was really clumsy. I could hardly walk. As soon as the mall opened, some moms with preschoolers came in, and the kids were all over me. I kind of panicked and tried to run away, but all I could do was waddle. The kids chased me like we were playing a game. I fell, and a kid jumped right on my big Barney head, knocking it off. I screamed, 'Goddam it! Get the fuck off me!' I laugh about it now, but I felt terrible. It was such a simple job, and I blew it after five minutes."

Jim, a 36-year-old working for a consumer products company, also considered swearing acceptable and had never been reprimanded for it. When his boss announced that he was leaving for a new job in Houston, Jim was convinced that he was next in line to be the head of the department. He had an excellent relationship with Parnell, the group vice president, and met with him to tell him he wanted the job.

"I feel I've proven myself. I know the business backwards and forwards, I've been instrumental in bringing in new customers, and you know that it was my initiative that changed some of the dumb-ass procedures in my department that had been detrimental to productivity."

Parnell acknowledged that Jim was contributing to the success of the company. They talked about specific projects and events, and Parnell was complimentary. But Jim wasn't hearing what he wanted to hear. Parnell was hedging. Jim pointed out his other strengths.

"As you know, Parnell, I don't mince words. I don't play games with people. I say what I have to say, I do what I have to do, and I get things done. Don't you agree? You've got too many chickenshit pussies around here who are afraid to stick their neck out."

"You're definitely aggressive, Jim, and you take chances," said Parnell. "You've made a few mistakes, but all in all, your ideas are exemplary."

Jim was still waiting to hear Parnell say he had the job. "You know I'm dedicated to this company, Parnell. I willingly give much of my personal time. Do you realize that, in four years, I haven't missed a day of work? Not one fucking day!"

Parnell paused a few seconds, then surprised Jim by saying, "Are you aware of how often you swear?"

Jim was stunned at first, then laughed. "You've got to be kidding. There's no one in the room but you and me. We've played golf together. We both swear. What's that got to do with anything?"

Parnell seemed reluctant to speak. "The words don't bother me, Jim, but they're a reflection of something else. You're right, you don't mince words, so I'll be equally candid with you. Consider this conversation an example. You referred to dumb-ass procedures. We've had them, probably still do, but someone thought they were good at the time. You made a big stink about them for a long time and disrupted other people's work by doing things your own way before new systems were in place.

"You say we have chickenshit pussies working here. My guess is that you've let them know how you feel. Not everyone is as daring and as innovative as you, but many of them are steady, cooperative workers. When you insult them, they are less likely to want to support your initiatives.

"I know you've never missed a day of work, even when you weren't feeling good or were exhausted. That's commendable, don't get me wrong, but you can be one nasty guy when you're not at your peak. I can think of a few days when the others in your department wished you had stayed home. On top of it, when others are out sick, you're the first person to accuse them of faking illness or blowing off a day to have fun.

"You're a great worker, a valuable asset to me, but you are only one of my employees. I need people with a variety of talents and ideas to make this business work, and I need managers who inspire them, motivate them, encourage them, and show them how to work as a team. If I make you the head of your department, I can count on you to kick some ass, as you might say. But there's a way to straighten out the poor performers without alienating everyone else, and I'm not certain you can do that. To get the respect you deserve, you have to respect others. You obviously don't."

Jim's confidence in his abilities made him blind to his poor people skills. He's lucky, because the group vice president was willing to point out his shortcomings, constructive criticism that managers are often surprisingly reluctant to offer in performance reviews. Jim blundered by failing to recognize the management style preferred by the executive with the authority to promote him.

Cindy's situation was much different: the president of her small company was the offender. She tried to do something about it.

"He swears because he's angry, or blaming somebody for something. Morale is terrible, and employee turnover is high, largely because of him. I wanted to tell him but didn't have the nerve, but I found a magazine article about the risks of swearing on the job and I put it on his desk. I attached a note that said, 'This might interest you,' and signed it. I was trying to help him and the company, but he stormed into my cubicle, screaming at me and saying he will say whatever he God damn feels like saying. He's a terrible person, and I have no respect for him. Nobody does."

"I Only Swear When I Get Angry or Frustrated"

Many cussers make this claim, often adding that it feels good to whip out a word that really expresses their feelings.

Okay, but how many times a day do you get angry or frustrated? Pick any day of the week, and try to keep track of events or situations that cause you to swear. If your work is so stressful that you would need three personal secretaries to record the causes of your eruptions, select one of your days off. Carry a pad of paper and a pen with you, or just make mental notes of what annoys you to the point of cussing, even if it is to yourself.

It's Saturday, free of workday stress. Nevertheless, your first offense might occur the moment you get out of bed if you didn't get to sleep in as long as you wanted, you partied too much the night before, or on the way to the bathroom you trip over the exercise device you never use. Next, the phone rings just as you sit on the toilet. You discover too late that no one replaced the roll of toilet paper. You cut yourself shaving. You realize you have enough errands to keep you busy all day, with no time to relax. You make three calls before you go out and get answering machines.

While driving through the traffic, you rack up a few good ones that could win a creative cussing contest. The hardware store doesn't have the vacuum cleaner bags you need. It's raining when you come out, you drop something in a puddle, service is slow at the fast-food restaurant, the bank closes just before you get there, and you forgot to stop at the cleaner's. That night, your favorite TV show is preempted by the "Religious Music Awards Show," and nothing good is on the other channels.

On top of all this, you might have serious problems, like not having enough money to pay your rent or mortgage, concern about losing your job, your child's poor health, your other kid's troubles in school, and the pain you've been getting in your side, all aggravated by your obnoxious neighbor's incessantly barking pit bull and its unsettling chewing sounds. These endless worries could be the underlying source of your testy temperament, but life must go on. Each day you have to tackle tasks you don't want to do, deal with things that go wrong, and put up with people who try your patience.

If you were by yourself the day you encountered and counted your curses, no one had to hear your stings but you. You didn't do much to enhance your own disposition, and your use of swear words only perpetuated your habit of using them, but otherwise, no great harm was done.

But are you certain you didn't swear loud enough for anyone to hear? Did you use profanity when the sales clerk said she didn't have what you needed? Keeping everything in stock is not her job, so why ruin her day by showing your irritation?

Did you have a child with you? Many a parent has had an experience similar to the one actress Ellen Barkin related on the David Letterman show. Her 6-year-old daughter was blamed for using obscenities that the other kids were repeating. The girl was sent to the principal's office and asked if she knew what the words meant.

"She had been calling everyone a bleeping bleep-hole," said Barkin. "She told the principal she didn't know what it meant, but her mommy says it every day to bad drivers."

When you swear in front of your children, the mistake is not just exposing them to curse words, but to your lack of emotional control and your inability to deal calmly with daily annoyances. They will imitate your words, but what's worse, your attitude.

If your spouse or significant other was with you on a day of cussing, it probably didn't inhibit you. Sad to say, when we feel relatively secure in our relationships, we take each other for granted. The courtship and the good behavior it requires are over. They chose us, and we feel they have to accept us for who we are, to allow us to be ourselves, to listen to our grumbling and our swearing when we feel like doing it.

"I love to swear, especially when I'm driving," a disc jockey in Ohio bragged on the air. "I swear at everyone in my way—truckers, bus drivers, little old ladies. It makes me feel good. And it's funny when my wife is in the car, because it drives her nuts."

You can be sure she's not nuts about him. His expletives are just the thumping of his bumper-car mentality that someday might put her through the windshield. Maybe he thinks his aggressive driving shows her that he will be her protector when faced with real danger, like when another driver decides to fight back, but he is far from being a noble knight when his shining armor is a Ford Taurus.

If you were alone when you had a particularly bad experience, you probably told someone about it. Maybe you are well mannered enough not to swear in public, but you don't feel satisfied until you have had a chance to complain to someone about the incompetence or outrageous impediments you had to endure. Spouses and significant others are usually the victims of such harangues. You are looking for sympathy, or you're explaining why you were delayed, but depending on the scale of your scathing attack on the rest of the world, you don't get much compassion, and you certainly don't engender love, affection, or admiration.

WE'VE BECOME WHINERS AND COMPLAINERS

A hot-selling doll in early 1999 was Amazing Amy, who has sensors and computer chips in her little body to help her say ten thousand phrases. To make the doll representative of the typical child of today, the programmers loaded her with hundreds of whines, nags, and demands. For example, if she asks for a cookie and a child feeds her one of the other chip-embedded plastic food items that come with the doll, she says, "I didn't want that. I wanted a cookie." If she still doesn't get a cookie, she is programmed to repeat the demand five times, ten seconds apart, each time in a slightly different way, crying and whimpering.

"I hate to think how this doll's 'mommies' are going to grow up," commented psychologist Dr. Joyce Brothers in the *National Enquirer*. "They'll be rude, overbearing, and demanding."

Dr. Brothers doesn't have to wait that long. The rude mothers are here, and many of the daddies aren't much better. In an earlier time, it seems a greater number of people were less demanding. They were more tolerant of daily challenges, more accepting of the fact that we live in an imperfect world, more dispassionate, and better equipped to cope. They didn't always like what was happening, but they fixed what they could and hoped for the best without cussing up a storm, particularly in public.

"I hate to say anything that sounds like 'Well, back in my day . . .' because the world does change, sometimes for the better, sometimes not," says Burt, a retired grocery store manager. "During the war, I had plenty to cuss about. I fought in Italy. I was scared half the time, uncomfortable most of the time, and being shot at just about any time. Everyone swore constantly, even when we weren't in danger. But I put all that behind me when I came home. I had to fit back into society, to act civilized. We didn't have much, but I was happy to have all my fingers and toes, no holes in my body, and to sleep through the night without hearing explosions. I raised three good kids, put them all through college. I never told them much about the war. I doubt if they ever heard me swear, but boy, I had been good at it."

Various forms of pop psychology began to blossom in the early 1970s that promoted emotional expression and focused on what was best for the individual's mental state. Slogans from this period in history set the pace: Let it all hang out. Tell it like it is. Don't hold back. Be honest with your emotions. Get in touch with yourself. Don't be afraid to be sensitive. You gotta vent, man.

A reluctance to communicate openly was considered a detriment to honest relationships, and pent-up fury and frustration was allegedly leading to stress, ulcers, and heart attacks. Men in particular were encouraged to say what was really on their minds. The strong silent types, the men who faced hardships straight on, who looked for solutions because a man had to do what a man had to do, began to shrink in number. In Hollywood and on TV, the lead characters as gallant heroes had to make way for protagonists who were villains, misfits, and antiheroes.

We also began to develop higher expectations. Technological advances, intense competition, and demands for continuous improvement were the driving force behind higher-quality products, exceptional service, lower prices, immediate delivery, and satisfaction guaranteed.

Now we have unparalleled quality, speed, and convenience. Automobiles last at least five years instead of three. We have drive-in restaurants, drive-in banks, and drive-in dry cleaners. Take a cell phone to the mall so you can make plans for the night. Nothing happening? The video store, with the latest films down to 50-year-old classics, is open until midnight. Need cash? Any ATM will do, twenty-four hours a day. There's one at the all-night supermarket, where you can find a huge selection of food that is well marked for evaluating its nutritional value. Use a credit card to buy a gift in the housewares section and have it shipped overnight, anywhere, guaranteed. Documents can be faxed or e-mailed instantaneously to the other side of the world. The information you once researched at the library is now immediately accessible in your home through the Internet.

Life has become easier, faster, and healthier, to the point that our expectations are unrealistic and we don't appreciate what we have. We are spoiled rotten! We want cars and computers to always do what they are supposed to do without breaking down. We want waiters and salespeople to be there when we want them there, and to be competent. We want phones to be answered within three rings, by a human, or we hang up. We hate waiting for anything, especially at drive-in restaurants and banks that boast about fast service, even if we aren't in a hurry. We want referees and umpires to see what we see, even though we see it in slow motion on the instant replay. We want the rain to stop, the traffic to go away, kids to be quiet, dogs not to shed, and sex to be fantastic instead of just great.

We shouldn't lose sight of the fact that we haven't created Utopia yet. Without being complete pessimists, it might help to approach each day with the assumption that Murphy's Law is still pertinent: Whatever can possibly go wrong will. With this outlook, you will be surprised and elated each time things go right.

A wiser route is to think positively. It brings contentment and brightens your personality. The only advantage to negative thinking is that it helps you prepare for a problem—or, in positive terms, rise to the challenge. When life gives you lemons, make lemonade.

THEM'S FIGHTIN' WORDS

"All right, who threw the first punch?"

When cops break up brawls these days, they no longer ask that question. Court cases have proven that the guy hurling the insults and verbal attacks was asking for a licking. More often than not, before the fists fly, the combatants began with profanity and name-calling as their weapons.

Fortunately, most of us don't get in scuffles that would qualify us as recruits for the World Wrestling Federation, but swearing can lead to physical violence. Any discussion that explodes into an argument and escalates to fisticuffs usually involves cursing. As emotions get heated, logic and reason give way to parts of the brain that think less clearly. An obvious sign is when someone becomes so upset over an issue that he or she drags up unrelated grievances and throws them into the fray. A brain scrambled with outrage is nearly incapable of thinking of meaningful words to duel with, but the cuss words—short, powerful, and generic—come easy. When the crude names hit their target, there's a boomerang effect that sends back similar words—or worse, draws a slug or a slap.

At Southport High School in Indianapolis, principal Larry Hensley-Marschand decided in September of 1998 to enforce the school's long-ignored policy of no profanity in the school. His objective was to improve the quality of the language, but he discovered another benefit.

"Every semester, we had ten or more fights in the halls, the cafeteria, or the gym," he reports. "The first semester that we forbid cursing and swearing, the fights were reduced to three."

Shortly after he announced the policy, Hensley-Marschand was also surprised at the number of students who came to his office or stopped him in the halls to say they were pleased that he was outlawing bad language.

"It was bothering some of the students, but they weren't about to tell their peers to put a lid on their trashy mouths," he said. "It had to come from authority. The change is perceptible. The atmosphere around the school used to be unpleasant, but it's not anymore."

Al, a software salesman, manages to use soft words when he gets into arguments, and he is convinced it helps him win. Keeping his cool either calms his opponents down or infuriates them to the point that they make fools of themselves.

"For several years, I dated a woman who frequently spun out of control. During the blowup that ended our relationship, she kept pacing back and forth, cursing me and blaming me for everything. I sat there, saying nothing. She said, 'If my cursing bothers you, you haven't heard anything yet!' I told her I believed her. I never insulted her or raised my voice. When it was over, I knew she would have to live with the barrage of insults she had thrown at me. I walked away at peace with myself because I had behaved like a gentleman."

Most of us have basic dispositions that can range from jocular to somber, and personalities that fall somewhere between Jim Carrey's and Joe Pesci's. Unless you are born with a cheerful nature, maintaining a pleasant mood when things are not going smoothly is not always easy. Through some quirk of nature or the influence of society, it is easier for many of us to be grumpy or downright belligerent than it is to be exuberant. We struggle with our emotions, often surrendering to anger and frustration and letting foul words fly because it's so much easier than controlling ourselves. It sometimes takes earnest effort, an internal pep talk, a compelling reason to put on a happy face, but it's worth it.

Points to Ponder

- If you don't enjoy being with people who have negative attitudes, listen to yourself to make certain you don't sound like them.
- We swear at situations, at objects, at ourselves, and at other people. Swearing at others is the most harmful, but no one enjoys hearing anyone swear about anything.
- Don't complain, unless the person you are talking to can solve the problem.
- Employers want people who are cheerful, cooperate, find better ways to do things, believe in teamwork, and have can-do attitudes. Chronic cursers rarely fit the description, or get the promotion.
- Accept the fact that we live in an imperfect world, that things go wrong, that you're going to be inconvenienced. Cope, don't cuss, then move on.
- Consider every annoying little task a challenge, and take pride in getting it done, especially if a family member or fellow worker will appreciate your effort and attitude.

JANE KRIWZI, 30, LIBRARIAN AND ARTIST

There was a time in my life when I didn't swear: age 5 and under. There was a lot of swearing in my house. My dad sure swore. He was trying to be a bohemian or beatnik. He was an artist and a pretty heavy drinker. Swearing was all part of the package. He was trying to be a tough guy, I guess. My mom is a librarian. My family was not religious at all. My mother's side was Irish Catholic, and my dad's family was Southern Baptist. His family was very poor. But Southern Baptists believe you're supposed to suffer. If someone gives you a nice gift, you have to wrap it up and stick it in the back of the closet. You have to suffer like the Catholics do, but with none of the incense or gold or velvets, none of the trappings of Christianity. Catholicism has art and music; it has a glamour. But some

Baptists are in a tent next to a river, hootin' and hollerin' and speaking in tongues. It's really dry. Nothing graceful about it, nothing to recommend it. Yeah, my father was descended from hardworking, simple people. Farmers.

I bonded with him really intensely. I adopted his mannerisms, including the swearing. Some of his friends were really bad swearers. They were jazz musicians, had drugs, you know, the whole culture of "we're so tough." What my dad was going through was a manifestation of pain. I don't want to perpetuate that crapola now. It was something about being tough. In order to be close to him I had to be tough and not girlie. I would like to shed aspects of that.

There was a lot more laughter in my mom's family. More physical affection, but plenty of alcoholism and some tragedies. It was not as dry and uptight as my father's experience. My mother's mother would say "Horseshit." Or "Jesus, Mary and Joseph!" Or "For the love of Mike!"

She was Irish. I guess in those days people didn't swear as much. Maybe they would just get drunk and beat each other up. Her husband, my grandfather, was Polish. He would say, "Hunchback Jesus on a unicycle!" It was like saying, "Holy Jesus!" He was a man of few words and would bust out with this stuff once in a while.

I'd say I swear once or twice a day. It's a tie between shit and fucking. I think my swearing is happening naturally, but the minute it's out of my mouth I sometimes feel really self-conscious. I feel as if I'm putting on an act or something. Like I'm trying to punctuate what I'm saying, trying to convey the intensity of my feelings. If I were more articulate, I could express what I'm saying without swearing. If I could do that, it would be nice. I think if I tried I could completely eliminate swearing, but it's not my top priority right now, although it's probably linked with my top priorities in a way I don't realize.

When I'm furious, I'll use words like motherfucking. Words like that make me feel I'm confirming the righteousness of my anger.

I'm usually not bursting out at someone directly. I'm talking to a third party. By swearing when I tell a story, I think I'm trying to encourage others to get just as angry as I am, hoping I'll get more sympathy.

I don't think enormous outbursts really solve things. I have this one relative who has been irritating me. When I talk to him on the phone, I think everything's fine. Then afterwards when I'm talking to my friends, I find myself calling him a fucking asshole. I am trying to release something, but I don't think it works very well. I just end up replaying a tape in my head, and maybe swearing about it makes me angry all over again. The language itself might be contributing to the anger. Maybe there is a connection there. Because I basically really love this person. I had to be driven very far to call him an asshole.

I remember someone visiting his household once who said "I was p-o-ed . . ." at their dinner table during a birthday party. And this relative's wife stopped the party and said, "We don't use those terms in this household." I guess he married someone just like himself. But I hear his mother was a very dried up and bitter and difficult woman. Maybe that's why he's supercontrolled. I have never seen anyone so unflappable. I remember his daughter telling me that she saw him do something out of control only once. She said, "Right after his father died he did this really weird thing. While he was packing, he ate an entire bag of miniature pretzels." And that is the most out of control he's ever been! He's into math and numbers and finances, that kind of thing. Maybe that explains it. Can you imagine if eating pretzels was the most out of control thing you'd ever done?

I think swearing can be unfeminine. Sometimes it's an affectation for a woman, like it makes her look tough and gritty and sexy. A young female attorney at the library where I work is the most obnoxious woman. She's young, thin, attractive, like a cheerleader. But she acts like a guy, you know, she's strident, she yells, she curses, she talks about how she wants to make the opposing counsel cry. It's all an act.

You can tell when people are comfortable with swearing. If the people around me are doing it, I will sometimes join in to try to assimilate. To connect. It might seem as if the people who don't swear are just boring people, but there are plenty of people who do swear who are completely boring. If I meet people like that now, I just go the other way.

There was a brief embarrassing interlude in my life when I was into pro wrestling. All that the fans of pro wrestling seem to do is drink and swear and watch wrestling. It was just a whole persona they cultivated. They'd sit around watching monster trucks, which is one rung below pro wrestling. They'd say, "Watch that pussy roll." I hate men who call things pussy. I totally think the world is full of these people who work in mundane jobs. They are maintaining whatever it takes to keep the stupid job. Then at night they go out and get drunk and become completely out of control. "The real me finally gets to come out" kind of thing. And you wouldn't want to know them at all.

Posers are, you know, people who are thinking they are so cool. When I was in high school, I wanted to get into broadcasting. I was an intern at one of the local radio stations. And there were these DJs and DJ hangers-on. They thought they were somehow in the music world, but they were just on the outer rings of the music business, and they thought they were so hot. Of course they would swear constantly, always trying to be supercool and telling these really rude jokes. "Why don't you come in here and take some dicktation." Or "Wanna see my tattoo?"

One of my friends worked there, too, and she swore like a sailor. I know she slept with at least one of the DJs. Some of those guys had these huge inflated opinions of themselves for being on the radio, you know. They were maintaining this facade of "we're so cool, we're such cutting-edge men." It was a persona they had to maintain. Or maybe that's who they really were. Maybe there was nothing more to them than all that swearing and being cool.

You know what I think it is? I think swearing is a really primitive attempt to take control of a situation. I remember in summer camp when I was 10 or 11. Swearing was the law of the jungle. You had to be tough or you'd be ripped to shreds. It's so weird. There are certain things we don't grow out of. And Lord of the Flies is one of them. That book is real.

Did I use the F word with the opposite sex in high school? I didn't even know the opposite sex in high school. I was totally innocent then. I didn't look innocent. I had a black crew cut and a mohawk. I was trying so very hard. I know you'd never believe it now, I look so wholesome and corn-fed. But one Christmas I decided I was just tired of who I'd been. I had been wearing my hair long and wavy and blond. I just cut it off. I got rid of all my preppy shirts and got my trenchcoat to try to look tough, and I cut my curls off and dyed my hair black. I was about 14 or 15 years old. I was so convinced of my ugliness and the idea that no one would want me or was going to like me, that I thought, "If they're not going to like me at least they'll respect me. Or fear me." It's terrible what we do to ourselves. I don't know what triggered the black hair all of a sudden. I guess I wasn't having enough fun. That was an intense swearing time for me as well. I remember telling my mother to "fuck off." My dad would fly into a rage whenever I swore at my mother. He could endure a lot of things, but not that. So I guess I had that power over him.

I would tend to say that my attitude toward swearing is indifferent, but in talking about it now . . . it's making me realize I like it a lot less than I thought. It's a very unattractive trait. It's a way of hurting people. And when I hear people swearing at each other in the street, I get scared. It sounds so angry. I think there is a connection between violence and swearing. If you grow up in an atmosphere where there's a lot of swearing, it's also an environment where there's a lack of respect. In that setting, a person with a wrong twist in them, or a predilection for it, could become violent.

FIVE
What You Say Is What You Are

BILL WORKS AS A security guard in a bank. One Saturday morning a suspicious-looking man walked in. He wore a shabby raincoat and an odd cap, even though it was a clear day and about sixty-five degrees outside. The man was black and appeared to be about 50 years old. Maybe a vagrant, Bill thought. He watched as the man helped himself to the coffee and cookies provided for customers. The man slowly paced through the bank, sipping his coffee, his eyes searching the lobby of the bank. He returned for another cup, then walked over to an unmanned customer service desk and sat down. Bill approached him.

"Good morning," Bill said. The man smiled and nodded his head, his mouth filled with hot coffee. "Are you here to do banking business?"

"Yes, I certainly am! I'll be making a deposit in my account momentarily," he said, with a cheery British accent. "I do hope you don't mind if I rest a bit. Is it inappropriate for me to be sitting here? I'm afraid I didn't notice any chairs available for visitors."

Bill was surprised by his accent and respectful manner. "No, you're okay here." Then, in an attempt to make conversation, he asked, "Have you been banking with us long?"

"Only about six weeks," the man replied. "I recently relocated from Miami. I'm the assistant librarian at the main library."

Just then Bill heard a disturbance at one of the teller stations. A smartly dressed and attractive young woman was speaking loudly and sternly to the teller. Bill heard her say, "It has to be a mistake by this goddam bank. It's not the first time you've fucked up my account."

Never judge a book by its cover, Bill thought to himself.

We all pass judgment on others, developing opinions based on what we see and assume. On the first encounter, we consider their physical appearance, clothes, body language, and even the kind of vehicle they arrived in. We have preconceived notions based on what we might know about a person—his or her gender, race, marital status, profession, hometown or neighborhood, and what others have told us.

It's frightening to realize we are judged right back, and equally frightening to know that we only get one chance to make a first impression.

As the preceding story illustrates, however, perceptions can be misconceptions. We've all heard the axiom that appearances can be deceiving. Most of us ignore this warning, claiming that our initial impression of people proves to be on target 95 percent of the time. But at what point do we form a sound opinion of someone? When are we convinced that we have a reasonably accurate reading on a person's character?

Our judgment only begins when someone briefs us on a person we are about to meet and takes shape when we see the person for the first time. But our various perceptions don't meld until after we have heard the person speak. What people say—and how they say it—is the determining factor in our view of them. Likewise, what we say is the determining factor in their view of us.

To prove the point, consider people you see but never hear. In pictures, for example. Lustful young men say they would not hesitate to hook up with any one of the beautiful models in the Victoria's Secret catalog or the sexy babes in *Playboy* magazine. Neither would lustful *old* men. They assume that attractive women have fabulous personalities, melodious voices, and sedate temperaments. They imagine that the only word these women ever say is yes.

Women are equally quick to assume perfection when a man has looks, presence, and signs of success. Try to recall every fairy tale you can that includes a handsome prince. Do you remember if the chap who kissed Sleeping Beauty ever said anything? Could it be that the prince searching for Cinderella had deep and disturbing secrets, like a foot fetish? Do we know for sure that Snow White's hero wasn't insanely jealous about her seven male roommates, all capable of looking up her skirt? Does it necessarily follow that the Queen's kid lived up to his name simply because she called him Charming instead of Charles? The creators of these dashing but dull fops didn't want to shatter the fantasy by giving them enough dialogue to reveal personalities of any kind.

A century or so ago, when people were even more apt to judge you on your station in life than they are today, speaking intelligently was a way for the poor folks to rise above their lowly status. Matronly ladies would respect a well-spoken lad, even a ragamuffin, and men in high positions would recognize his potential. Language was considered the social equalizer, the pathway from poverty to success.

Nowadays, language is still a social equalizer, but the highbrows speak the language of the lowlifes, rather than the reverse. Even the F word appears without shame in magazines such as the once venerable *New Yorker* and *Vanity Fair,* which profiles rich and famous people whom you might expect to have more elegant language.

"I never used bad language until I was in my fifties," laments Margaret, an active 78-year-old writer who has a master's degree in English literature. "I say *shit* more often than I care to. I picked it up from my children during the 1970s, when swearing became very much out in the open. They were young adults, and I guess I was trying to relate to them in a new way, to show them that I was hip. Now I'm stuck with this acrid word."

Police officers feel they need to talk rough street talk to let the thugs know that they mean business. Some college professors freely use *damn, hell, pissed,* and a smattering of other borderline bad words in and out of the classroom. Coaches scream profanities at their players with the assumption that it motivates them. Strangers in a bar strike up a conversation and let the cuss words flow like beer on tap. Everyone at all levels speaks the same language.

They might be succeeding in a misguided approach to be intelligible, but it doesn't promote the perception that they are intelligent. Cops run the risk that the general public will view them as former thugs themselves, randomly recruited off the street, sent to the police academy, and handed a uniform, a badge, and a license to carry firearms.

When I was appointed the chief of police, I made it my policy that members of the force were not permitted to swear while on duty. I always felt that police officers, as professionals and public servants, should not stoop to the lowest level. Some would tell me it was necessary to swear to secure compliance, but in rough situations, a gun and the tone of your voice is all you need when you tell someone to put their hands in the air.

TV programs and movies do not accurately portray life on the police force, but some officers want to behave like Clint Eastwood's Dirty Harry. They wouldn't swear in an affluent area, and it is equally inappropriate for them to swear when dealing with people of a lower-income status. Respect is one of my tenets, and we are to treat everyone with equal dignity and respect.

—Goliath J. Davis III, Chief of Police, St. Petersburg, Florida,
in an interview for this book

Our culture emphasizes looks over language. Once we are out of school, no one pressures us to expand our vocabulary or to mind our grammar. We are guided by the style gods, convinced that sharp-looking clothes with the brand name prominently displayed say more about us than we could ever verbalize.

Looks are critical for the formation of a favorable image, whether they are natural or manufactured. We have beauty products to highlight our best features and hide our bad ones, tinted contacts for our eyes and caps for our teeth, hair removers for women and hair restorers for men, liposuction and facial contouring for both, health clubs and exercise videos, breast implants and Wonder bras, and a host of other tricks that almost match the artistry of airbrushing and computer-enhanced imaging.

But wait! Despite all the get-buff-and-beautiful quick tricks, most of us don't have the time, money, energy, or bodily basics to look beautiful. We don't qualify, and neither do most of our friends, relatives, and neighbors. The fact is, even if you happen to be a Brad Pitt look-alike or a dead ringer for Claudia Schiffer, the initial attention you get will dwindle quickly if you have a sour attitude and a trashy mouth to go with it.

BEAUTIES CAN BE BEASTS

Most of us rely on our personalities to find friends, jobs, and lovers. Our personality is quickly revealed through the words we use, our vocal volume, the tone of our voice, our expression, and our ability to connect with the people to whom we speak.

Unfortunately, most of us receive no formal training in this area. It's supposed to be common sense. Manners and etiquette, which include how we speak to each other, are conventions we develop with input from our parents—if we have a complete set and choose to listen to them. As we pass through the maturing years, we also learn from teachers, from friends, and from occasionally putting our foot in our mouth.

Boys have always been slower in this arena, often badgered for being crude clods, but girls are sinking to the traditional male level. Institutions once known as finishing schools for young ladies are, well, finished. Charm schools are also part of history.

Dorothy Shreve, who has operated a number of charm and modeling schools in Southern California, says teenage girls are so eager to become models that they insist on taking the quick course. "They don't even want to take the time to learn how to walk," Dorothy says. "They don't even know what charm means."

If their modeling career never takes off, most of them no longer have the residual benefit of style, manners, and presence formerly stressed by training schools.

If both genders fail to learn as youngsters, it is up to them to decide how to talk and behave as adults. By the time they are in their early twenties, the only person nagging them is likely to be a boyfriend or girlfriend, and many find it easier to find new partners who don't sound like their mothers. No one likes being told how to behave.

When it comes to cursing, constructive criticism is not only unwelcome, it's not taken seriously. "I can control it when I have to," is the usual assertion. "I only swear around people who aren't bothered by it." But how do they know who is bothered by it and who isn't, and how can they tell who accepts it and who merely tolerates it, if no one ever calls them on it or voices a complaint?

Men's Health magazine reported back in 1996 that 81 percent of women cite vulgar language as the biggest turnoff in a man. This statistic has to be a surprise for most men, especially the X-generation gents who assume women's language isn't much better. They remain oblivious, perpetuating their stereotype as insensitive louts. In all likelihood, a survey of men would probably find that they are just as turned off by women whose language is excessively vulgar.

"I was at a busy hotel bar by myself, when I spotted a good-looking lady at the other end of the bar," says John, a 42-year-old bachelor. "She was with another woman. I went to the bathroom, but just so I could come back and sit closer to them without being too obvious. Up close, she was even prettier than she was from fifty feet away. But then I heard her conversation. She said *fuck* four or five times in less than a minute. I use that word myself, but I don't like hearing a pretty woman talk the way I do. It's stupid of me, because at least we had that in common! But I didn't like it. I moved back to where I had been sitting."

Profanity is so pervasive that, in most cases, the listeners use the same words as the talkers, and the negative impact is likely to be minimal, if it exists at all. Yet, if you swear openly, you have no way of knowing how many opportunities to make a new friend you might have squelched, or how often you alienated someone or lost a degree of respect through your lackadaisical use of foul language.

Peter, an advertising copywriter, is an unabashed curser and says everyone swears at the agency where he works, both the men and the women.

"The only thing that bothers me is the boss swearing," he says. "It doesn't seem right, maybe because he's in his fifties and everyone else is like 35 or younger. He should be setting an example or something. I bet if he didn't swear, you'd hear a lot less swearing from everybody else."

You might be convinced that your moderate use of profanity goes unnoticed because you captivate people with your personal magnetism, your jovial manner, your magical charisma. You might be right, but you might not see yourself as others do.

Shawn was a successful salesman who took it upon himself to be the life of every party. At six-foot-three and barrel-chested, he stood out in a crowd. He supplemented his physical presence with a strong voice and hearty laugh. More than once, at gatherings where the guests knew him well, he would burst on the scene and shout, "Let the madness begin!" He made the rounds, somehow managing to speak to everyone he knew and to meet those he didn't. He always had something to say. If he encountered a quiet group of men or women who appeared bored with themselves, he would entertain them with the latest joke. More often than not, the jokes were tasteless, but the way he told them and his own infectious laughter seemed to make it acceptable. If he wasn't one of the last to leave, he practically announced his imminent departure as if to signal that the party might just as well be over.

Because of his excellent track record in sales, his company transferred him to a region on the opposite side of the country that needed to be rejuvenated. He was replaced by Martin, a straitlaced but knowledgeable salesman who had worked for a competitor.

"I understand I have a tough act to follow," Martin said when he called on one of Shawn's largest customers.

"Shawn was okay, but sometimes I gave him an order just to shut him up and get him out the door," said the customer.

At sales meetings and in informal chats with other sales personnel, Martin learned more about what others thought of Shawn.

"The guy came on like a steamroller. I think he demanded that customers buy from him."

"At conventions and social events, he really was the life of the party, but I'm glad he is gone. He dominated the room, and took charge of every conversation. Everyone seemed to like him, so I guess I never wanted to admit that he annoyed me."

"It was so nervy of him to tell dirty jokes to us," said one woman. "I laughed to be polite, but now I regret that I never told him he was out of line. Someone should have taken him aside and clued him in, but he probably never would have listened."

A colleague agreed. "Half the time that he bragged about getting sales, he would insult his customers in the crudest way, saying things like, 'I got that guy's pecker in my pocket,' or 'He's such a wimp, I think he squats to piss.' Speaking of a very dignified woman customer, he said, 'I've got her tits in the ringer and I'm reaming her up the rear.' It was hypocritical, and you wondered what he said about you behind your back."

"I always felt sorry for his wife," said a secretary in the sales department. "He flirted with all the women, thinking they all loved him. I thought he was a big-mouthed scum."

So Shawn went on to a new challenge, happy with himself and building sales in his new territory, unaware of the impressions he left behind.

Without question, Shawn had strengths that kept him going and overshadowed his boorish behavior. But not everyone can get away with crudities. He had a presence that demanded attention, but most people are far less dynamic. Shawn could cuss in a clever way, always with a big smile, while others lacked his ability to pull it off.

"I was a pretty popular guy in college, always joking around, but when I joined the corporate world, I was afraid I'd have to be real proper," recalls Jason. "But Shawn was totally uninhibited. I liked his style, and he was a leader and a top sales guy, so I tried to be like him. I thought everyone wanted to be like him, but they just didn't have it in them, but I did. After he left, I began to realize that he was an anomaly. Everyone else was very businesslike, and became more so when Shawn wasn't there to influence them to act differently. At first I tried to be his replacement, but I caught on quickly that no one wanted him replaced. I picked a bad role model."

HAVING CHARACTER OR BEING ONE

Another sad reality is that our society seems to prefer people who are characters rather than have character. We want to be entertained, to hear gossip, to witness others defying rules that we are afraid to break. Men and women with character are admired but considered bland. They do what they are supposed to do, stay cool-headed, and mind their manners. Typically, they don't even swear.

A young man wrote to an advice columnist about a woman he loved and wanted to marry. The woman was torn between him, an honest and hardworking guy on a career track, and a volatile ne'er-do-well whose affection for her was as unstable as his job history and mental condition.

Finally she chose the other guy and told her lovelorn second choice that, if she was ever in need, she knew she could count on him. Why, he wanted to know, would she consider him second choice when she knew he would be far more devoted and reliable?

Some women prefer the excitement of the unpredictable, the columnist answered. For what it was worth, she added that women who go the route of the lout often regret it later.

Both men and women with character have the satisfaction of knowing they are doing the right thing, but they must avoid being sanctimonious. Fortunately, people with character usually have the maturity to avoid boasting about their diction and conduct.

The nonconformists and rule breakers prefer to be in the limelight. They take pride in their flippant or defiant attitude and are more concerned about impressing people with their outrageous behavior. They flaunt their audacity and push the limits on what they can get away with. They are rebels, and they dare to be different, and for that they are often admired.

One of the most visible rebels with an attitude in the 1990s was basketball player Dennis Rodman, who frequently got in scuffles on the court, was ejected for unsportsman-like conduct, missed games for unexplained reasons, swore in public rallies, and even wrote a biography proudly titled *Bad As I Wanna Be.* He was an example of a manufactured personality, from the rainbow hair to the cross-dressing to his brief marriage to Carmen Electra. His antics and his verbal attacks on his own teammates got him kicked off the Los Angeles Lakers shortly after he joined the team, ending his basketball career.

The opposite of Dennis Rodman was his teammate on the Chicago Bulls, Michael Jordan. There was nothing boring about Michael. Which one gets the prize as the best role model?

You can create or fake a Bad Boy attitude without too much effort, but building character requires real work, sacrifices, and self-control. If you believe it takes guts to buck the trend and defy popular conventions, you're right, and that's exactly what people with character and principles have to do.

> *I've smoked since I was 12, but dammit, I want to breathe in my lifetime once. Then I'll get rid of cussing, and I'll be done. . . . I just want to get rid of all the bad things. Cussing is really addictive. . . . I'm sick of being a smoking, drinking, cussing . . . of being that person that everyone says, "Yeah, there she is."*
>
> —Actress, singer-guitarist Courtney Love, interviewed by
> *Chicago Tribune* rock critic Greg Kot, May 20, 1999

THE TOP TEN REASONS TO STOP

Are you getting the point here? Does it make sense yet?

It all boils down to one thing: *What kind of person do you want to be?*

Forget rich, gorgeous, and talented for a moment, and focus on your basic character. Do you want to be known as someone who is thoughtful or thoughtless? Hospitable or hostile? Kind or cruel? Accommodating or intimidating? Cultured or crude? Mannered or macho?

The choice is yours. You can still strive to be rich, but it takes hard work. You can exercise every day to develop the perfect body, but it requires time and discipline, just as it does to nurture and refine a talent. There are hurdles and outside forces that challenge you on the road to achieving what you want in life, and you might need help along the way. But after a certain age, anywhere between 13 and 21, you alone become responsible for your character. Why not put some energy into becoming a nice person? It's not that difficult, it's admirable, and it's gratifying. It is also a quality that you can hold on to easier than talent, looks, and money.

Cut the cussing and the tasteless language, and there's a good chance that you will:

1. Sound more intelligent.

More often than not, nonswearers don't just seem smart, they are smart. You can be among their ranks by talking in a simple, direct manner.

You don't need to use ten-dollar words to sound intelligent. Compare "I suspect that Bill doesn't have all the information he needs to make that decision" with "Bill is a stupid bastard who will fuck it up because he doesn't know shit." Who's the stupid one?

2. Communicate more clearly.

What does it mean to say something looks like shit? Suppose you are talking about a house. Is it brown? Poorly designed? In need of paint? In disrepair? If you refer to someone as an asshole, will others know what you mean? Is that person loud and obnoxious? Dishonest? A bully? Irresponsible? A women hater? Be specific, especially if you are trying to alert others to keep him out of your fifty-minute car-pool trip.

3. Be more pleasant.

Coarse language doesn't sound nice. Any argument with this one? You might be used to hearing it, but if you think about it, words that represent body waste and violent sex acts are harsh and bitter. Besides, people who swear often tend to be disagreeable, critical, cynical, angry, argumentative, and unhappy complainers. If you don't enjoy being with people who are sour-sounding sad sacks, don't be one yourself.

4. Have greater control of your emotions.

Nonswearers are often calm, rational, mature people who control their anger and deal with daily annoyances. Cursing doesn't make the traffic go away, the waitress move faster, or the spilled milk dry up. Don't blame others or curse about your bad luck. Learn how to deal with the matters that make you swear.

5. Avoid offending others.

Your friends might speak the same lewd language as you, but others overhear you, like a friend's wife or husband, his or her children, the new secretary, the women at the next table, whomever. If you don't care, that says something about you that's not very admirable. Maybe you aren't a complete turnoff, but there are people who won't appreciate you because of your foul mouth.

6. Earn more respect.

For starters, if you do items 1 through 5, you will earn respect. Reflect on the people in your life whom you admire, and list their best qualities. If they swear, more than likely you are a little disappointed that they do. If you are in any sort of leadership position—a parent, a teacher, a coach, a police officer, a supervisor—people will expect your behavior and manner to be bit superior to theirs. Even your younger brother or sister expects more of you.

7. Improve your relationships.

Maybe swearing does make you one of the "guys," but ask yourself if a toilet tongue has done anything to improve some of your more important relationships, like with your parents, your spouse, or your children. How about with your supervisor, or with his or her boss, who might have a better job for someone with a mature, can-do attitude? Or your fellow workers, or your customers? If you think your swearing isn't a problem with anyone, ask yourself if your relationships could, perchance, be even better if you didn't swear.

8. Avoid conflict and hostility.

When you disagree with individuals, you are challenging their judgment and questioning their intelligence. You have to argue rationally and diplomatically to win them over to your way of thinking. Maybe you haven't had much luck with "You're full of shit!" Or maybe you tried "For God's sake, pull your head out of your ass and see the light." If neither approach worked, or resulted in a bloody nose, try Plan B next time.

9. Be a happy person.

Are you cussing because you are crabby? Is your job or your entire life miserable? Change what you can, and try to accept what you can't. Often, the trick is to change your attitude. If you hate serving customers, challenge yourself to make them happy, and their gratitude will cheer you up. If you think people don't like you because you are unattractive, develop a cheerful, attractive personality. Everyone has problems, but look to the bright side.

10. Contribute to a better society.

The widespread use of profanity and vulgarity is a factor in the deterioration of civility, good manners, the English language, morality, and decency. Don't add to the slop. Do the opposite. Consider it your responsibility as a citizen to do your part to clean up the verbal environment. You will feel better about yourself, and other people will feel better about you, too. Besides, it's something you can do by yourself that is easier than trying to solve the drug problem, end violence, prevent child abuse, or save the world.

Points to Ponder

- The way we speak can determine who our friends will be, the amount of respect we will get from our families and coworkers, the quality of our relationships, how influential we will be, whether we get the job or the promotion, and how strangers respond to us. Other than that, it doesn't matter.
- It's not just the words you say, but how you say them. Be nice.
- Not cussing won't necessarily help you become rich and successful or good-looking, but the top ten reasons for cutting your cussing might strike you as having real value and meaning. Review them again.
- The best way to know if your family and closest friends think your language is sometimes offensive, or that it reflects an unpleasant negative attitude, is to ask them for an honest assessment.

TWENTY-FIVE REASONS TO STOP SWEARING

Cursing Imposes a Personal Penalty

It gives a bad impression.

It makes you unpleasant to be with.

It endangers your relationships.

It reduces respect people have for you.

It shows you don't have control.

It's the sign of a bad attitude.

It's a tool for whiners and complainers.

It discloses a lack of character.

It's immature.

It reflects ignorance.

It sets a bad example.

Cursing Corrupts the English Language

It's abrasive, lazy language.

It doesn't communicate clearly.

It's the sign of a weak vocabulary.

It neglects more meaningful words.

It lacks imagination.

It has lost its effectiveness.

It represents the dumbing down of America.

Cursing Is Bad for Society

It contributes to the decline of civility.

It offends more people than you think.

It makes others uncomfortable.

It is disrespectful of others.

It turns discussions into arguments.

It can be a sign of hostility.

It can lead to violence.

TIM WINTER, 29, INCARCERATED

I was 27 when I came to prison. Years earlier I was on medication for back pain and became addicted. My crime was repeatedly impersonating doctors on the phone, calling pharmacists to place prescriptions that I would pick up. I was a clean-cut, blond golf pro from a very upscale community on the North Shore of Chicago. I went to New Trier High School, one of the best high schools in the country. As soon as I was jailed, everybody came up to me wanting to be on my good side, but they all had a motive. They wanted things I could buy for them from the commissary. In prison you almost starve, so food from the commissary was important. In exchange for my buying them things, they promised to protect me.

I work in the officers' kitchen cleaning up and serving. Each shift has about forty-five people, and I am one of the three white men. Most of the men in prison are black, and they all swear. They can hardly even speak. When they do speak, it's more like a grunting dog. They all speak in incomplete sentences, and the person who talks the loudest and swears the most is considered a leader, and that's the one that people respect the most. Even if I have good ideas, the other inmates are not interested unless I really raise my voice and talk really, really loudly. If I raise my voice and swear, people will say, "Yeah, yeah, you're right." If I just speak in my usual soft tones, nobody listens.

The inmates have no morals and no manners. They are very disrespectful to each other. The inmates swear out of anger and fear. They have a lack of education and don't really know other words to use. Their education ended abruptly, so they have no real language to draw on. They have a lot of deep-seated issues, and most of them are chemically dependent. Chemically dependent people need to be accepted. They all swear to fit in. So do I, but I have different words to describe things, they don't. People notice that I have proper language and they say how I talk is really good, but addicts have this acceptance issue, so after a while, I have to start talking like them.

There is no mental stimulation in prison. The weight room is a lot more popular than the library. Some people go to Bible study classes. Often, they go because their grandparents knew the Bible really well and had tried to teach them the gospel. They are really good at quoting the Bible, but they talk the talk, they don't walk the walk.

One of the worst parts about prison is the noise, because everyone talks so loudly. When people talk to you, they are demanding. People say, "Let me in with you." If you have something that they might want they say "gimme." No one asks for anything. There are no manners at all. They might say, "I'm gonna sit with you," not "May I sit with you?" They say what they want, and everything sounds like a stickup. "Gimme this, gimme that." Anyone with a clean mouth really doesn't get very far. It's really not a correctional facility, but a place where you become socially demented.

SIX

Why Don't These People Swear?

NANCY HAIMBAUGH, 50 SOMETHING,
ENTREPRENEUR, EMPLOYMENT COUNSELOR

I was a well-mannered, well-behaved little girl. I never thought of swearing because I didn't know most of the swear words. When my parents sent me to a boarding school in Wisconsin, I learned all the nasty words. We liked to say them as loud as we could without getting caught. When I went to college at Miami of Ohio, I stopped swearing. I left after two years and got married to a very traditional man. We lived in a traditional little town, and I was the model housewife. I was even named the Woman of the Year in our town, and the local newspaper did a beautiful full-page spread on me.

In the early 1970s, I decided to complete my college degree. I went to Northern Illinois University at the age of 31 and discovered a different world. Everyone smoked pot. Everyone supported a cause, and I became a big supporter of the women's liberation movement. I even went on marches in Springfield. I began to swear again, and often, believing that the curse words were harmless words that helped liberate me. I was angry, convinced that I had been living in a box under the control of a male-dominated world. My husband hated my swearing. He said his mother never swore, and he didn't respect any woman who used foul language. My response was, "I don't give a fuck."

I swore so freely around the house that I wasn't certain my kids could distinguish good words from dirty words. But somehow my 4-year-old son knew. I was in the kitchen and he came up to me with his cherublike face and said, "Mommy, I know you like to say fuck and that's okay, but my friend Johnny is coming over today, and his mommy doesn't like that word. Would you please not say that word in front of him?"

I suddenly realized all of the negative energy I had been generating. I gave him a great big hug, and that day began changing my language.

WES STRAUSBAUGH, 33, EXECUTIVE RECRUITER

I don't like the sound of swear words. What bothers me the most is when people say, "Oh, God." Sometimes I say to them, "You mean gosh." But I don't go around telling people not to swear. That doesn't fit my approach to people, which is to be nice to everyone. I don't care if he's a parking lot attendant or an executive I'm trying to recruit. Everyone has his or her own problems, so I smile and try to bring a brief moment of humor or joy into their lives.

I can't pinpoint my reason for avoiding curse words. I guess my Catholic upbringing has something to do with it. Maybe I swore when I was in grade school, but I don't remember. Did my parents swear? I don't know. I had a hard upbringing and have very little memory of my youth. I was adopted and raised in Savannah. Both my parents were alcoholics. They got divorced and both got remarried, and I didn't care for either my stepmother or stepfather. I went to an all-boys Catholic military school in Georgia because the military schools provide the best education in Georgia. I can't remember if the students swore very much.

I went to University of Georgia Southern on a football scholarship. After freshman year, I went with some friends to an audition being held by a modeling agency. We just wanted to meet girls, but we were told we couldn't stay unless we were there to audition. So I did and was signed up on the spot. I got jobs right away, and the agency sent me to Paris for two years. I did some modeling in the Orient, and in New York. I stopped modeling when I was 23.

Everyone gets mad once in a while, including me, but anger isn't part of my nature. I have a good disposition, which I guess I was born with. I was always hyper, moving around, doing things. There's not much for me to get mad about. I don't drive, so I'm never stuck in traffic. If I go to a restaurant and there's a long line, I just go somewhere else. I get frustrated more often than angry, like when a deal falls through. I take a deep breath and relax.

The truth is, I don't consciously do anything to overcome frustration and avoid swearing. I don't think about these things. Do I ever say damn? I don't know. Damn. *I don't know. I really don't know.*

FLINT COFFEY, 59, BUILDING MAINTENANCE MAN

I grew up in the rural community of Pulaski, Tennessee. My parents never swore. I had a few uncles that swore, but most people didn't swear. We had a lot of respect for our parents, and what they taught us stuck. In high school, nobody swore very much. I remember my grandparents saying dangnabit, *and* ijax. *I didn't know what those words meant, but I thought they must have been cuss words.*

We didn't have any racial problems where I lived. The schools and restaurants were segregated, but all the black kids and the white kids played together. When the schools decided to integrate in 1959, we just did it. There weren't any problems. It wasn't an enforced integration, and it didn't need to be. Everyone was told that they could switch to another school if they wanted to.

I moved to Chicago when I was 18. I didn't like the big city, so I moved to the northern suburb of Glencoe. I was married, had kids, and usually worked two jobs. I worked with a crew laying concrete for remodeling projects and home additions. Some of the guys had terrible language, with every other word a cuss word. It didn't bother me much, but sometimes I would tell them to keep it down in front of the owners of the homes where we were working. They would be so loud, and so insensitive.

I'm a big guy, but I'm like a teddy bear. I don't think I ever get angry. If I start to, I just turn around and it's gone. I feel that life is a blessing, and if I spend a day angry, I'll miss out on that day.

Sometimes I get irritated in traffic, but then I say to myself, that's the way it's meant to be. Some guy might honk at me and give me the finger, but he drives on and I forget about it.

I guess I'm lucky that I've never lived any place where people would hassle me. I am easygoing, I like to smile a lot and be friendly to people. They sense that right away. When I was in high school, I was part of a program working with the grade school kids. I really enjoyed that. There would always be a crowd of kids around me. Years later, when I would go back to Tennessee, everybody knew me or remembered me and wanted to say "hello." That made me feel good.

I have had some bad times, but I believe that God doesn't put more on a man than he can bear. When my wife was pregnant with our fourth child, she told me she wanted to go home. I thought she meant for a week or two, but she began packing up everything. Her parents never thought I was good enough for her, and they had convinced her to come home. We got divorced, but I used to drive all the way to Tennessee on the weekends. I think we still managed to raise great kids.

A couple of years ago, my youngest daughter died after an epileptic fit. She was married with two kids, but she was always working hard. I guess she wasn't taking her medicine properly. It was hard on me, but you have to accept what happens to you in life.

I remain cheerful, and I am not phony about it. Some guys don't like to smile and shake your hand, but I always do. I can get people to warm up. Lots of people in my neighborhood take their kids on vacation during the holidays and spring break, but some of the older teenagers want to stay home. Friends will ask me to stay with the kids, and they like it when I do. I don't let them get away with things they are not supposed to do, yet they like having me around.

I guess I am lucky to have a good disposition, but I just don't understand why some people are always angry, or do things like hold a grudge. Life's too short.

TONY KOSCHMAN, 19, COLLEGE STUDENT

My family moved from Orlando, Florida, to New Hampshire when I was 12. In high school, lots of the teenagers swore as if it was common language. They wouldn't give any thought or meaning to the words. It seemed inappropriate to me. The girls weren't as bad, but when they were in groups or cliques, the language was slanderous.

I go to a small college in a small town. Some students swear, some don't. Some do it for no reason, as if they don't understand what they are saying. But I heard a guy and his girlfriend fighting in the hall one night, and it upset me. It wasn't just the bad language, but the intensity. When I hear something like that, I get concerned about the outcome, the emotional stress, crying, that sort of thing. Maybe it would get physical. It really bothers me.

I prefer not to swear. I try not to, but I do once in a while. A few weeks ago we were playing touch football, and I kept dropping passes. One time I said the F word. It just came out.

I chose not to swear when I was a kid. My parents told me not to, but they were pretty lenient. They taught me other principles and ideals that probably influenced me more. I also learned a lot about how to live through the Boy Scouts. I started as a Cub Scout when I was 5, and eventually became an Eagle Scout. So did my brother. I've heard that only two or three scouts out of every hundred become Eagle Scouts. Most of the boys drop out before they get to the stage where they have a chance to become Eagle Scouts.

I was also in Police Explorers when I was in high school. I also participated in Granite State College, sort of a Jeopardy game sponsored by New Hampshire and shown on cable TV. I think I always tried my best as a student. I passed, I graduated.

PENNY CURRIER, 45, PROFESSIONAL HARPIST AND FORMER MISS AMERICA CONTESTANT

I didn't have much exposure to swearing in my upbringing, so when I hear it on the streets and buses in Chicago, I'm appalled.

It's as if our young people don't seem to understand the definition of the foul language they're using or that they simply enjoy the coarse sound of it. Maybe their habit of swearing impairs their ability to think of legitimate words to describe anything.

When I hear profanity, it's like someone smacking me on the back of the head. It's so offensive. I remember watching the first episodes of the TV show NYPD Blue *when I heard the word ass-hole. I couldn't believe I was hearing it on television. Fast-forward a few short years, and you can hear profane words on so many of the programs.*

I was raised in a suburb of Denver, Colorado. My father was both an attorney and an engineer, and my mother was a legal secretary and homemaker. They never swore, and it was not allowed in our home. If any of us seven children used a bad word, they would correct it on the spot, so swear words never passed through my lips. I was a music major at the Eastman School of Music at the University of Rochester in New York. I played the harp, violin, and piano. Eastman was very strict, very intense, very serious and disciplined and so were the students for the most part. I don't remember anyone swearing much.

When I was 22 and had my degree, I achieved a childhood dream of becoming Miss Colorado and participating in the Miss America Pageant. It was 1975, and I enjoyed a year of travel and appearances of speaking and performing on the harp. I was admired and always treated with respect by men and women as I traveled the state. When I arrived in Atlantic City for the Miss America Pageant, it was—wow! The women were so accomplished, I couldn't think about competing with them. I simply concentrated on doing my personal best in each category. I think every girl took the same approach, because they were all friendly. When the top ten were announced on live television, I was just as disappointed as the other girls who lost, but no one was cursing backstage after they were cut. Some were only 18 or 19, but they were all mature, polite, gracious women. They didn't get there on beauty alone.

Since then I have been enjoying my career as a professional solo harpist performing at parties, corporate events, and weddings. I wear a long flowing gown and project an angelic image. It's important for me to maintain a dignified presence at all times. When I take a break, I can't go to the bar and order a beer. Most of my work is at formal events for sophisticated people, so it's rare for anyone to say vulgar things in front of me. I recently performed at a large hotel for a corporate reception that was mostly men, and the group's conversation at the nearest table was F this and F that. I thought, come on, guys, I'm not deaf. But they were just businessmen trying to be relaxed and less formal with each other.

I never used swear words until I started working. Like everyone else, I have pressures and sometimes difficult clients who upset me, but the only swearing I do out loud is within the walls of my home. I consciously try never to swear in public. It's ugly and it's ignorant.

TONY SCOTT, 47, SOUP KITCHEN OPERATOR

I have been operating the Good News soup kitchen for eight years. It's affiliated with the Good News Church next door, and I go there. I'm not a Holy Roller or anything, but I know God wants me to be a good person. I swear now and then, but sometimes I apologize even when no one's around. When I hear people swearing around the church or around my kitchen, I ask them not to. People have learned that I'm here to help them, not hurt them.

Most people who come here are polite and grateful, but I do get troublemakers. Sometimes they've been drinking. I have to ask them to leave, or I throw them out, or call the police. I've even gone to court to get restraining orders to keep some from coming back.

One time I had a lady come into my kitchen who was cursing at everybody. I had to put her out. She kept cussing, and I said, "You're being ugly, and God doesn't like ugly." Just then she slipped, right in front of the church, and fell on a broken bottle and cut her hand. She looked at the church, then looked at me, as if she knew God was punishing her. It was just a coincidence, but she behaved herself for about two months. Then she was back at it again.

I grew up in Chicago, where you have to learn to take care of yourself. When someone would confront me, I would puff up and not back down. If you show you are weak, they go after you. But I never did much cursing. Cursing only makes matters worse, and usually a fight comes next. I've seen it happen.

I never swore until I was a teenager. It started off as a game. One guy would see how many curse words he could say in a minute, then the next guy would do it.

I don't get angry very often, but when I do, it's usually at myself, not other people. When I see other people get angry, I think it's humorous. You know, it's like when someone slips and falls. You laugh, but you wouldn't laugh if you were the one falling.

I get annoyed at people when I'm driving, but I know no one intentionally gets in my way. Their mind is on other things, or they're just not thinking. I do it myself. Sometimes, someone will flip me off and honk at me and I just honk back and laugh.

WENDY LEMAN, 27, EDUCATIONAL CONSULTANT

I grew up in Granite Bay, California, north of Sacramento. My mother swore once in a while, but not as much as my father. He only swore when he got angry, and it scared me. I was probably more upset from the anger, but he was responsive because he wanted to stop. We made a deal that he would give me a quarter every time I heard him curse. I made him give me a dollar when he said the F word, because I didn't like that word at all. One day we got in an argument and he swore at me, and I said, "You owe me a dollar-fifty for that one." It had an impact. He never swore at me again, but he never paid me either!

I don't use curse words because I feel it's not effective. My parents didn't raise me with any specific religious beliefs, but I used to go to church with my friends, no matter what religion they were. I wanted to know who God was. I always liked church, and today I go to a nondenominational church.

I remember the first time I swore. I was in sixth grade, at the swing set during recess. I forget the specific situation—I think I swore at another girl for taking my turn. What I recall is saying to myself, that was dumb. Instead of getting my way, I alienated the other girl. I realized, even at that age, that trying to be mean or threatening doesn't accomplish much.

Kids swore all the time at my high school. The boys more than the girls, I'd say. The kids from wealthier families were just as bad as the kids at the other end of the scale, with maybe less swearing among the average-income students. The fact that I was a non-swearer probably went unnoticed because I didn't make an issue of it. I knew lots of different people because I was involved in swimming, gymnastics, cheerleading, drama, and other things. No one ever commented on my reluctance to swear.

I've made a choice about my language and about my lifestyle, and other people make whatever choice is right for them. I do notice when people unconsciously pepper their sentences with swear words. I wouldn't hold it against them, but I don't enjoy it either. It's important to remember that words have whatever meanings we give to them.

I also notice when people are angry. Anger isn't a bad thing; it's what you do when you're angry that can be destructive. I say that I'm angry, or why I'm angry. Other people swear, thinking it is a quick route to let someone know how mad they are, but I don't like the message it sends. It's linked to false power, or an effort to exert power. Sometimes it's a way to show off, yet I consider it ineffective. There are so many other verbs and adjectives to use.

I got mad at work the other day. I was on the phone, and when I hung up, I said out loud, "I can't believe he did it again!" My coworkers laughed, and one said, "I never heard you talk like that before." It must have been the tone of my voice, because I didn't *swear. I try to be patient, and I'm naturally even tempered, but everybody has moments or experiences when they are completely frustrated or impatient. I find that expressing my feelings and making them particular to the situation helps other people understand me better.*

If you asked me, "Do you ever want to swear?" the answer would be, yes, sometimes. People curse all the time—casually in their speech, in anger, at God. It seems to empower them in some way. At some level, we all want power and control over our circumstances. I'm no different. I don't like it when I swear and on the occasions that I do, it's usually alone and when I'm at my wit's end. In those situations I pray and collect my thoughts—reminding myself that focusing on the situation and not cursing it will ultimately resolve whatever has transpired.

JIUN HO, 26, INTERIOR DESIGN CONSULTANT

When I left Malaysia to attend college in the United States, I didn't speak any English. I learned very quickly that swearing was part of the English language, but I didn't like it. Both my parents were schoolteachers, and swearing was not allowed in our home. Even when I was upset, these words would not come to my mind. Mandarin, my language, does not have many swear words. Several of the languages in Malaysia have no such words. When I was a teenager, the students who spoke Cantonese would swear occasionally. Cantonese and Mandarin are the same in writing but pronounced completely different.

I studied design in Chicago, then got a job in San Francisco for a company that designed interiors for hotels around the world. Many of the people I worked with were from other countries, mostly Asian, and I didn't hear much swearing from them.

Many of the American friends I have made in the San Francisco area work in computer technology firms. They work hard, are under pressure, and swear a lot. I am surprised, though, at how often they swear when they are not angry or frustrated. They don't consider it bad or impolite. The words just come out. I still get offended and uncomfortable. I tell them to excuse their language, and some don't care. Others try not to swear in front of me, or change the pronunciation, like friggin'. To me, it's the same.

I'm getting used to it now. I hear it so much, that sometimes when I'm upset I will swear, but I feel bad that I do.

JAMES MACK, 69, MUSICIAN AND MUSIC INSTRUCTOR

English is a great language. I love words and always have. I still remember many of the poems I was required to memorize at the Corpus Christi Catholic School I attended in Chicago. Even as a child, I was fascinated with the sound and the flow and the way the words worked together. I also studied Latin and was translating Caesar's Gallic Wars into English while in grade school.

I developed an appreciation for etymology, and even when I am teaching music, I explain the roots of words and their related words to students. I have no trouble communicating my thoughts in standard English. If I want to emphasize a point or show strength, I can speak in sharp, biting English in a very low voice and still be effective.

I would like to say that there is a philosophical, noble reason or a significant lesson I learned in life that prevents me from using bad language, but there isn't. I just don't do it. I never did. I never in my life heard my mother say "damn." She didn't preach to me about language but did want me to be polite and proper. I always said yes, ma'am, or thank you, sir. To this day, I still open doors for women and take off my hat indoors. I discourage my students from wearing hats in class.

Although my family lived on the south side of Chicago, I went to St. Phillip's Catholic High School at Kedzie and Jackson. St. Phillip's recruited me and several other black students. I took a test, passed, and got in. I was there in the 1940s. Everyone was very polite. There was never a single fight. Throughout my youth, I don't remember being exposed to much swearing.

Everyone was always very nice to me, and I don't remember even once being the victim of a racial insult. Personally, I could never direct an insulting remark to anyone. I love people and I love life.

I think I am constitutionally unable to hate. During the war, people hated the Germans because of Hitler. When I thought of Germans, I thought of Mozart, Brahms, Bach, Beethoven—all of the other great German composers. How could I possibly hate them? The same with the Jews. They have contributed so much to society.

Throughout college and my army years, I don't remember being exposed to much swearing. I received a grant from the Ford Foundation to study music at the University of Chicago. When I was in the army, I played in a band, and remained stateside.

I guess I send vibes that make people want to be nice to me. It's my style, my manner. I'm always upbeat. I don't think about negatives, even illness. Years ago, during my early involvement with the recording industry, everyone smoked pot. Each person would take a drag and then pass it to the next person, but they always skipped over me. Nobody said anything, they just knew that I didn't want to participate.

Everyone was on a first name basis, too, but they referred to me as "Mr. Mack." I said, "Why don't you call me Jim?" and they would say it just didn't sound right. No one would ever claim that I am stiff and formal, just the opposite. But, for some reason, people have always respected me.

Many times in the music world I would hear comments like, "That guy's a real jerk, a miserable person, but he's a great tenor." That's all it took for me. And usually when someone receives praise and recognition for being good at what he does, he stops being a jerk.

My life has been filled with kind and loving people, people who have gone out of their way to reach out. There are as many such people now as there ever was, but we hear a lot of negativity. For example, there seems to be a whole industry built around bashing Bill Clinton. There are controversial athletes like Mike Tyson and TV personalities like Jerry Springer who are promoted for the sake of entertainment. When I hear swearing on television, especially when it comes from women, I am astonished. I'm not critical of it, I'm just astonished.

I confess that I will say "damn" when I get angry, but I usually say it to myself. My philosophy is to do whatever I can to solve my problems, then get a good night's sleep. If a problem is too big to solve in one day, I turn my attention to something else that I can solve.

BEVERLY BLANK, 58, HAIRSTYLIST

You're brain dead when you use bad words. You're just telling the world you have no imagination. When I was younger I used to swear, but I didn't want my daughter to take after me, so I found a way to keep us both in line. I made a deal with her. When she was about 5 or 6 years old I told her that if she ever heard me using a bad word, she could swat me one. People used to say, "You let your daughter hit you?" I'd say, "Well, I get to do the same to her if I ever hear her imitate a swear word. That way we're both covered." Of course, it was just a pat we gave each other, not a whack.

I was always very independent. I never gave in to pressure by my peers to talk a certain way, or do a certain thing. I remember once going out with this boy who had a reputation for expecting a lot from the girls. We went into the city, and in the car he started making passes at me. I said, "What kind of girl do you think I am?" "A good girl?" he said. I said, "Right." He never took me out after that, but I didn't want to go out with him either. You have to stand up for yourself. You make your own destiny.

I don't judge other people for swearing, I just don't really like hearing it. And I'm not the only one. I work at a beauty salon, and we have some elderly customers here and sometimes they don't come back because they hear an employee using that language.

I don't like it when my boyfriend swears. He's Latin, and he loves that F word. I tell him I don't like to hear that kind of talk from him. He says, "But, honey, is your language." I say, "I don't care, just don't talk that way around me." I'll just leave the room if he and his friends start talking like that. I'm not angry, I just don't like hearing it. He comes and asks me if everything is okay, and I say, "Yeah, I'm fine, I don't mind sitting in the other room for a while." He swears in Spanish, but I don't understand what he's saying. Besides, everything in Spanish sounds good to me!

I saw this movie recently, Trading Places. *It's one thing to hear Eddie Murphy swear. It's such a part of him you hardly notice it, and he's so funny about it. But what really bothered me about this movie was that these old-time stars—Don Ameche and Ralph Bellamy—were in this movie and they were swearing just like Eddie Murphy and it sounded terrible! Sounded like they were just trying to keep up with the younger actors. It was a good movie, but that really was awful. It wasn't appropriate to them at all. Swearing is either part of a person or it isn't.*

My daughter's friends used to come over and sometimes use those words. One time one of them said, "Mrs. Blank, how come you never say anything to us when we talk like that?" I said, "Well, it's up to you. It depends on what you want me to think of you. I'm not going to force you. If you want me to respect you, you won't use those words." I treat kids like adults. I show them respect, they show me respect.

JON KOMAREK, 19, COLLEGE STUDENT

I'm from a village south of Buffalo, New York, and went to high school with kids from farms and the rural areas. I'm surprised that I don't swear more than I do, because I've always been very active in sports. I played on soccer, tennis, volleyball, golf, and hockey teams. Hockey was the worst, with lots of swearing in the locker room and in the games. I had a friend on the team who never swore at all, and I remember times when he was real uncomfortable with all the swearing going on. He'd just step away and be by himself.

It got rough when we played schools in Buffalo. The players were so cocky, and really vulgar. You felt threatened. My younger brother plays now and it's the same, with fights on the ice. I know that's part of the game, but these are 16-year-olds. They don't need to do that.

My parents taught me not to swear. If I was the kind of guy who swore, it would be a reflection on how my parents raised me, and I don't want to give them a bad image. I respect them.

They never told me why swearing was bad but just said don't do it. I guess I can't explain why I don't. It's been a personal choice. Swearing isn't necessary. There are so many other words. Swearing is like saying you don't care about the people around you.

I'm not real bothered by guys who swear, but sometimes it's one word after the other. I think, that's enough. But I don't say anything. The girls in my high school never swore much. There were a few sketchy ones, but we didn't hang around with them.

I hear more swearing now at college. People are just screaming it. I don't think they realize they are saying it, it's so much a part of their vocabulary. It's too much and offends a lot of people.

If adults want to swear on their own time, I guess I don't have a problem with that. But I don't like it when they swear in front of their kids. That's like telling the kids it's okay for them to swear. The movies that go too far are the same thing. The stars are role models and definitely influence the audience.

SYLVIA ARUFFO ORKIN, 50 SOMETHING, HEALTH CARE BUSINESS OWNER

My parents were Methodists, but they didn't make me fear God or threaten to punish me if I used dirty words. Cursing was simply something you didn't do. When my father mentioned it at all, he would say, "Swearing shows the poverty of the person's vocabulary."

I was also strongly influenced by Mrs. Wolters, my teacher in fifth grade and again in eighth grade at a public school in Detroit. She made us diagram every sentence, cover to cover, in our grammar books and showed us how to "have fun" with the dictionary. She read aloud to us, instilling a love of the sounds of skilled communication. We learned new words every day through rigorous drills, contests, book reports, and weekly spelling quizzes. My best friend from those days and I were reunited in 1997. After a thirty-five-year separation, we recited, in unison, without hesitation, every auxiliary verb in the English language, just as Mrs. Wolters had taught us.

I was in high school in the mid-1960s, studying architecture and design at Cass Technical High School. It was a huge public school with thousands of students who all had passed a competitive review of tests and application essays to be accepted. A common after-school activity was a club related to your major. I took supplemental design classes on Saturdays. My friends tended to be more serious than social. I only remember two who swore.

During the summer of my freshman year at University of Michigan, I worked in the advertising department of the Detroit Free Press. *The men there swore but would drop their voices and look both ways before they did. This tended to reinforce the idea that swearing was not normal speech, so I never picked it up.*

When I was at Michigan, my undergraduate adviser was a world-famous professor of linguistics, Kenneth Pike. He strengthened my awareness of words and languages. The campus bristled with the issues of the day: protests against the Vietnam War and marches for civil rights. Brick tossing and public profanity were all part of the commotion. I actively worked for several causes but didn't march with profane placards or confront police screaming, swearing, or making demands. That's just not my style.

While spending twelve years as a designer and illustrator, I pursued my love of language by learning Spanish, French, German, Portuguese, and even Hausa, an African language I could use in my work with the Peace Corps. I went on to earn a Ph.D. in linguistics and an MBA at Northwestern University so I could go into international business. It is amusing that in order to do official translation and interpretation, I had to learn all the profane and vulgar words in Spanish and French because parties in legal actions use them frequently.

I have always enjoyed theater because of my artistic sense. My children and foster children were always involved in school plays and community theater. The language in plays can be earthy, but I don't object if I perceive the artistic rationale. However, in most cases swear words do not contribute as much to the plot, theme, or character development as skillfully selected vocabulary would. I enjoy dramas like Law & Order *that use words in unexpected and tightly crafted ways.*

Mass media affect the way people communicate, adding new vocabulary like "Yaddah-yaddah." It can also add new meanings to old phrases, like signaling a lie by slowly saying "That's the ticket," the way the Saturday Night Live *character did. If popular stars swear, their fans will also. Before mass media, people kept journals, wrote letters, and made speeches using more formal language. In fact, one of the challenges in producing a historical screenplay is that the communication style actually used in the period is unacceptable to today's audience as "real" speech. Language evolves. Cursing is now used regularly simply because the person hasn't been trained in a broader vocabulary or may use cursing for shock value or to vent frustration. I enjoy the artistic and linguistic challenge of communicating those attitudes in other words. Perhaps equally important is that, although I get mad and upset at times, I seldom lose control. I tend to dive into solutions without having to "vent" first—unless it is a computer crash. You will hear an unmistakable "shit" before I restart the machine.*

But such reactions are not common. I had a dinner party not long ago. I was carrying in the spaghetti sauce when I tripped and dropped the bowl on my light blue carpet. I shouted, "Oh my goodness! Oh my goodness!" My guests laughed and commented that, had it happened to them, the air would have been as blue as the rug. But it was a lot less stressful to simply laugh with the guests, pick up a wet cloth, and start scrubbing.

KAREN, 53, PHOTOGRAPHER

I try not to swear, because I think it's uncouth. It has a negative effect. But it really depends on the circumstances. If you're talking to a good friend who also swears and the topic is something objective, then it's okay. But if you are angry and using it against someone, that's not good.

I never swore as a kid. I just didn't get upset. I fought with my brothers, but I don't recall really getting too upset about things. My parents didn't swear. Every once in a while my dad would say, "Oh hell," but my mom would just slam the kitchen cupboards if she felt angry. Religion was an influence. One of the commandments was that you couldn't even say, "Oh God."

Having polio didn't seem to upset me that much, unless I've blocked it out. I just don't remember being that upset. My parents took good care of me. They redecorated my bedroom and made it nice for me. Polio never stood in my way, though it may have made me a little less outgoing. I did develop a strong sense of independence, probably because of the school time I missed when I had to have operations. I missed all of first grade, part of seventh, all of eighth, and part of eleventh. I had private schooling at home during those years. I probably was a little less socially adept because of the circumstances. I just dealt with it. That's how my parents taught me, I guess. You just do what you have to do. That's how I deal with work, too. I just focus on what I'm doing and try to do a good job. I try not to focus on what someone else did or didn't do. Not that people don't irritate me. I don't like inefficiency, or controlling behavior, and I do get upset. But as I said, I try not to swear.

My brothers don't swear too much, either. One of them, if he gets really involved in a game on TV and his team loses, he'll blurt out the F word. But then his three children go running to their mother and say, "Mommy, Daddy's using the F word!" Sometimes they repeat one thing my dad used to say, "Oh garsh. Oh golly, oh garsh." I guess that's a cross between gosh *and* darn.

In high school I don't remember having anything to swear about. College was difficult. I had to work hard. It was my first time away from home, living with people I didn't know. But I don't recall anyone around me swearing, and I know I didn't. I attended a Jesuit university that had just converted to coed a year or two before I arrived. Some of the teachers resisted that change, especially some of the priests. They would ignore the women in their classes. They didn't want us there. But I was happy not to be called on.

It was only after college, when I started teaching, that swearing became more common. The teachers would all get together and complain about the politics of teaching. Even I started to swear a little then. I probably picked it up from the kids!

Where I work people swear. And sometimes they're talking to clients! I find it unsettling to listen to them. I can't tell if they're angry or just excited. They sound angry. But otherwise it doesn't bother me too much when others swear. I think it does help me professionally not to swear. If you do—and I hate to say this because maybe it's snobbish—it sounds like poor upbringing. When I get angry, I say "Oh rats," or I clam up.

Driving annoys me more than anything, even the three-mile trip from my house to work. The other day some guy in a sports car wanted to get around so he scoots into this area to the right that isn't even a lane, then he screams at me because I'm trying to park there. My car windows are tinted so people can't see me, and I yell at them, "Go home!" If they have out-of-town license plates, I yell, "Go back to where you came from!" But of course they can't see or hear me.

ED PAVLO, 49, SALESMAN FOR FINANCIAL SERVICES

I grew up in Linden, New Jersey, which is a blue-collar town. You'd expect swearing to be prevalent there, but I don't recall hearing much of it. My parents were from Czechoslovakia, and if they swore, it was in a language I didn't understand. I'm a Catholic, but I went to public schools. In high school, I played baseball and I was the quarterback of the football team. The term "locker-room language" didn't apply at this school. We might have been tempted at times, but coaches and teachers were always around, so we resisted. Outside of school, we might pepper a sentence with a cuss word or two for emphasis, but in general swear words were not part of our vocabulary. I don't know how it happened, but I managed to get involved with a good group. Most of my friends from high school went on to become doctors and other professionals.

I went to college in Montclair State in New Jersey where I was a running back on the football team. I started swearing along with everyone else. I guess it was one of the many ways of expressing the freedom of being away from home. After a while, though, I said this just isn't me, so I stopped for the most part. Today, I'll use a swear word now and then, but it's rare.

I'm in sales, so I don't swear in business. I don't swear at home, particularly since I have an 11-year-old son. He has used a swear word at times, I think, to get a reaction from me. I don't make a big deal about it. I'll ask, "Do you use that word in school?" I don't want him to think that curse words are powerful words, because then he will use them for impact.

When someone swears a lot, you really notice it. It's a distraction. Not long ago, a fellow salesman asked me to accompany him on a sales call to a dealership in North Carolina. The owner's language was amazing. Every third or fourth word was a swear word. I've never heard anything like it. We walked away wondering if we even wanted him as a customer.

I really don't know what words I use in place of swear words. Son of a gun, maybe. I just don't have a lot of occasions to swear. Emotionally, I try to keep at an even keel. I also dump data from my mind, not dwelling on things that annoy me.

ROCHELLE KOPP, 34, CONSULTANT TO JAPANESE BUSINESSES IN THE UNITED STATES

I've never given much thought to swearing. I don't do it, and my friends in school and in business have not been the type to use curse words. My parents didn't swear. In fact, my father made a point of correcting my English, trying to get me to stop saying "like" and "you know." If I had gone so far as to swear, I'm sure it would have been an issue.

I went to Highland Park High School in Chicago's North Shore, a nice area. You heard swearing in the halls, but the kids who were serious about school and involved in activities didn't swear much. At least not the ones I knew. I was one of the "nice kids" with a goody two-shoes image. I worked on the school paper and the yearbook. I remember swearing once when I worked on the paper, and everyone ran over to me to see what was wrong. They were so shocked to hear me curse that they thought something terrible had happened. I don't remember what the problem was or what I said, but it make me realize that cursing has more impact if you don't do it often.

In college, no one swore very much, as far as I recall. I went to Yale. I was a coxswain on the rowing team. We didn't swear, but I suppose that's because rowing is a preppy sport. People at Yale were achievers and smart enough to know that their behavior, not just their brains, would determine their success. People who go to Yale are a pretty serious bunch. They're thinking of their futures and are also very image conscious. I remember a girl with a really strong Long Island accent. She got rid of it.

I worked in Tokyo for two years and went to the University of Chicago for my MBA. I worked for management consulting firms before starting my own firm, Japan Intercultural Consulting. I work with Japanese companies doing business in the United States. Often, I'm training Japanese on how to communicate successfully in the United States. I have to maintain a good image to earn my clients' confidence and set the example, and I have to be sensitive to what's offensive in different cultures, because I'm essentially a diversity consultant. Sometimes, Japanese businessmen yell at each other in a way that would not be acceptable here, and Americans occasionally use crude language that wouldn't be acceptable to the Japanese.

Resolving diversity issues has helped me develop tolerance for all kinds of people. Politically and socially, I lean to the liberal side. I admit I'm a bit of a conflict avoider. I consider myself shy, but I doubt if anyone knows that. You can't be shy in my line of work, and I have plenty of friends.

Swearing just hasn't been an issue for me. I have an excellent vocabulary, which I began developing in my high school reading lab and while studying for the college entrance exams. I think that swear words aren't as interesting or useful as some of the other words in the language. I don't get angry very often. Things bother me, but I have good emotional control and a generally sunny disposition. I remember screaming at a dry cleaner once when they lost one of my suits and wouldn't admit it. I was really upset, but I didn't swear. Those words just aren't on the tip of my tongue.

SHELLY KIMEL, 61, CORPORATE TAX ACCOUNTANT

I don't swear and I never did, because I don't like the sound of it. I think swearing gives a bad impression. I can't think of anyone in particular who influenced me. It was a personal decision.

My friends in high school swore, but it didn't bother me. If they wanted to speak that way, it was their choice. I don't remember anyone commenting about the fact that I didn't swear. I lived in Chicago and commuted downtown to DePaul University. I went to class, then came home. Many of the students lived at home, so there wasn't much socializing. If swearing was commonplace, I wasn't aware of it.

I've been with the same corporation for over thirty-one years. Everyone's very professional. I don't hear any bad language. I drive to work, leaving home early in the morning because I don't like to be rushed and I like to get to work early. I drive defensively and no longer honk at people. I take my time, lay back, relax, and listen to the radio during my long commute to and from work. Listening to the radio takes my mind off driving and any bad drivers who might otherwise annoy me. I'm on time or early for everything, so I never get upset and start cursing people who are in my way.

If I get mad, it is usually at myself for making stupid mistakes. My usual reaction to annoyances or problems is "darn," or "shoot." If something or someone is really bothering me, I give signs rather than say anything. The silent treatment, I guess. I sulk.

Some people think they are being cute when they swear. I never hear anyone telling someone else not to swear. Nobody cares much. Why bother bringing it up if the majority think it's okay?

MARY WILSON, 65,
DEALER OF NEW AND USED CLOTHING

Swearing is ugly. It lowers you. It's ignorance, so if someone swears at you, don't swear back. Someone has to be of a sound mind. People look down on you if you do a lot of swearing. It classes you as scum. I wish people who swear would see a big mirror of themselves doing it. It's ugly, very ugly.

I grew up here in Birmingham. I had very Christian parents and five brothers and four sisters. My mother was very strict, but my father let us have our way. Neither of my parents ever swore, and neither did I. When I was a teenager, you had to keep up with the gang, and if you didn't swear, you had to be tough. We had fistfights, *but no guns or knives. There were lots of gangs in the 1950s. I lived on 12th Street and if gangs from the other streets came over, there would be a gang fight. This was our turf. We swore at each other, pulled each other's hair, threw stones and bricks. We thought we were big, but it was ignorance. After high school, we grew up.*

When I came to Chicago, my first job was a cashier at the John T. Shane furrier. The boss was always swearing at a Polish worker for no good reason. It was very unbecoming of a boss to do that, and at times I felt like walking out the door. The Polish man didn't say a word, he just dropped his head and turned red. All the employees felt bad about it. One time, several furs were missing and the boss suspected the Polish man of taking them. But a few weeks later, he sat near the store after hours, and his own cousin broke in. It was an inside job. He never apologized to the Polish man.

If someone swears at me, I want to hurt them. They're asking for a fight. I would not tolerate anyone swearing at me. I would have to jump on them and go to jail. I am very temperamental. If I had a date who swore at me, out the front door he would go.

I don't think swearing is appreciated anywhere. Whatever the conversation is, I can talk without swearing. You can make any point you want to get across without swearing. You have to treat people the way you want to be treated.

If I'm angry with someone, I just try to avoid them. That's the best medicine. Whatever I don't like, I avoid. I stay as peaceful as possible. If my family annoys me, I go into hiding for six or seven months. I don't call on anyone. If they call me, I make it short. I keep a low profile. I'm a loner, and that way I stay out of trouble.

CHRIS ROBERTS, 29, RELIGION EDITOR FOR A TV PROGRAM

I probably swore as often as most kids did when I was in high school, depending on the situation. My father was the pastor of a Baptist church, so a few of my friends had a preconceived notion of how I should speak and behave. Some of the members of my youth group were very conservative, and swearing in front of them was my way of declaring I was part of the real world.

Bravado is a factor in every teenager's language, so I outgrew it. There was a time when I would stub my toe in the privacy of my own bathroom and curse repeatedly. Today, reacting that way doesn't occur to me. I still curse now and then, usually out of frustration.

I didn't consciously reduce the frequency of my swearing, but I haven't spent much time in an environment where swearing was common. I went to Yale. Afterward, I spent two years working with Bill Moyers, producing documentaries that dealt with ethics, values, and choices. That experience influenced me in many ways, including my decision to pursue a graduate degree in theology. I earned my degree at Oxford. In 1997, I was part of the crew that launched Religion and Ethics NewsWeekly, *the television program where I'm now the religion editor. You don't hear much profanity around here.*

I don't like to hear anyone cursing in public. It's inconsiderate of others and adds to the coarseness of our culture. Depending on who is cursing, it can sound irresponsible or even silly. I expect people who are well educated to employ a more expressive vocabulary. My tendency is to consider people who swear openly, at least the ones with a background where they were taught to know better, as less generous, less charitable. Maybe that's a loose connection, but that's how I feel.

I consider swearing more acceptable when it's used among or by people with backgrounds different from mine. For example, I worked on a farm one summer and wasn't surprised or offended by the way another worker spoke.

Why did Tina Brown introduce profanity to the New Yorker? *She intentionally offended many of the magazine's readers, apparently to attract other readers. The movies reach a different audience, but when I see one that's filled with cuss words, like* Pulp Fiction, *I'm embarrassed for the director. It often reveals a lack of imagination.*

HOWARD HELMER, 60, SPOKESPERSON
FOR THE AMERICAN EGG BOARD

My job takes me all over the country promoting eggs and giving cooking demonstrations. Swearing seems to be common everywhere I go, but I think I hear less of it in smaller towns versus the big cities. I'm aware of swearing because my family doesn't swear at all. My parents were Russian immigrants. We lived on the south side of Chicago in a neighborhood of fellow immigrants. All were like one big family, in and out of each other's apartments. Swearing was banned. Of course, being immigrants, my parents and their friends probably didn't even know American swear words. It was a cloistered environment so even my language was protected—and monitored—by my parents.

Speaking properly was part of the family policy of being a mensch, *the Yiddish word that loosely means a gentleman. The word is not gender specific, so it applies to women as well. I raised my own children that way, and they are raising their children in the same way. We don't even say "shut up."*

I think that swearing and the behavior that often comes with it has no value. It really doesn't get you what you're after. For example, if you swear at a waiter who hasn't performed in some way or other that you like, will he be nicer to you? Not likely. He's more apt to spit in your soup before he brings it out to you. In my travels I often see people at an airline ticket counter all but swearing at the agent for something gone wrong. I know that agent won't accommodate that person nearly as well as they might because of it. That poor traveler's mouth is going to get him or her second best treatment from that agent, you can be sure.

I'm a very laid-back person, but I do get angry like everyone else. I can't hide my ire, my rage. Sometimes that translates into becoming testy. But you won't hear me swear. I'm not prone to it. All right . . . maybe "damn" will spill out. But whatever I hope to accomplish, being a gentleman—a mensch—usually works. On the other hand, I suppose my anger has impact among people who know me because it's so rare.

I think that people who swear when they're upset are less effective because their foul language is so offensive that it dismisses what they are really trying to say. They might intimidate others into doing something, but certainly not out of respect. Their victims just go through the motions. Even in a calm conversation, if a person is really crude it distracts me from what he is trying to communicate. People who think that cuss words punctuate what they're saying are mistaken.

Maybe it's a socioeconomic issue. Maybe it's also a part of what I think is the general deterioration of many elements of society. In some societies it could be associated with being tough and might help establish an individual's rank in that society. Living in New York City you tend to get jaded. It's a great city, really, but a big city, so you're exposed to everything bad as well as good. People whose vocabularies allow them to spit out swear words as a matter of course are part of the bad. That's my opinion.

DOROTHY KOLSCHOWSKY, 35, CANDY SALES REPRESENTATIVE

I swore when I was in high school and in college, but never around my parents, who were good Catholics. Just about everyone at school swore. I was a cocktail waitress for a while at the University of Illinois and heard plenty of foul language.

I got married at 20, and now I have four children. My first child was born prematurely, and her birth and survival seemed like a miracle to me. I made a conscious decision to live my life for God, to live by His standards and to set an example for my children. Actions speak louder than words, and I didn't want to tell them how to behave without behaving that way myself. I was influenced by my parents, who always told me to be a role model for my two younger sisters.

It was no problem for me to stop swearing. Even when I was with friends and away from my children, I didn't swear, and still don't. Earlier I might have mentioned to my friends that I was offended by bad language, or maybe some of them sensed it, so no one swears in front of me.

I try to be a person of character. I have a passion for history and enjoy reading about the great men who founded our country, who made such great efforts. They inspire me to do my best, to be a better person.

I am honest, because we all pay in the end when others cheat the system. People might steal from stores, forcing prices to go up. They cheat on their taxes, so the government needs more from everyone else. I don't even take paper clips from work or use the phone for personal calls. It's immoral.

I don't talk about people behind their backs. If I do, the people I'm speaking with might think I say bad things about them, too. There are people I don't care for, people who annoy me, but I see no good purpose in hating them. Everybody has weaknesses, including me, and maybe I annoy some people. We all struggle with our flaws.

I'm learning to be patient, to not get angry. When I'm mad, I speak louder rather than swear. I tend to react with a question, like, "Why did I do that?" or "Why did you do that?" I could say darn *or* shoot, *but those words really aren't in my vocabulary either.*

I try to learn something every day, even something as simple as cooking something different, exercising, or consuming fewer calories. I learn things from my children. I don't wait until I reach my goal to be satisfied. Life is a journey, and you have to appreciate small steps along the way.

JOHN HAGNER, 71, STUNTMAN AND ARTIST

I heard so much swearing from my father when I was a kid that I decided I wouldn't do it myself. I loved my dad, but he smoked, drank, and cussed a lot. He was never mean, but his behavior scared me. He was a strong German type, made his own beer and drank it before it had time to get cold. He had a serious stuttering problem, but for some reason he never stuttered when he swore. Sometimes when he couldn't get a word out, he would swear to get the words flowing again. We were Catholics, and the priest would come over to visit, and my dad would swear in front of him. The priest knew why, and probably put up with it because otherwise he would be there all night waiting for my father to finish what he was trying to say.

I moved from Baltimore to Los Angeles in 1958 to work as a stuntman. I've spent half my career as a stuntman and half as an artist, mostly doing portraits of actors for publicity purposes. I still do both. I haven't noticed a big difference in the amount of swearing on the set over the years, but that's because it was bad from the beginning. It's part of the language. I worked on the movie The Greatest Story Ever Told, the story about Jesus Christ, and the swearing between scenes was no less that usual.

I resisted picking up the bad language. I never smoked or drank either. I didn't mingle much or play cards when we had to wait around. I was sort of an oddball, doing my scenes and going home.

I was aware of who swore and who didn't. I didn't like it, but I never confronted anyone about it. I wouldn't say I had less respect for guys who swore, it's more like I felt sorry for them.

I don't remember actors like Gregory Peck, Walter Pidgeon, or Charlton Heston swearing. I was in a lot of movie and TV westerns. Gene Autry and Roy Rogers didn't swear, as far as I know. These people didn't have to swear. They had a sense about themselves. Chuck Connors, who was the Rifleman, swore some, but he was a wonderful friend.

A typical scene for me was a fistfight or falling off a cliff. Sometimes I'd accidentally take a real punch and be knocked out for a few seconds. There was no reason to swear about it. One time I fell off a horse and broke my toe, but I wasn't acting at the time! Other than that, I never had a serious injury.

In 1973, I founded the Hollywood Stuntmen's Hall of Fame in Los Angeles. I moved it to Moab, then to Portland, Oregon, but had to put it in storage when the city wanted the building. Movie people liked to stop in when they were up here making movies, like City Slickers II. *Jack Palance was here, Kris Kristofferson, Ernest Borgnine, and others. They are all good people. I was in* Geronimo, *which was filmed here in 1993, with Gene Hackman and Robert Duvall. They can play tough guys, but they're kind and don't swear like they might in a movie. Duvall was with a boy he was sponsoring who was dying of cancer. I had Duvall make a footprint in cement for the Hall of Fame, and he had the youngster put his handprint in as well. It was great! Sadly, the boy died a short time later.*

LYNNE HERBSTRITT, 57, SALES ASSOCIATE
AND FASHION DESIGNER

Just about everyone I know swears, men and women. I didn't have much exposure to bad language until I was out of college, and I remember being shocked to hear women swear. I was a child in the 1950s, and we were taught that swearing was wrong. My parents didn't swear, and I don't remember my brothers or sisters ever swearing. Maybe the boys swore at Oak Park High School, but not in front of me. After high school, I went to a nearby girls' college and lived at home.

I always associated vulgarity with a lack of education, or with people from a low socioeconomic class. I guess I still do. If I know someone has a good background but his language is bad, I can't help thinking that he was the offspring of uneducated parents. Maybe people with backgrounds similar to mine feel that swearing liberates them. Personally, I don't feel restricted or deprived, thus excluding the need to swear. I believe what I was taught and need to be true to my beliefs. I recognize that the world changes, but the increased use of bad language coincides with the decline of the

English language in general. Proper grammar and usage is no longer stressed. I think it's a shame.

How you present yourself to others is important, and I think a favorable image requires control. I have control of my language and my emotions, and I love the sense of power it gives me. I rarely get angry. I get frustrated, I feel pressured, but I know I have to deal with whatever problems I encounter. What's the point of swearing? It doesn't solve anything.

I've raised four children, and now I work full time. I'm on my feet serving customers all day at a department store. My job requires me to be polite and cheerful, to make the customer happy. I do it not only because that's what I'm paid to do, but because it makes me feel professional and satisfied. I sincerely want to make the customer happy. I take great pride in who I am, a person who does what she has to do, and if I fake it, I'm not being true to myself. I don't go to the back room and act differently. To me, that would be like swearing in private but not in public. It's hypocritical.

At the end of the day, the salespeople are supposed to make certain their departments are in order, with the clothes folded and stacked neatly for the next day. Sometimes I'm tired and eager to leave, but I do it.

If I ever question whether or not I'm doing the right thing, I remind myself that I've been honored as the top salesperson. What my instincts tell me to do for my employer helped me earn recognition, self-respect, and the confidence that my way of thinking and acting is worth something.

I admit that I am motivated at work by the fact that I need the job. Since I have to work, I make the most of it. I don't take anything personally. I know how to get along with people. When there's a problem or conflict, I find a positive way to interpret it. My philosophy is to do what it takes to come out a winner.

SEVEN
Cut the Shit, Now and Forever

"WHAT WORDS DO I use instead?" is the first question asked by anyone who wants to stop swearing. Alternative words are assumed to be the solution to the problem.

Substitute words are only part of the solution, and some sound just as sour. The real remedy for offensive language is to change your attitude. Why? Because the tone of what you say has far more impact than your words. It's essential to recognize this. Just as a harsh tone intensifies the offensiveness of a word, the soft tone of a whimsical remark can make the same word almost innocent.

By adjusting your attitude and learning to control your emotions, you can significantly reduce your use of the words and phrases that make you sound disagreeable, caustic, grating, cynical, resentful, and not very nice. And it works both ways. If you train yourself to avoid using certain vulgar and negative words, you will actually feel better and be less of a grouch.

An attitude adjustment doesn't require a complete personality overhaul, unless vulgarity is such an integral part of your personality that your friends would think your body was occupied by an alien. If you can at least cut back the bad language, pruning off a word here and a word there by controlling your temper or resisting the urge to complain, your friends are likely to appreciate the change. If you eventually manage to soften your disposition, your friends might even increase in quantity as well in quality.

Casual swearing, or the lazy habit of injecting cuss words into your conversation as easily as you butter your potato, is an excellent starting point, a place to practice. It will help cleanse your vocabulary, getting those words off the tip of your tongue where they are always perched in eager anticipation of a chance to poison the air. It is much easier to eliminate or find substitutes for casual cuss words than it is for causal cuss words because you aren't under any emotional pressure to blurt out your usual expletives.

For example, if you find a box from UPS at the front door, it is easy to say "What's this?" instead of "What the hell (shit, fuck) is this?" The coarser question signals your suspicion that your spouse ordered something expensive and unnecessary. Don't sound ready to accuse him or her of wasting money until you know the facts. The box might actually contain a present for you. It might even be something you had said you needed, and it was thoughtful of him or her to get it for you.

If you discover the box contains three leather-bound and illustrated volumes on the retrieval and display of moonrocks along with a receipt for $700, you now face the challenge of resisting causal swearing.

You might feel you lack the vocabulary to replace your swear words, or fear other words will sound pompous and phony rather than natural for you. Most swear words can be replaced with simple words or expressions suitable for anyone. Words that are more sophisticated exist, but this book is not designed to boost your vocabulary to academic levels. The objective is to help you say what you mean, and say it nicely.

WIPE THIS WORD OUT OF YOUR VOCABULARY

Shit. If we did it as often as we say it, the city sanitation department couldn't hire enough people to shovel it. It is the favorite word of consummate cursers, applied in every possible syntax and context, but it should be kept in the toilet rather than kept handy. It's a wonder that it has become so popular. It doesn't even have a nice flow to it, as do softer S words like *shine, shimmer, sheen, serene,* and *sleep*.

The F word is only a runner-up to the S word in frequency and distribution. Both words describe private acts that provide pleasant sensations and comforting gratification, but both are also distasteful terms. People are more comfortable with the S word than with the F word, even though the subject matter of the F word is prevalent in books, movies, and TV while bathroom scenes are almost nonexistent. Going to the bathroom is an essential activity for humans of all ages but has zero entertainment value for all but the truly sick and depraved. Scatological humor tends to focus on humiliation and degradation.

Anthropologists and Freudian psychologists will argue that excrement is grossly misunderstood and unjustly maligned. Freud, famous for his anal fixations, believed our unfavorable treatment of feces as a disgusting and foul-smelling substance is a conditioned response. In literature and philosophy, it symbolizes life and death. Manure, the most obvious metaphor, is the remnant of life-sustaining animal feed used to fertilize the fields and replenish the food supply.

According to *Scatologic Rites of All Nations* by John G. Bourke, published in 1891, various cultures have used poo-poo in everything from religious ceremonies to—perhaps more fittingly—witchcraft. Tribes have used it in initiation rites, smearing it on bodies of young warriors to instill endurance and courage. In the heat of battle, it was probably more effective than basic body odor at repelling attackers.

Amazingly, some cultures used it in medicines and as a seasoning, which took the bite out of telling each other to eat shit. Although we consider fecal matter to be malodorous and repulsive, women of early civilizations used it in cosmetics and perfume and combed it into their hair. However, historical records fail to indicate how often these women managed to get dates.

For contemporary men and women, the past and present uses for excrement and its poetic connection to all things living and dead "don't mean shit." The exceptions are farmers and X-generation suburbanites raising vegetables organically in their backyards. We are talking about swear words here, something that people like to toss around without regard for their real meaning or value.

The word *shit* has been around for more than a thousand years and is derived from a number of European languages, including the Middle English verb *shiten,* to void excrement. Only rarely did it appear in print until the middle of the twentieth century, even though it was widely spoken after World War I. Today, it appears to be as common as the commode, a permanent fixture in the vocabularies of men, women, and children everywhere.

Some of its applications were clever and imaginative at first, but the exhaustive employment of the word has eliminated any chance that future linguists and degenerates will find creative new ways to put it to use. The time has come to head in the other direction, to reduce the use of this word and find fresher ways to express ourselves. Unfortunately, most of us aren't verbally inventive, which is one reason why we rely on old standbys.

The technical and acceptable words for the real thing include *excrement, feces, fecal matter, body waste,* and *stools.* (Whoever thought of stools must have used a dried-up pile of it to reach the top shelf in his cupboard.)

A few terms relating to farming are *manure, dung,* and *guano.*

Euphemisms include *number two, droppings, doo-doo, poop, night soil,* and *butt muffin.*

Crap is a euphemism, but not a nice one. It is true that Thomas Crapper was the inventor of a valveless flushable toilet in 1882, and it's fun to believe his name was the origin of the word, but the word has been around for centuries.

About the only acceptable verb for going number two is *defecate,* but one word is plenty to describe something we don't enjoy describing.

REPLACING THE EXCREMENTAL EXCLAMATION

Used alone as an exclamation, the word *shit* is a solitary expression of disgust. It has evolved to serve as a suitable expletive for any negative mood, and even a few chipper ones. The first-choice alternative for its use as an outburst of emotion is *shoot,* a logical substitute because it is a mere vowel away from what you really want to say. Yes, it lacks the power, but keep in mind that you are accustomed to using and hearing the swear word. Eventually, as you focus on developing a distaste for *shit,* anything will sound better.

No one will laugh at you for using *shoot.* They probably won't even notice, unless the people you are with are trigger-happy cops, crooks, hunters, or snipers. It was selected as an option decades ago because the beginning and end of the word sound similar to *shit,* and the single syllable is equally easy to spout off. Any mouth, even a big one, should be able to handle this adjustment without too much effort.

A second option is *shucks,* which cleverly connects the front end of the S word with the rear end of the F word. While *shoot* still works, *shucks* has become a bit too sappy for most folks, but it might be worth a try.

Here are a few more oldies but not so baddies that you can use as substitutes. You will notice that *these words are substitutes for other expletives as well.* It is very important to note this.

Nuts!	Darn it!
Curses!	Blast it!
Cripes!	Oh, man!
Yikes!	Man o man!
Criminey!	Oh, brother!
Egad!	Dang it!
Mercy!	Dangnabit!
Good grief!	I don't believe it!
Holy cow!	Gadzooks!
Holy mackerel!	Nerts!

An exclamation is an exclamation—a meaningless utterance; a verbalization of an emotional reaction; an expression of surprise, shock, frustration, or anger—so you can choose to say any swear word, euphemism, silly expression, and made-up word you want. You will learn more about this in chapter 10, "Finding Alternative Words."

If you are looking for a substitute for every specific curse word you use as an exclamation, you need to pick words that sound similar, like *shoot* and *shucks* for *shit.* Keep in mind that no option will satisfy you at first. Swearing is a habit just like any other habit, and you won't be comfortable changing your pattern. Smokers don't get the same fix sucking on hard candy as they do a cigarette. However, their mouths will be sweeter, and so will yours. The people around them won't be offended, and neither will the people within earshot of you.

ELIMINATION FOR SIMPLIFICATION

This lesson is intended to make the purification of your soiled tongue as easy as possible. For some common uses of the word, eliminating it entirely is easier than searching for a substitute that approximates the length and sound of the S word.

The first several uses of *shit* listed in chapter 1 are examples of expressions that don't need *shit:*

> Who (the shit) knows?
>
> Who (the shit) cares?
>
> You're (shit) out of luck.
>
> Don't give me that (shit).
>
> What (the shit's) wrong?
>
> She thinks she's hot (shit).
>
> He had a (shit) fit.
>
> You're up (shit's) the creek without a paddle.

Easy, huh? If you feel you are weakening a statement, consider the tone behind some of these pronouncements. "What the shit's wrong?" is a way to show anger or annoyance rather than concern.

When you tell someone he or she is shit out of luck, or up shit's creek, you're not expressing a great deal of sympathy. In fact, you might sound like you are gloating, almost pleased with the bad news. If that's the case, how do you benefit from rubbing someone's misfortune in his or her face? If it really makes you feel better, at least be subtle so the person can't tell whether or not you're glad about the situation. Dropping the S word helps.

Saying "Who cares?" is milder than saying "Who the shit cares?," but you can go a step further to avoid being abrasive. Who are you to speak for the whole world? Somebody out there cares. In fact, the person who raised the issue with you apparently does, but you are indirectly telling the person that he or she is a fool, the only person wasting time thinking about it. If you don't care, say "I don't care," or "That doesn't matter to me," and let others speak for themselves.

DON'T DEGRADE WORDS THAT WORK

There are dozens of expressions with simple words that work fine without us trashing them up. Don't substitute the S word when a more common word will do. For example you can refer to a number of objects as *stuff,* another single-syllable word that starts with the letter *s.* It is a worthy alternative, as in "What's all that stuff doing here?"

As an exercise, cover up the words on the right in the following lists, then read each sentence on the left, thinking of alternatives to the S word. Many of the answers border on being clichés, so you shouldn't have much trouble thinking of the options provided. Maybe you will think of a different but appropriate word. Write it down next to the suggested alternatives so you don't forget it.

If you can't think of a good substitute for as many as nine of the sentences (one-fourth), your working vocabulary is seriously deficient, probably from a reliance on the S word.

It's a shithole.	(dump, shack)
It's a piece of shit.	(junk, trash)
She doesn't know shit.	(anything)
I have a shitload of stuff.	(load, ton, pile)
Tough shit.	(luck, too bad)
No shit.	(kidding, I know)
We were shooting the shit.	(breeze, bull)
I nearly shit in my pants.	(soiled)
He scared the shit out of me.	(daylights, dickens, life)
He kicked the shit out of the guy.	(daylights, tar, stuffings)
I was scared shitless.	(to death, silly)
He's a dipshit.	(nerd, geek, loser, simpleton)
He's a shithead.	(jerk, dope, mean person)
I'm in deep shit.	(trouble, a fix)
Shit happens.	(things, stuff)
He's full of shit.	(it, hot air, gas, beans)
He's a bullshitter.	(liar, phony, untrustworthy)
That's bullshit, horseshit.	(nonsense, untrue, baloney, bunk)
Are you shitting me?	(kidding, teasing, serious)
I'm tired of your shit.	(excuses, arguments, behavior, nonsense)

What a lucky shit.	(guy, girl)
Same shit, different day.	(stuff)
Holy shit!	(cow)
I took a lot of shit from him.	(grief, abuse)
Oh, what the shit.	(heck)
I'm really getting my shit together.	(myself, act)
He drank until he was shitfaced.	(drunk, wasted, hammered, out of it)
Don't be a chickenshit.	(chicken, coward, baby)
That's really bad shit.	(news, stuff)
I'm on his shitlist.	(hitlist, bad side)
Those guys are real shitkickers.	(farmers, country boys)
He's got that shit-eating grin.	(devilish, satisfied)
He went ape shit.	(crazy, nuts, berserk, insane, raving mad)
He had a shit fit.	(temper tantrum, coronary, cow)
It's not worth jack-shit.	(anything, a plug nickel)
Today's lunch is shit on a shingle.	(chipped beef on toast)
I got the shitty end of the stick.	(short)
I got stuck with the shit work.	(menial, difficult)

Many of these statements aren't very polite, even with the substitute word. If you often find yourself making derogatory remarks, other chapters will help you overcome that habit. The objective here is to get you started by at least eliminating the vulgarity.

And don't feel using clichés is beneath you. A cliché is defined as a trite or overused expression. That describes almost every phrase that includes the S word.

Metaphors and similes are clever ways to make a point, adding interest to the way we communicate. The following metaphors are effective, but the imagery is not something you want to dwell on. Changing a word or two would only diminish the impact of these statements, so a better solution is to rephrase the sentence or create a more respectable metaphor.

Shit or get off the pot. (Do something or go away.)

He thinks his shit doesn't stink. (He thinks he walks on water.)

She sticks to him like shit on a shovel. (She sticks to him like a leech to flesh.)

They're as happy as pigs in shit. (They're as happy as two birds in a nest.)

The shit hit the fan. (The boss went berserk.)

Even when the S word is used literally, it doesn't sound nice, as in, "I have to take a shit." Such a statement would warrant the otherwise cruel and curt response, "Who cares?" If you have to explain where you are going, "to the bathroom" is universally understood and accepted. Or be original and say something like, "I have to drop the kids off at the pool," or "I have to make waves." The truth is, what you do there is your business and of great interest to no one but you, so keep it a secret. Doors were put on bathrooms to provide you with privacy and protect others from sights they would rather not see, so spare them the specifics.

Actually, to say you have to take a shit is not a literal expression. George Carlin points out that this declaration is incorrect. "You don't take a shit, you leave a shit," he explains to the unenlightened. "If you really want one, take one of mine. I won't be needing it."

WHAT DO YOU REALLY MEAN?

Suppose you meet a friend and offer the standard greeting, "Hi, Susan! How are you?," and she answers, "I feel like shit." What does that mean? Is she physically ill, feeling guilty about something, or emotionally distressed? Did her boyfriend just treat her like shit? And what does that mean?

We expect this word to convey a clear understanding of so many things, including how we feel, look, taste, smell, and hear:

This coat feels like shit.

The room looks like shit.

The food tastes like shit.

He can't hear shit.

This place smells like shit.

You would think we spend a substantial amount of time with our bowel movements, developing a keen awareness of the texture and varying fragrances so that we can offer comparisons that are quickly grasped by all our fellow feces handlers and examiners.

But when we say an edible item tastes like shit, are we implying we know because we have eaten shit? When we say a room looks like shit, do we mean it is brown? And what, exactly, does shit sound like? Are we referring to noises that occur during expulsion?

Of course not. We've made a judgment and are making a terse statement of disapproval. We have every intention of elaborating but want to make our views known immediately. One word seems to do it.

One word. Nothing wrong with that. But here are a few that do a better job, each with a distinctive meaning:

This coat feels (coarse, flimsy, stiff, itchy, damp, heavy, loose, tight, long).

The room looks (dirty, dark, small, messy, cluttered, crowded, tacky, disorganized).

The food tastes (raw, overcooked, sour, salty, rotten, spoiled, dry, soggy, cold).

He can't hear (me, you, anything, sirens, conversations, the television, insults).

This place smells like (garlic, onions, gas, paint, glue, a sewer, a locker room).

Pause for a second or two before you bark the poop word, and determine what you really want to say. By being specific in your complaint, someone will know the cause, be able to explain it, or do something about it. Also, you won't be expressing a wholesale rejection. The style of the coat is okay, it's just too small. The room isn't terrible, just cluttered.

Maybe a different slice of the meat wouldn't be so rare or salty. If you speak up instead of mumble, Grandpa will be able to hear you. And if you open the windows and cover the paint can, the room won't smell.

The vagueness and discordant sound of the word *shit* can make you appear arrogant, snobby, and demanding. Focusing on the real problem will soften the attack, perhaps allowing others to consider your remark an observation rather than a complaint.

MAKING A POSITIVE OUT OF A NEGATIVE

"What's this pile of shit doing here?" a college student asks his roommate.

"That's my good shit," comes the reply. "I put my bad shit in the hall."

When you use the word *shit* to be mean good and to mean bad, almost within the same breath, you are not saying much to help your listener know the distinction. Finding good in the bad is commendable, but it's cheating when all you do is reverse the meaning of a bad word.

"That movie was funnier than shit," a man tells his friend. Is shit funny? Could it be that some people seeking a good laugh look in toilet bowls? He meant to say the movie was the funniest movie he ever saw. It was hilarious, hysterical, uproarious!

"He really knows his shit." Now there's something to be proud of. Maybe this talent is akin to knowing the back of your hand, but knowing your business, your trade, your craft, your area of expertise, or your topic is far more impressive.

"I love this shit. It's the best shit I ever had." This level of appreciation is hard to reach, unless you are on drugs. If you really love something, you should be able to reveal its true identity.

"What a babe," comments a guy looking at pictures of Jenny McCarthy. "She's built like a brick shithouse." While Jenny admits to some construction work, she's softer and rounder than the average latrine. And why would anyone want to compare a beautiful woman to an outdoor bathroom? This simile was assembled simply because of the flow of the *i* sound in *built, brick,* and *shit.* The repetition of similar vowel sounds is called assonance, but this example is asinine. How about saying she is shaped sweeter than a sugar jar, an unbelievable stunning structure, an impressive frame? Claiming she has a fabulous figure or a great body isn't original, but it's more appealing than a pile of bricks.

FUNNY SOUNDS

Assonance, alliteration, and rhyming words tend to be amusing. With a little effort, you can make a few up.

> He has (bricks) for brains.
>
> She doesn't know (granola) from Shinola.
>
> I've got the (Hershey squirts).
>
> That scared the (shirt) off of me.
>
> He thinks his (pits) don't stink.
>
> Everything I touch turns to (trash).
>
> I was knee deep in (a dung heap).

These expressions are cruel and can be fighting words. Avoid them:

> Eat shit and die.
>
> She's a fat shit.
>
> The guy's a shitbag.
>
> You're full of shit.

That last statement deserves closer examination because we use it and variations of it all too often. Someone makes an outrageous statement, an accusation or a claim that you disagree with. You're convinced the person is wrong, and your ego is not going to allow him or her to think he or she can deceive you. So you say, "That's a bunch of bullshit."

But the person you've said it to has an ego, too, and doesn't appreciate the direct attack, especially if other people are present to witness the ensuing verbal battle. You've made it a personal issue by implying the person is a lying scum, rather than questioning the accuracy of the statement. Your bold accusation will only strengthen the speaker's will to hold his or her ground, even if the person knows he or she was stretching the truth.

What could you have said instead? You have several options:

A. "That's a lie."

No good! It's not swearing, but the effect is the same, providing evidence that alternative words are not necessarily better.

B. "That's a bunch of baloney."

Or *bunk, nonsense, rubbish, malarkey, hokum, balderdash,* or *fiddle faddle.* You are still challenging the speaker, but with words that are less vicious. Silly words, such as *balderdash* and *fiddle faddle,* might generate a laugh and avoid some of the tension.

C. "Right. And Princess Diana's death was faked and she is living on a private island with Elvis."

This or any other ludicrous statement is an attempt to dismiss the other person's remark as so untrue that it can't be taken seriously and isn't worthy of further discussion. It might work if it is delivered with humor, and the person accepts the fact that he or she got caught fibbing about something that really isn't important. Otherwise, it could be taken as mockery.

D. "That sounds like an exaggeration."

Embellishment works here, too. You aren't discounting the remark entirely, just implying that it is slightly off. Also, you aren't making a definitive statement, but letting the person know you, personally, are somewhat skeptical. It is even less accusatory than "You're exaggerating," because you're not directly charging the speaker with the exaggeration.

E. "I find that hard to believe. Where did you hear about it?"

This softer approach is the best option. It questions the source rather than attacks the speaker. Also, you are asking a question, giving the individual the opportunity to think about his or her source for the information, and to decide if he or she might have been misinformed. The person has the opportunity to blame someone else for misleading him or her.

The differences might seem subtle to you, or require quicker thinking and more diplomacy than you are accustomed to. Maybe, but now that you have heard a more tactful way to confront a suspected liar, try it when you get the chance.

If you prefer, you can pick a single word that sounds right for you, and get in the habit of using it every time you are tempted to say *bullshit*. If you choose a word that begins with *b*—like *bunk, baloney, booshwah,* or *balderdash*—your mouth might be headed in the wrong direction, but your brain will have a chance to steer it to a more gentle word.

Something like *balderdash* might sound ridiculous or old-fashioned, and *bovine fecal matter* is too confusing, but corny comments often prompt laughter that takes the tension off, turning the confrontation into a calm conversation about the veracity of the claim that was made.

You also have many adjectives at your disposal with different depths of meaning, such as *silly, ridiculous, absurd, preposterous, groundless, outlandish.* You don't have to remember all these words, just the ones you feel comfortable with.

The point is, if you really want to cut back on your cussing, you have to start somewhere. You can pledge to yourself that you will avoid saying *bullshit* in the future. If you think all of the options lack the power and the force of *bullshit,* it's because you are conditioned to think so. Any of the other words gets your message across, and you can intensify your objection if you wish by the tone and volume of your voice. But don't overlook the value of toning the message down so that you sound reasonable and polite rather than like a belligerent hothead who is quick to call someone a liar. Besides, there is always the chance that the statement is correct, making you look like the fool.

Points to Ponder

- Most swear words can be replaced with simple words or expressions, or be dropped from your statement. What's left might lack intensity, and in most cases, that's good.

- Language that attacks or insults gets you nowhere. Be tactful and diplomatic, not emotional, and others will listen.

- We have made *shit* a multipurpose word. Consequently, we can't expect to find one word to substitute for every application.

- The word *shit* has existed for more than a thousand years. If alternative words and phrases sound like clichés to you, the worn-out and overused S word is the biggest cliché of them all.

- To break the habit, get accustomed to using the logical substitutes. *Shoot* is just one vowel away from the word you really want to say. The word *stuff* works fine to describe various *things*.

- Although they are decent alternatives, *stuff* and *things* can be lazy and meaningless words. If you want to communicate intelligently, take a second to think of what you are describing, then say it.

MICHELLE, 33, ARTIST

I swear sometimes, but usually just to myself. I don't want to offend anyone. Many people are offended by it. I don't want to be crude or crass. To hear it doesn't bother me too much, but I don't like gratuitous swearing, like in movies when every other word is F this, F that.

In the first grade I got in trouble for swearing. Some boy was bugging me and I called him a fucker. *He said, "Oohh, you said a bad word! I'm going to tell the teacher!" I had to go sit in the principal's office. She was very stern with me. So I learned public swearing isn't okay.*

But my initiation into swearing came when I was 3½ years old and I met my stepdad for the first time. It was Easter and my mother took me over to meet her boyfriend. I wanted to show him my Easter basket. I remember when we got there he wasn't even up yet. He came out of his bedroom through these double doors and the first thing he said was, "Shit, man!" He wasn't even interested in my Easter basket. So after that my mom couldn't exactly tell me not to swear, when her new husband did.

My mother didn't swear though, and neither did her parents. We all went to Sears together once, and I suddenly had this terrible swearing episode. My grandparents couldn't shut me up, so they ignored me as if I didn't belong to them. This was around the same time that I'd been exposed to my stepfather's swearing.

But my father's family, they were all heavy swearers. I went to my grandfather's memorial service, forgetting that everybody on that side of the family talked that way. Afterward, my grandmother, this elegant old lady with white hair perfectly done, was sitting on a sofa and in comes one of my cousins, saying, "That little shit," and plops down right next to her. She just sat there with this relaxed, pleasant smile. A little later I heard her talking about somebody and saying, "Those goddam sons of bitches." I later learned that her husband had taught her to swear on their wedding night. He was against anything taboo and always had to do the opposite.

Those grandparents took me to Hawaii when I was 9 years old. I was in the pool and my grandfather was standing there like a drill sergeant barking orders at me. "Keep swimming, keep going!" I was dying in the pool but he kept pushing me. My grandmother was lying on her chaise lounge and she finally got up and said, "God damn you, stop, stop!" but he kept it up. "Swim!" he kept shouting. All the polite ways to tell him to stop weren't working. Then I just remember snapping. I swore at him. But I didn't know how to swear that well, and I got the words completely out of order. All of a sudden he stopped. He looked stunned. Later when I was older he liked to talk about how I got the words out of order. But he had this twisted sentimentality and when he talked about what I said, he put his hand over his heart and said, "You said that to me . . . to me!," like he was remembering something touching I had done for him. On that side of the family they had a lot of things turned around. They had some family history that most people would have swept under the rug, but they would frame it and put it on the wall. It was like that with swearing, too.

In spite of this influence, I would say I rarely swear. Only with certain people, or when I'm in a dangerous situation. I remember my second stepfather would swear at me when he got drunk. He would do repulsive things. I'd just swear right back at him. So I only swear on specific occasions, with specific people like that.

One time I was driving across the Golden Gate Bridge in my grandfather's truck during a bad rainstorm. I had two friends with me, sisters from a pretty old-fashioned family. I was having trouble switching lanes; no one would let me in. It was a hazardous driving situation, no visibility, that kind of thing. I kept swearing. This one friend would gasp every time I swore, as if she'd never heard those words before. I kept apologizing, but then the next word out of my mouth would be a better swear word. She was totally shocked, like she'd been brought up in a bubble. I kept swearing, she kept gasping, I kept apologizing, I missed the toll booth and the exit and had to go up, turn around, that kind of mess. Ordinarily I wouldn't have used those words in front of that kind of person.

In college—I went to art school—kids didn't swear too much. We were too busy concentrating on our work, I think. We went to comedy clubs where the comedians swore, but that didn't bother me. Sometimes we had baseball games, but it was ridiculous, artists playing baseball. They argued about the arbitrariness of the lines on the field. That kind of thing.

I accidentally swore in front of an aunt of mine once. I was always very careful to be proper around her. But her daughter said, "Don't worry about it. I broke her in."

I think not swearing has helped me to get along in society. I usually keep a cool head, even in an emergency. And I try not to get too stressed out.

EIGHT
The F Word:
Stop Me Before I Say It Again

> *I'm not going to say that word anymore. I mean it. Every time I say it, I'll put up $100. Let's be honest. It's a stupid word. It's stupid and it's silly and I've said it so much in my life, it's just ridiculous. I've done a lot of stupid things in my life that I probably won't do again, and using that word is one of them. I just want to be a good example for people. Maybe I want to be the person I ought to be for a change.*
>
> —Mike Ditka, coach of the New Orleans Saints, in an interview for
> *Sports Illustrated*, July 20, 1998

THERE ARE TWO INTERESTING theories about the origin of the F word involving acronyms—words formed by the initial letters of other words. One claims it was a badge worn by convicted prostitutes and adulterers and stood for either Forced Unsolicited Carnal Knowledge or For Unlawful Carnal Knowledge. The other theory is that it meant Fornication Under Consent of the King, a plea by the King of Someplace to repopulate the country after a plague.

Rubbish, say the scholars. The first written record of the word was around 1475. Acronyms were rarely used until the twentieth century, and these two theories seemed to surface around the 1960s. Like a popular dirty joke, someone came up with these clever and convincing explanations and will never get credit for them.

The word might have existed long before the 1400s, but it wasn't documented, presumably because it was always a vulgar word and was considered what might have been called "unpenable"—before printing was invented and it became "unprintable." It first appeared in a dictionary in 1671. Samuel Johnson left it out—along with all other words regarded as vulgar—of his highly regarded dictionary of 1755. John Ash included it in his *New and Complete Dictionary of the English Language* in 1775, defining it as "To perform an act of generation, to have to do with a woman." It disappeared from dictionaries not long after that and didn't reappear for nearly 170 years when it was included in the 1965 edition of the *Penguin Dictionary.*

A reluctance throughout history to record the F word makes it difficult to trace its origins, which really shouldn't matter beyond curiosity, except to explain its early and continued usage as a violent word. Two of the suspected origins of the word, the Middle Dutch *fokken* and the Germanic *ficken,* both meant to copulate, but they also meant to strike. The hard *k* sound is found in other striking words, such as *hit, kick, poke, pork, crack, knock, sock, spank, clank,* and *peck.* It is also common in other curses and derogatory words such as *cock, cunt, dick, prick,* and *suck.*

Sexual intercourse is arguably the finest physical pleasure known to man or woman, so it seems that you would be wishing someone well by telling him or her to get fucked. Instead, the word *fuck* most fittingly refers to rough sex or an act of pure animal self-indulgence, void of love and romance. In commonly used terms of contempt such as "I really got fucked over," and "Fuck him," it borders on having the same brutal, humiliating, and demeaning connotations of rape, an act of violence rather than sex.

A faction of the feminist movement in the 1970s wanted to replace the hard-sounding F word with the softer term *swive,* an Old English word meaning intercourse, but it didn't catch on. Instead, liberated women latched on to the F word and began using it as if they were not on the traditional receiving end of the activity. Statements by women gradually regressed from "Charlie and I made love last night" to "I let Charlie fuck me last night" to the more aggressive "I fucked Charlie last night." It's another example of equality of the lowest quality between the sexes.

Defenders of this word believe it is hypocritical to exclude it from our vocabulary since everyone is either having sex with some degree of satisfying frequency, wishing that they were, or thinking about it more often than food, sleep, money, or a good foot rub. Comedian George Carlin points out that, in the daytime soap operas and *Melrose Place* genre of evening shows, everyone is fucking someone else, so why not say the word? Good point, up to a point, but that's like saying intriguing and passionate romance should be replaced with the raw sex of pornography, or that a seductively semiclad woman is less appealing than a woman spread-eagled for a gynecological examination.

If it's true that sexual intercourse ranks high among the few of our favorite things, even more so than bright copper kettles and warm woolen mittens, the F word still does not qualify as an acceptable description because of its many violent applications. You would never lash out at someone by saying, "Go make love to yourself," or "Get copulated," or "You're an intercoursing son of a bitch." No way. There is only one word strong enough to deliver a brutal and hateful verbal attack. Consequently, it's ludicrous to think the often vicious F word can become a mainstream appellation for life's most sublime, private, and passionate pleasure.

"More commonly today, the F word is used to express not desire but derision, not heat but hostility," wrote Elizabeth Austin in *U.S. News & World Report* in a plea for all good citizens to abandon the word. "When used as a kind of verbal space holder, a rougher equivalent of 'you know,' it carries a rude message. It is both a gauge and an engine of our ever plummeting standards of civility."

WHAT'S LOVE GOT TO DO WITH IT?

Proponents of unleashing the F word argue that it often has nothing to do with love or even sex. It's just a word that sometimes has a mean meaning, sometimes has a happy meaning, and sometimes is completely meaningless. The problem with its multiple functions is that the listeners don't always interpret it to mean what the speakers intended.

"There was a time when, if you said 'F you,' they were fighting words," believes Scott Stantis, who creates the family comic strip "The Buckets." "Now that phrase is used so casually it can mean hello or it can mean good-bye."

Oprah Winfrey can attest to that. "My career began in a newsroom in Baltimore. It wasn't unusual for someone to greet you in the morning with 'How the *uh* are you?'"

Phil is a father who didn't care for any of the meanings behind the word when he was exposed to several of its applications one day at the ball game. He isn't a big fan of baseball. In fact, he had only been to three or four games in his life when his 10-year-old son asked him to take him to see the Chicago Cubs. They were already in their seats when two guys, Phil guessed in their early twenties, took the seats directly in front of them. One was wearing a white T-shirt screaming on the back in fat red letters, FUCK YOU.

"There was no way I was going to sit there for nine innings with my son, staring at this incredibly hostile message," said Phil. "I've used that expression, but I couldn't believe somebody would broadcast it in bold letters to every person who came up behind him that day. I was surprised his friend wasn't wearing one of those T-shirts that says 'I'm with stupid.' Do you think he made any new friends that day? It's more likely that he got beat up. I didn't stick around to see."

Phil told his son the man was blocking his view, and they managed to find seats a few rows over. Everything was fine until well into the game, when several sun- and beer-soaked fans began cussing out the other team's players, hurling the F word in the direction of the players with all their vocal might.

"They used the word maliciously, but later used the same word as they laughed and joked among themselves. It took the fun out of the day for me, even though the Cubs won and we saw Sammy Sosa hit a home run. I sensed that my son was uncomfortable hearing that language with me. It's a shame a dad can't take his son out to the old ball game without hearing and seeing this kind of thing."

On the street after the game, a car came to the curb to pick up some teenagers too young to drive. One kid screamed to the driver, "What a fucking fantastic game that was!"

"The word *fantastic* wasn't strong enough for him?" Phil pondered. "As I walked away, I hoped the person in the car he was talking to was an older brother, not a father. These days, it might have been his mother."

A constantly used four-letter profanity is special in Hollywood for at least three reasons. First, many screenwriters sprinkle their scripts with it because they lack the talent to write convincing dialogue without it. Second, studios prefer to make films containing violence and foul language because they earn an R rating and thus attract teenagers who shun PG and PG 13 films, seeing them as a sign of immaturity. Third, and perhaps most important, many moviegoers use profanity in their own speech and don't mind when it crops up on screen. Profanity is now so accepted in American life that it's creeping into prime-time TV shows. Not only is this inexpressibly tacky, it also cheapens us as a nation and a people.

—Walter Scott's Personality Parade column in *Parade Magazine,*
September 28, 1997

VERSATILITY OR PERVERSITY?

The F word is praised by legions of men and women for its versatility and its ability to communicate so many things, even though it is one simple syllable. These same people probably think salt makes everything taste better. They fail to see that it's just a lazy way to spice up a sentence. And while it does communicate quickly, it also confuses because it can mean good or bad or happy or sad, depending on the context. A friend could send you a note that reads "I got fucked on Friday," and you wouldn't know whether to congratulate him or recommend a lawyer.

This word rose in popularity and began developing more uses than baking soda during World War I. It was so overused by British soldiers that, as some contemporary cursers fear might happen today, it actually lost its power. John Brophy wrote in *Songs and Slang of the British Soldier* in 1930: "It became so common that an effective way for the soldier to express his emotion was to omit this word. Thus if a sergeant said, 'Get your ____ing rifles!' it was understood as a matter of routine. But if he said, 'Get your rifles!' there was an immediate implication of urgency and danger."

Soldiers not only introduced the F word as a modifier for every conceivable object and action, they inserted it into the middle of perfectly good words. An example of this word rape from World War I still heard today is *abso-fucking-lutely*. This is one of many terms that youngsters hear at some point in the corruption of their diction and gleefully use it the next chance they get, thinking it is an innovation.

Not surprisingly, the F word and all its variations grew in prominence during World War II. Not because the men liked to talk rough and dirty when ladies weren't around, but because they were away from home in wretched conditions and frightening situations, experiencing every physical discomfort and emotional trauma imaginable, not to mention the agony of not having their ladies around. Voicing the F word was an expedient way to express their frustration, depression, fear, anger, anguish, horror, and misery, and sometimes get a good laugh.

Pick a war, any war, and the dastardly dialogue is the same. Situations that are brutal and unbearable, tense and terrifying, bring out the worst in what we say.

Why is it then, that in times of peace and prosperity, when our daily conflicts have more to do with winning games and jackpots than with winning wars, we are using a word once reserved for the worst of all possible human conditions?

In modern-day life, the emotion that provokes this vile word the most is probably frustration. We hate things to go wrong, and there is something sadly gratifying in using the F word when we have exhausted our patience.

For example, in the movie *Trains, Planes and Automobiles,* Steve Martin encounters one obstacle after another in his efforts to get home from a business trip. Exacerbated and on the verge of exploding, he demands a car from a woman rental agent who is offended by his manner and his language.

"I really don't care for the way you are speaking to me," she says.

"And I really don't care for the way your company left me in the middle of fucking nowhere," replies Martin bitterly, "with fucking keys to a fucking car that isn't fucking there. And I really didn't care to fucking walk down a fucking highway and across a fucking runway to get back here to have you smile at my fucking face. I want a fucking car, right fucking now."

She pauses, gains her composure, and asks, "May I see your rental agreement?"

"I threw it away."

"Oh, boy."

"Oh boy what?" he snarls.

She stares at him, then barks, "You're fucked!"

The humor is in the revenge the woman gets by putting Martin in his place with the same unsavory word he used to offend her. The audience, while sympathetic to Martin up to this point, enjoys her zinging retort. She was not personally responsible for his troubles, and even though he had no one else to blame or to complain to, she didn't deserve such shabby treatment.

Aside from the obvious provocations, a mouthful of peculiar uses of the word have surfaced in the last few decades. In one of Eddie Murphy's best movies, *Beverly Hills Cop,* a person he just met makes a few casual statements that both amuse and surprise Murphy. "You're fucking me, you're fucking me!" he laughs.

Michelle, a young lawyer, was frightened when she misinterpreted her cousin's outbursts at a large family gathering.

"I was in the living room, and one of my cousins was in the hallway talking to his ex-wife, who was there with the children. His back was to me, but I heard him react to something she said by shouting, 'Fuck you. Fuck you!' He said it several times as she kept talking, each time a little louder. I was very distressed that they were starting to argue at a family event. It turned out she was telling him she landed a great new job. He was thrilled and impressed but was expressing his joy in a manner I had never heard before."

Finding new ways to use the word could be considered inventive, but it adds to the confusion about its meaning, neglects excellent existing words, and is more crass than creative. Random House published a directory in 1995 called *The F Word,* edited by Jesse Sheidlower. It contains more than two hundred pages of terms and their definitions and euphemisms that suggest, in sound and meaning, the word itself. Although a few are clever enough to be amusing, most are terms of contempt, mistreatment, disgust, violence, and animosity.

Sheidlower's book includes compounded variations and phrases that are in actual use, primarily in the United States, but many of them are too rare or restricted to the military to bother considering alternatives for them. Many fit into an animal or creature category, such as *bearfuck* (confused undertaking), *goat fuck* (fiasco, mess), and *bugfuck* (insane), while others refer to specific sexual acts. Most of the terms are not of the variety that could fit into your everyday conversation, or are likely to slip through your lips unintentionally. People who use the more creative, complex, and crude terms spout them off consciously to amuse others. If they so choose, they have time to prevent themselves from being gross and obscene.

You Need an Attitude Adjustment, Not Alternatives

Perhaps surprisingly, the F word differs from the S word in that there aren't many common phrases in which it is used, or phrases for which there is an obvious alternative word or two. This word is used most commonly as an exclamation—a stand-alone expression of anger, frustration, surprise, or a host of other emotions—or as a meaningless modifier, an adjective added purely for emphasis. Consequently, finding ways to eliminate it from your vocabulary requires more effort than selecting and getting into the habit of using optional words. The essential first step is to convince yourself of three realities:

1. Fuck *is a truly bad word.*

You have to tell yourself this, disregarding the fact that millions of people use it every day. Don't succumb to the growing evidence that it is overcoming the bad reputation it has had for years. The everybody-does-it argument is a generalization and an excuse. A good percentage of the population—a percentage that is good—still considers the word to be foul, violent, and uncouth. The evolution of the language might someday make the word *fuck* as acceptable as the word *flower,* but we're not there yet. Don't risk offending someone or doing harm to your own image. Condition yourself to cringe every time you hear the word, particularly when it comes from your own mouth.

2. It isn't necessary.

There are men and women who have never used this word, and, believe it or not, they lead normal, productive lives. They go to work, raise kids, have friends, get angry, and even make love without using the word. You know it's possible, because you've been in situations when you couldn't use the word and you managed to control yourself and say what you had to say with fuck-free sentences. You might think that, at times, especially moments of anger, no word works as well for you. Common sense should tell you that's a matter of conditioning. You allowed yourself to start using the word until it became a gratifying habit. You can find at least one word suitable for an exclamation and one word to replace the adjective, and develop the habit of using them. Eventually, they will work most of the time.

3. It doesn't do you any good.

Think about this. How do you benefit from using this word? You don't need to say *fuck* to be friendly, forceful, or funny. In almost every situation you can think of, your ability to communicate is more effective if you don't degrade your message with this wicked word. If it really makes you feel better shouting it out when you are outraged, indulge yourself, but try to do it when you are alone. If others hear it, they might not be bothered by it, but no one is going to feel better about you.

What to Say Instead

The act itself is sexual intercourse, plain and simple. *Copulation* and *fornication* are what were known as the dictionary words—that is, words that were acceptable because they were in the dictionary. That rule no longer holds, since many of the nastier words are now lexicon entries. These words are also referred to as the clinical terms, but that implies that sex belongs in a laboratory.

The euphemisms for the sex act (there's one) are often criticized. Some are lame attempts to disguise the real word, and the profanity purists prefer that you not pussyfoot around. Either say it loudly and proudly, or let someone else say it for you.

Don't listen to the purists. They want you to wallow in the muck with them. Any word is more acceptable than *fuck*. It's true that using some euphemisms is almost like trying to lose weight by having a diet soft drink to offset your cookie. You're not fooling yourself or anybody else, but at least you're trying. Even this book uses the euphemistic term *F word* instead of sticking with the real word. That's because, at times, the reference or context makes the term *F word* more appropriate. Besides, using the obscenity over and over is as tiresome as the people who use it again and again.

We need polite ways to describe a delicate subject, even if they are flawed:

- *Having sex* is the best term to use. It means having intercourse to most people, but Bill Clinton debated the definition and made it apparent that many people, especially men, feel they are not having sex unless they *go all the way,* an expression that definitely qualifies as a euphemism since it can also mean traveling long distances. Of course, some people are willing to go any distance to have sex.

- *Making love* has a tender and romantic ring to it, but to some people, it is simply kissing and hugging.

- You can *sleep with* or *bed down with* a lover, but you can do the same thing with your brother or your dog, so those terms are polite almost to a fault, but still preferable to the F word.

- *Getting laid* means only one thing, unless you live on a chicken farm. It sounds somewhat unpleasant and involuntary, sort of like getting laid off.

- A British obscenity that we threatened to borrow as a euphemism is *shag,* which made its American debut with the film *Austin Powers: The Spy Who Shagged Me.* Fortunately, it never caught on.

- To *screw* someone once meant to have sex, but now its popular meaning is to cheat someone, or to get cheated, as in "I got screwed." A similar term is "I got *hosed,*" which is milder and more amusing because it hasn't been overused.

One of the peculiarities in the way we communicate is that we are more likely to use one of the preceding terms instead of the F word when referring to sexual intercourse. It's ironic, but most of the common uses of the F word have nothing to do with sex. Example: "Yesterday was such a beautiful fucking day that I said fuck it, left work, and went to the beach. I met this girl who was fucking gorgeous, and we talked the whole fucking afternoon, then went to her place and had sex."

Our use of the F word not only has very little to do with sex, it has very little to do with anything. It makes you wonder why we say it instead of some of the other action words with a hard *k* sound. When we have an outburst, maybe we should yell "Crack!" or "Kick!" or "Knock!" There are no restrictions, really. You can even make up a word.

The euphemistic focus has been on words that begin with *f* rather than end with *k* since it is easier to catch yourself at the beginning of a curse and fabricate a different word. It's the easiest method if you can't go cold turkey on the word, and it's not a bad starting point:

> *Fudge*
>
> *Fiddlesticks*
>
> *Phooey*

These substitutes for the stand-alone expletive definitely lack power, but you might be comfortable with one of them on occasions when you are only mildly mad or annoyed. *Fudge* is the weakest, since it is widely recognized as a candy-coated disguise of your true sentiments. *Fiddlesticks* is archaic but lighthearted, so it won't offend anyone or frighten your children. *Phooey* is almost embarrassingly simple, but you can use it and most people won't even notice. After a while, it will sound okay to you and to the people who grow accustomed to hearing you use it.

Optional words for the stand-alone expletive are the same substitutes for the S word or any other exclamation. (See page 119 in chapter 7.)

For verbs, *fool, foul,* and *fuss* are good words because they actually mean something. They work so well that, in most instances, they don't come across as substitutes for the nasty word. There are also other suitable alternatives for these common expressions that don't begin with F:

Don't (fool, futz, mess, meddle, interfere) with that thing.

Stop (fooling, fussing, fiddling, futzing, messing) around.

The project is all (fouled, botched, goofed, mixed) up.

He (ruined, wrecked, bungled, muddled, destroyed) the project.

The chapter on the S word identified several common expressions in which the word could be dropped rather than replaced. We sometimes insert the F word in these same expressions to make them even nastier, just as *shit* provides a stronger tone than *hell* and *heck*. You really don't need any of these words, but select *heck* when you feel you need to punctuate:

Who (the fuck, shit, hell, heck) knows?

What (the fuck, shit, hell, heck) is wrong?

I don't (give a fuck, shit, damn, darn) care.

What the (fuck, shit, hell, heck, deuce)?

How (the fuck, shit, hell, in blazes) should I know?

I don't know what (the fuck, shit, hell, heck, blazes) he was talking about.

WAYS TO AVOID THE MEANINGLESS MODIFIER

Other than barking out the F word in moments of emotional stress and occasionally glee, the most frequently used format is *fucking,* both as an adjective and an adverb. If you use this word often and don't know the difference between an adjective and an adverb, don't worry. That's the least of your problems. You should be more concerned with the negativity of your language. Most of the time, you are casually jamming the word in front of a noun or other adjective for intensity or to draw attention to the point you are making. Unfortunately, you are probably expressing disgust, repulsion, disapproval, annoyance, disagreement, or anger—all negative emotions that aren't much fun for the people you are with. Be aware of where and how often you do it. Sounding like Steve Martin at the car rental desk will get you about as far as it got him.

In addition to sounding sour and bitter, using this word reveals your inability to think of a more meaningful and intelligent word. The alternatives you use won't necessarily replace the negative tone of your statement, but they won't be as harsh, nor will they reflect as badly on your character and disposition.

Here are five suggestions for overcoming your use of this infamous adjective:

1. Don't use any adjective.

Your goal should be to get in the habit of leaving out negative adjectives whenever possible. For example, if someone asks you why you were late for an event, you can say the . . . bus broke down, the . . . highway was backed up, you couldn't find a . . . cab. Just give the facts. No one asked for your commentary. They will know it wasn't your fault, so don't feel obligated to preface each noun with a negative adjective to show you're not happy about being late. You've reached your destination, so forget the hassle you had getting there. Apologize if you inconvenienced others, and enjoy the event.

You might feel like you are leaving a gaping hole if you drop the adjective, but if you are wondering what people who never swear say instead, it's nothing. They don't see a hole. You can rely on the power of your voice, adding inflection to words and syllables. Examples: What DIFFerence does it make? I was inFURiated!

The least you can do is avoid using the word casually, those times when you add the word for no particular reason. The less frequently you use the word, the more likely it will gradually drift away from your vocabulary.

2. When desperate, use the euphemisms.

Realistically, you can't be calm and in control of your emotions all the time, so you need to say something. If you stick with the f formula of euphemisms, you don't have to stray very far from *fucking*:

> effing
>
> fricking
>
> frigging
>
> freaking

These words almost sound like the real thing, and the first three have no other meaning, so you're really not covering up very well. They, too, are meaningless modifiers. Nevertheless, if you feel you need the satisfaction of almost saying the cuss word, these options are certainly more polite and acceptable. In a previous century, frigging used to mean masturbating, but no one seems to know that, so don't be squeamish about it.

3. Use words that end in ing.

Another way to wean yourself of the adjective form of the F word is to substitute words that end in *ing*. Your brain and your mouth don't have to make major adjustments. Words that have only two syllables also approximate the adjective, providing some degree of gratification.

Try *stinking*. It has the *ing* as well as the *k,* two syllables, yet somehow doesn't sound like a euphemism. Here are some others:

> bleeping
> disgusting
> revolting
> sickening
> nauseating

4. Use words that mean something.

You can do better, though, with modest effort and maybe some practice. It doesn't make sense to refer to the fucking car, the fucking test, the fucking weather, or the fucking whatever. How about the worthless car, the impossible test, and unbearable weather? As an exercise, think of other adjectives that really do describe these three common annoyances before you read on.

Another common annoyance is your work, or certain aspects of it. You spend lots of your time there, and the inevitable aggravations sometimes push your patience to the limit. You might say you hate your fucking job, but plenty of people would like a job if it involves fucking. Maybe you intend to say you hate your horrible, miserable, stressful, exhausting, difficult, ridiculous, demanding, demeaning, meaningless, mundane, arduous, unsatisfying, tedious, or boring job. The best advice, frankly, is to take a minute to determine if you really hate the job, then take more time to find a new job. Admitting that you feel stuck in a bad situation reflects poorly on your ability to deal with it or get out of it.

5. Accept the fact that there is no single substitute.

The options you choose for *fucking* are frequently going to depend on the context of what you are saying. No one word will work in every situation. If any word comes close, it is probably *stinking.* Other simple adjectives for contemptible objects and situations are *dumb, stupid, crumby,* and *lousy.*

It is impossible to provide a list of all the adjectives that fit every annoying experience you might have, but when you hear an adjective that sounds hard, powerful, or even funny to you, or for some reason has a sound you like, make a mental or written note of it, and try it out when you need to. The context in which you use a word is important, but here are a few that you actually might enjoy using when they fit the occasion:

odious	sinister
detestable	diabolical
contemptible	devilish
despicable	villainous
atrocious	wretched
ghastly	pitiful
appalling	dismal
outlandish	dilapidated
tawdry	vile
trashy	heinous
shoddy	insipid
sleazy	abhorrent

ABOLISH THE TRULY CRASS, CRUEL,
AND ABRASIVE EXPRESSIONS

When someone pushes you to the edge, when you just can't take the abuse anymore, there is nothing you can say that expresses your ire and your feelings toward that person more than the ever reliable, "Fuck you!"

And since nothing says it better, it's better to say nothing.

It doesn't end an argument, and it's not the last word you or your adversary will get in. Instead, it brings any confrontation to a higher and more dangerous level.

If you say it half jokingly to a friend who is teasing you about something minor, it can be as innocuous as, "Get lost," or "Take a hike." In which case, you might just as well use one of those terms. You should get rid of all of the lazy and crass expressions you might use with this word, such as "Get fucked," "I got fucked over," "He's a fucking asshole." Why not be smarter and more imaginative? Better yet, why not be nicer, calmer, and more positive?

Making the rounds on the Internet is an alleged office memo suggesting alternative ways to express your feelings without offending sensitive employees. In reality, the alternatives offered are what most people typically do use, while the gruffer terms are what they wish they could say. The true-feelings versions might make you feel better, but the diplomatic variations will get you promoted faster. Here are a few examples of good versus evil:

> Try: I'll stay late and get this done.
> Instead of: When the fuck do you expect me to do this?

> Try: I'm not certain that's feasible.
> Instead of: No fucking way.

> Try: I wasn't involved in that project.
> Instead of: It's not my fucking problem.

> Try: Are you sure this is a problem?
> Instead of: Who the fuck cares?

Try: Let's get everyone involved and discuss it.

Instead of: Not another fucking meeting!

Try: The boss can be very insensitive.

Instead of: The boss is a fucking jerk.

Try: With some training, you could master that skill.

Instead of: You don't know what the fuck you are doing.

Take a second to reread the negative statements. Notice that all of them can be said without the F word. It is extraneous. The meaning remains the same without substituting any word. The statements still aren't polite, but they are less vicious.

If you are convinced that the F word is as attached to you as your tongue, and that it would be easier to give up sleep than to stop saying it, persist! Don't get discouraged and say "Fuck it." Instead, say "Forget it," which will make you realize there *are* other words that work. Your initial objective should be to cut back, to reduce the use, to have other people feel better about you, and for you to feel better about yourself. If this word is so important to you, save it for special occasions. Don't wear it out.

Points to Ponder

- Even though it is widely used and often has no sexual connotations, the F word is not an acceptable word because one of its basic meanings is hostile and sometimes violent and brutal.
- Like the S word, it can express every emotion from anger to jubilation. Consequently, it does not communicate clearly, and its intention is often subject to interpretation.
- The F word is not a necessary word. Saying it might make you feel good, but it makes you sound bad. You can lead a normal, productive life without it, as do millions of other people.
- If you can't think of a better adjective, don't use any adjective. The best substitute, if you need to fill a verbal void, is *stinking*.

Tiffany Van Hoffman, 33, Corporate Consultant

Even if you are just casually swearing you can pollute the atmo-sphere for the people around you without realizing it. But directly cursing at someone definitely agitates people. I firmly believe it can lead to violence. If someone verbally attacks me I try very hard not to get drawn into their state of mind.

It just compounds the problem if you fight back. It mushrooms. One time I was out running and I passed these two fellows who said something quite revolting to me. It was so heinous, I won't even repeat what they said. All I think of to defend myself was to say, "Fuck you." I thought it would send the message "Don't mess with me, you lower life-forms." Well, I didn't know they knew where I lived. We had this huge white garage door. I woke up the next morn-ing and there, in red spray paint, big as life, huge red letters on the door, F U C K Y O U. I felt as if I'd been raped by these characters.

What was even more disturbing was my husband's reaction. He was the kind of guy who would get hugely offended if someone looked at him the wrong way. He loved to act like king of the road in his Mercedes and would start a cursing match with other drivers if they got in his way. I never knew when he'd pick a fight with someone. But you know, he was almost happy about this F U C K Y O U on our garage. He just whistled a little tune and got out his paint can and painted it over as if it were all perfectly hunky-dory that someone had abused his wife. I am not always an angel myself, but I didn't deserve that. I felt completely annihilated. It was as if he were just out in his deck shoes doing a little touch-up on his yacht and all was right with the world. Others had validated his cherished view that I was a person of no value. Hum de hum dee dum.

Such is the destructive power of strong words. I guess that's why we resort to them when we feel powerless. I learned a lot from this incident. First, that the saying is true: "Curses, like chickens, come home to roost." And second, that it was time for a divorce.

NINE
Names Can Really Hurt

FROM *ASSHOLE* TO *ZOMBIE,* we have been calling each other names since language was invented. The first derogatory term allegedly came about way back when cavemen could barely do more than grunt sounds like "ugh." A caveman was chewing on a raw fish—centuries before sushi was fashionable—when an obese and hairy cavewoman approached him. He took one look at her and growled, "Ugh! Leave!" Thus, the word *ugly* was born. As she left, she mumbled something like, "Sexist male chauvinist pig!" Her words would have become the world's second derogatory term, but they went unrecorded since nearby cavemen could not decipher what she said.

The unkind epithets men have for women and women have for men represent only a fraction of the abusive terms that have been devised through the centuries. New names continue to be crafted to accommodate, for example, New Age techies and computer geeks. Many times it's all in fun, mere teasing among friends, and the words aren't always crude. Cute terms can be modified to be made crass, and vice versa. The level of offensiveness is often a matter of context, tone, and the familiarity of the people involved.

Consider the assortment of "head" names. Some you can't take too seriously because they sound funny, such as *beanhead, cementhead,* and *dunderhead.* Even *butthead* has gained comical connotations, thanks to the cartoon character and his buddy Beavis. But if someone calls you *airhead, blockhead, bonehead, meathead, fathead,* or *knucklehead,* you are more likely to take offense. And you're not exactly flattered when someone calls you the vulgar versions—*dickhead, shithead,* and *fuckhead.*

If someone compiled a list of all the disparaging names we have for each other, the list would undoubtedly require more paper than a roll of Charmin. The good news is, the majority of them would not be classified as dirty words—maybe, say, just ten thousand or so. The bad news is, many of the "clean" names are far more beastly. Someone who is calamitously overweight would prefer to be called a *bastard* instead of *fatso* in front of a crowd. A Hispanic person would rather be called a *son of a bitch* than a *greasy spick*. Words that draw attention to a sensitive person's physical shortcomings or ethnic origins can cut deeper than sticks and stones.

The devastating impact of clean but cruel name-calling should make it brutally clear that finding alternatives to cuss words is definitely not the answer. Although this book focuses on reducing or eliminating profanity, obscenity, and blasphemy, ridicule is a broader crime that you need to seriously consider avoiding, especially if you intensify such slurs with a vulgar or profane adjective. When you are judgmental and openly intolerant of others, you are not only being unkind, but making yourself unnecessarily grouchy and irascible.

Face-to-face name-calling ranks at the top of the list of offensive ways in which we use profanity. When people get angry and yell expletives in front of you, you might not like it, but you can deal with it. If they swear at themselves for making mistakes or swear at objects in their way, their frustration doesn't involve you. But when an irate neighbor, boss, family member, or stranger directly insults you, attacking your character and calling you insulting names, it hurts and angers you, especially when they use profanity.

You are probably beyond deriving satisfaction by replying to your verbal assailant, "I know you are, but what am I?" Nor will you have much luck trying to disarm him or her by saying, "I'm rubber and you're glue, everything bounces off me and sticks to you." Those smug attempts to preserve your self-esteem and avoid altercations don't apply in the adult world. After a puzzled pause, your assailant will probably smack you with another belittling insult. You are more likely to react with equally vigorous insults, perpetuating a battle that no one ever wins.

So, if nasty names thrown in your direction only infuriate you, why would you want to insult someone else? They aren't going to like it, they aren't going to like you, and the repercussions will last much longer than they would if you had handled the confrontation with greater maturity.

In our current culture of political correctness, we have somehow determined it is a greater transgression to deride someone about their ethnic descent than it is to call them a genital word in an ungentle way. As evidence, consider the surprising initiative taken by the editors of the newest edition of the Random House *Webster's College Dictionary*. In front of words that insult ethnic or religious groups, they have added warnings that begin with: "This term is a slur and must be avoided. It is used with disparaging intent and is perceived as highly insulting."

We have come a long way here, especially since dictionaries historically have been objective suppliers of definitions, not promoters of polite behavior. Society's relatively successful effort to eradicate racial slurs from our everyday language, even convincing a dictionary publisher to flag insensitive slang, is significant. If ethnic slurs can be depopularized, perhaps the crudest cuss words can also be canned, cut, or decreased.

Unfortunately, we seem to be going in the opposite direction, resigning ourselves to the fact that curse words, like flies, are annoying when they are in our face but eventually go away. *Webster's College Dictionary* identifies obscene names as *vulgar slang* but does not provide the same statement of caution it does for ethnic slang. The introduction counseling against the notorious N word, on the other hand, is 110 words long and declares that *nigger* is now "probably the most offensive word in English." This could be considered a major blow to folks who would have voted for *cunt* or *motherfucker,* or maybe even *butterfat.*

Condemned for years as the most vile of insults, *motherfucker* was popularized by a segment of the same African-Americans labeled with the N word. In an ironic twist in the evolution of words, *motherfucker* has lost a significant amount of its power and nearly all of its shock value within the rougher side of the black community. In fact, both *motherfucker* and *nigger* have been used as terms of endearment. This is a dangerous trend, since the language of blacks is often duplicated by all of society's younger generation.

"Black people now call each other nigger, whore, and bitch in the rap music that reaches deep into the white community," says Peter Ebling, a TV scriptwriter. "The white kids pick it up, but they don't get it. They use it in the wrong way."

Some of this casual name-calling among African-Americans was common prior to rap music, but they were more cautious about letting non-blacks hear it. A more public display is perceived as contributing to the decline of civility as well as self-respect.

BACKBITING BACKFIRES

If face-to-face name-calling is the worst kind of swearing, a close second is behind-the-back bad-mouthing. You could argue that it is even more malicious because it is cowardly, not allowing the person attacked to respond or defend himself or herself. It is also more common because it is safer. You can spread titillating gossip or completely destroy someone's reputation without enduring a direct confrontation, immediate reprisal, or a punch in the snoot.

Nevertheless, you pay a price. The child's retort that I'm rubber and you're glue is true, in a sense, because maligning another person can sully your own reputation. If you have a habit of castigating other people, you might suffer consequences without even knowing it. Several things can be happening every time you vilify somebody:

1. *You are speaking to someone who happens to admire the person you are berating.*

2. *You are speaking to someone who agrees with you, but who will be cautious around you for fear that you will bad-mouth him or her when you get the chance.*

3. *You are revealing a lack of maturity and acceptance of someone's shortcomings.*

4. *You're implying that you are superior or have no faults of your own.*

5. *Later, if you are polite to the person you maligned, you are considered a hypocrite.*

6. *Others will consider you jealous, bitter, unkind, insecure, unhappy, petty, and mean.*

Kevin, today a successful salesman, said he is grateful he learned his lesson early in life. He went to high school and college with George, but they didn't become the best of friends until their junior year at the University of Maryland.

"The two of us were having beers one night, and got into one of those candid and philosophical discussions about ourselves, and George said, 'You know something? I didn't like you in high school.' I was slightly stunned, but asked why. He said, 'A couple of times when we were in groups, like having lunch in the cafeteria, you'd be bad-mouthing other guys who I thought were your friends. I wondered what you said about me when I wasn't around.' He was right, and I realized at the time that I still had a tendency to label people, viciously sometimes, even if I liked them. George made me aware of what I was doing, and I was able to change."

Fred's case is different. He didn't catch on until he was 42 years old. He worked in the marketing department of a midsized corporation and always felt at odds with another man in the department named Robert. Fred was quiet and methodical, whereas Robert was boisterous and unstructured.

"There was no open animosity, but I felt he didn't respect me, and I considered him obnoxious," recalls Fred. "I was always grumbling about him and relished telling others about his mistakes. I eventually left the company and forgot about him. About a year later, while doing my Saturday errands, I ran into him. I asked him how things were at the company and got a surprising response. He opened up to me, like I was his best buddy. 'I've been there twelve years and I think it's time to move on, but I can't imagine another company would want me,' he said. He was really depressed, questioning his abilities, and I not only found myself feeling sorry for him, but trying to boost him up. 'Robert,' I said, 'you've got guts. You take chances, and you've survived mistakes because the company likes risk-takers. You're smart, energetic, and you've got a sense of humor.' I went on and on, and suddenly realized that what I was saying was absolutely true. I had never acknowledged his strong suits because I had focused on his style, which conflicted with mine."

After the encounter, Fred gave it more thought. Robert was admired by many people at the company, he had friends there, so what value had there been in bad-mouthing him? Fred couldn't recall if anyone ever agreed with his negative comments about Robert.

"I wondered what others had thought of me when I was making remarks about Robert. Apparently, and thankfully, it never got back to him. Maybe now he was being candid with me since we no longer had a professional relationship, but I sensed that I had misjudged his opinion of me all along, and felt terrible."

Fred's initial attitude toward Robert was a classic example of how we sometimes thoroughly dislike someone when, in fact, it's only something they do that offends us. If Fred had made an effort to identify and appreciate Robert's strengths, he would have had a more productive working relationship with him and would have been more comfortable around him. Quite possibly, Fred would have eliminated some stressful moments and enjoyed his job more.

DON'T BE IN A RUSH TO JUDGE

There are some basic lessons here that maybe no one ever gave you, or if someone did, you should remind yourself of them every so often. They will discourage you from scourging others and, at the same time, improve your self-contentment:

- Separate a person from his or her action.

Everyone has good qualities and bad qualities. Sometimes the foibles are more noticeable and annoying, but you have to look past them, find a person's strengths, and focus on them. Recognize what is more significant, the way a fellow employee interrupts you and sprays saliva in your face when he shouts out his ideas or the fact that most of his ideas are brilliant and his enthusiasm infectious. Learn to be amused by people's quirks and idiosyncrasies. If that doesn't work, just be grateful you don't have them.

- The fact that others aren't like you doesn't make them bad.

If everyone thought and acted the way you do, life would be boring for everyone. Stay open-minded, and learn from others. If you disagree on political or social issues, gather more facts so you can have intelligent discussions, not arguments. If you are detailed, organized, and morally rigid, be proud but not self-righteous. Rather, admire less structured people for their ability to be relaxed and carefree. Instead of criticizing someone as irresponsible for devoting too much time to sports or a hobby, be happy that they have something to be passionate about. We should all be so lucky.

- Every jerk has a reason for being one.

We all have problems that influence our moods and our behavior. If you deal with certain characters you wish you could mutilate, or who tempt you to cut your own wrists as the only escape, find out from them or others what makes them tick, what family matters they have to cope with, the financial pressures they are under, what their fears and phobias are. Maybe you will only learn that they suffer from painful hemorrhoids. Whatever. You might not care at first but will see them in a new light that will make their behavior more acceptable. If obnoxious individuals simply lack good breeding, that might not be an adequate excuse for boorish behavior, but an awareness of their upbringing explains their actions and can increase your tolerance. Egotistical people are often insecure. If nothing else, recognizing that their arrogance is an act will diminish the feeling of inadequacy they try to force upon you.

- Empathy makes everyone less of a jerk.

Discovering that an enemy has problems and anguish might give you vengeful pleasure, but if you really believe you are a better person, a more mature and nicer human being, you will look beyond the immediate glee of your discovery and find sympathy and compassion. Knowing that other people have troubles of their own humanizes them, especially if you can get them to talk about their ailments or dilemmas. If a person senses that you honestly care, and can even offer helpful advice, your attitudes toward each other will improve and your interactions will change. You will continue to have conflict, but it won't be as intense. You can remain competitive, but if you can at least reduce the desire to discredit or destroy each other, you will also reduce your anger and frustration.

- Never be mean to anyone less fortunate than you.

Do you get angry at "old farts" who move too slowly? "Dumb bastards" who can't figure anything out? "Fat shits" who get in your way? "Ugly fuckers" you can barely stand to look at? Stop that! Sure, it can be great fun making jokes about bumbling senile citizens and funny-looking people, and it's probably normal to do so. But you wouldn't want people to be critical of your smaller imperfections, be it fat thighs or a wart on your nose. Instead of insulting people who have less going for them, you should be especially kind to them. Old folks can't help it if the food doesn't always make it to their mouths, unattractive people didn't choose a face that terrifies children, and most overweight people didn't know how fashionable it would be to look anorexic. Give them all a break.

And remember, we are all stupid at times. Maybe you're a cunning lawyer, but can you read a map? Maybe you know every player in the National Football League, but can you name the congressmen and senators who represent you in your state and in Washington?

- Don't be mean to anyone *more* fortunate than you.

We can always find reasons to resent rich people. Many women have an intense dislike for other women who are beautiful, and some guys are convinced that truly successful men lied and cheated their way to the top. Don't be jealous, be happy for them, and give them some credit. Even people who are born with looks, brains, and money have to work at keeping what they have, and their blessings often bring problems you don't even know about. Envy no one. You probably have something they wish they had, even if it is more time, a less stressful job, a simpler life, or close friends. Do the best you can with what you have, and don't compare yourself with others.

IDENTIFYING GENUINE JERKS

You might have a coworker or a relative you really don't like. No matter how hard you try to accept him and recognize his good qualities, you can think of only one word to describe him: *asshole.*

It's a convenient word, indeed, that sums up a host of horrible qualities in two simple syllables. When others who know him suggest he be on your team or join your staff, you can say, "Forget it, he's an asshole," and they will understand.

But one person might not be too sure—cousin Eddie maybe, who asks, "What's that got to do with it, as long as he knows his stuff?"

"Because he's a fuck-up who will ruin it for the rest of us," you reply. You expect that to end the discussion, but cousin Eddie persists.

"Look, I know he drinks too much, beats his dog, needs to use soap more frequently, and tells really long jokes that are about as funny as tofu, but he's good at this. So what if he's an asshole?"

You think about it for a while, then say, "It's not just that. He's a jagoff, too."

Everyone laughs, except persistent cousin Eddie. "Tell me more."

Now you have to get serious. "Okay. He is not a team player. It's his way or no way. He doesn't follow the rules and will get us all in trouble, then deny everything. He'll take all the credit for the victories, blame others if things go wrong. If he gets discouraged, he'll just walk off. I can give you four or five incidents where it's happened."

"You mean he is a cheater, a troublemaker, a liar, an egomaniac, a faultfinder, and a quitter?"

"You got it."

"So why didn't you say so in the first place?"

The point is, if you feel it is necessary to exclude someone from the group, or to warn others about his or her behavior, you have to be more specific. You don't want to scandalize someone, and it's better to let others make their own judgments, but you need to be more descriptive and factual if you want to prevent your boss from hiring an embezzler or save your sister from marrying a guy who drills peepholes into bathrooms.

It is difficult to like everyone, perhaps impossible. Even people you love, you can't like all the time. Many a joyful bride, on her blissful wedding day, has called her new husband unflattering names for the embarrassing statements he made at the reception, or was damned by her day-old spouse for making them miss a flight or forgetting a suitcase. You can adore your own child and want to strangle him minutes later for pouring chocolate syrup on the platter of spaghetti. So it becomes a serious challenge to like a neighbor's teenager who bangs the drums poorly, a manager who demands a report by tomorrow and reads it three weeks later, a stranger in a Monster Truck who cuts in front of your Volkswagen, or a competitor who tries to put you out of business. Vicious and hateful names seem to have been created just for them.

Fortunately, one of life's defensive measures is humor. Long after most of your maddening moments of injustice and mistreatment, you can relate them to someone else and you both laugh about them. You can curse and cry after someone on Rollerblades knocks you off your bike into a mud puddle, but millions of people would howl if they saw it on *America's Funniest Home Videos*. And if your coworkers annoy you and your manager is an imbecile, you chuckle when you see your own sorry situation in the "Dilbert" comic strip.

You might be one of those rare people who immediately senses the humor in actions of people who are demanding, insensitive, ignorant, or simply different from you. If not, you can lighten up and try to see the comedy in your crises. You will succeed once in a while, which is better than never.

When this approach fails, you can still find some gratification in name-calling that makes a point without being profane or vicious. There are alternative nouns and adjectives that are condemning but also amusing because they are old-fashioned, British, sound funny, or are unexpected when they come from you. The next chapter tells you how to find such words, but here are a few suggestions, which don't even include the broad range of adjectives available:

Mistreats women: cad, cur, heel, bounder

Seeks money dishonestly: chisler, extortionist, shyster

Poorly bred:	pagan, savage, ogre, clodhopper
Lacks morals:	reprobate, miscreant, ne'er-do-well, rapscallion, pariah
Lazy, not bright	slacker, slug, deadbeat, dolt
Takes advantage of others:	maggot, parasite, vulture, vermin, weasel
Dishonest:	rogue, scalawag, scoundrel, viper
Unpleasant woman:	shrew, harpy, vixen, Queen Bee
Easy woman:	tramp, tart, harlot, wench, floozy, strumpet
Bratty kid:	rascal, scamp, imp, rug-rat
Lacking manners, style:	oaf, loon, kook, buffoon, nincompoop, lummox
Oversized bully:	goon, thug, mongrel, galoot

Even more effective and humorous than single words are clever and imaginative put-downs, a skill mastered centuries ago by Shakespeare and his buddies. Today, put-downs are the entire act of some stand-up comics, a routine first done successfully by wisecrack artist Don Rickles. Now in his seventies, Rickles has not only managed to escape getting beat up, but still has people paying to be insulted by him. Louis Safian, author of *The Giant Book of Insults* (Carol Publishing Group), says the insult gag helps you blow off steam while adding luster to your reputation as an astute wit. Some examples from his book:

He's so conceited, he has his X rays retouched.

He follows the straight and narrow-minded path.

He must have gotten up on the wrong side of the floor this morning.

She is so indecisive, she has a 7-year-old son she hasn't named yet.

He will never be too old to learn new ways of being stupid.

The best part of his family tree is underground.

It is not easy making up your own clever insults, and surprisingly difficult to remember the good ones you hear and to use them as ammunition. Give it a try, but try even harder to deal with difficult people in a more mature and patient manner.

INSIGHTS INTO PERSONALITIES

The more you understand people and their motives, the easier it will be to deal with them. Probing deeply into their personal lives isn't always possible, but neither is it necessary if you know how to read the signs that explain their behavior and predict what they will do next. A psychological system called the Enneagram is based on the premise that everyone fits into one of nine basic personality types. Each type has a point of view toward life and reacts differently in times of security and during periods of stress. If you understand the traits of each, you develop greater tolerance for the way people behave.

Also, if you know your own personality type, you understand and accept your own behavior without getting overly frustrated. You will relax when you realize your expectations are common for your type, but perhaps not realistic or as important as you suppose.

Following is a brief description of the predominant characteristics of each of the nine Enneagram personalities. As you read them, you will see people you know and will also find one that fits you closely. To some degree, you will discover that you possess some of the desires and motives of other types. By contemplating these characteristics objectively, you can look at yourself rationally, calm down, and learn to control the stress, anger, and disappointments that not only provoke swearing, but make you unhappy.

Type One: The Perfectionist

This type is preoccupied with errors and is always seeking perfection. Perfectionists work hard at getting things in order, are demanding of themselves and others, and become angry and sometimes lose sight of what's really important. They often resent people who let things slide without caring or feeling guilty. They can be jealous when others are praised for good ideas, get promoted, and are well liked. They want recognition for what they do. With some, an outlet for their passion for perfection is involvement in social or political causes. They also suffer from the conflict of wanting to do something that they know is not the proper thing to do.

Type Two: The Giver

Givers are helpful and supportive, sacrificing their time and energy to help others succeed. They know how to make people feel good about themselves, taking a deep interest in their lives. They enjoy approaching and helping difficult people and earning their appreciation. They don't seek glory, but they do want approval and recognition for their role, to be considered indispensable, and to benefit with some form of special treatment. If they don't get it, they get angry, and work harder at giving in order to get approval. They believe knowing the right people is important, and they serve as the link, introducing people who can benefit from each other. They become a source of information and valuable contacts. They satisfy their own needs indirectly, working behind the scenes, but their own image and reputation for their contribution is important to them.

Type Three: The Performer

Performers believe in success, in being winners, but more important, being perceived as winners. If they aren't successful in the eyes of others, then they feel they are nobody. Consequently, performers promote their image and status, even if it involves deception. Their values are based on what others expect of them, often accumulating and displaying material assets and possessions, convinced that affluence brings happiness and respect. They project self-confidence. What they do is more important than what they feel, so they become intense competitors and pursue several things at once. They fear being idle or unable to work. However, they strive to be appealing in personal ways, such as being a perfect spouse or great lover. Their goal is to be loved for what they do, not for who they really are.

Type Four: The Tragic Romantic

Something in the lives of tragic romantics is missing, while everyone else seems to have it. They have been abandoned, denied the relationships that others enjoy. They become melancholy, envious, and desperate, unable to appreciate another person's happiness. Uncertain of what they really want, they pursue objects, status, love, and recognition that is often unattainable and reject what is available to them. If they come within reach of a goal, they experience disappointment and walk away from it, often desiring it once again. This cycle frequently repeats itself. Socially, they are embarrassed by their lack of success and their failure to be included, and they become reclusive.

Type Five: The Observer

Observers need private time to think, preferably alone in their home or apartment. They simplify their lives by avoiding desires, needs, and obligations. They become frustrated when they develop a desire to have something because they take pleasure in the simpler route of having little and doing nothing, thus avoiding responsibility and personal entanglements. Even if they are prosperous, they are stingy. Their pleasure comes from intellectualizing and observing who and what influences popular culture. The mind and information are sources of power.

Type Six: The Trooper

Troopers are suspicious of authority and cautious about everything. If they have any uncertainty about an action they need to take, they typically expect the worst or examine every possible downside. Their fear leads to procrastination or inaction. They lack trust in others, suspecting ulterior motives. Most of them can barely function without support groups, seeking a common bond and security in numbers. They become preoccupied with finding trustworthy people and ideals they can believe in. They often fear people and overcome their insecurities by building their physical strength and appearance, and by seeking power through intellect.

Type Seven: The Epicure

This type is an optimist who seeks action, adventure, and pleasure, moving away from troubles. Life is full of opportunities and interesting people. Many things excite epicures, and they plan more activities than they have time to do. When things go wrong, they get excited over the options and move on, often unable to sympathize with others in trouble. They don't believe in limitations and ignore rules that slow them down. At work, they prefer to do things their way. They surround themselves with people who think the way they think and like what they like. They stay in touch with old friends, looking for stimulating news. Having a monogamous relationship can be a struggle. They are survivors, always looking forward to life's next adventure.

Type Eight: The Boss

Bosses firmly believe that the strong dominate the weak, and life will be good if they have complete control. Their mission is to do what it takes to succeed and stay on top, to avoid emotions that respond to the needs of others over their own. They use every resource available to achieve objectives and refuse to believe obstacles can't be overcome. They love power struggles and respect anyone who remains committed to what they believe in. They will be honest and open with anyone who qualifies for their inner circle. Satisfaction requires territory and plenty of possessions. They fear being deprived and know where and how to get everything they need.

Type Nine: The Mediator

Avoiding conflict and tough decisions are signs of a mediator. They are not certain what course to take, so they follow the direction of someone who convinces them what is good or important. More often, they know what they don't want rather than what they do want. They are hesitant to give in to others but have trouble saying no. They prefer to work in a group in order to feel included and to share responsibility. They avoid essential decisions by busying themselves with other details and escape by indulging in simple pleasures.

You might want to make the effort to explore the complete profiles of the nine personality types, which are far more extensive than these summaries. You can also investigate other theories that not only help you understand and tolerate other people but also improve the way you communicate with them. The Jungian theory, for example, identifies only the following four major personality types.

Directors. They accept challenges and love to take charge and move fast, but sometimes without planning, listening, or giving consideration to the feelings and attitudes of others. They are efficient but overbearing and self-centered.

Socializers. They love to be involved with people and projects, offering ideas and loads of enthusiasm. However, they are not always practical, ignoring the facts and unable to finish what they start. They are often perceived as flaky and out of touch.

Relaters. Close relationships are important to relaters. They avoid risks and hurting others, so they make decisions slowly. They want to know what others think before they proceed. They are friendly and good listeners but easily give in to others.

Thinkers. These people are systematic problem solvers. Everything must be right, so they gather all the facts before acting. They prefer to figure things out by themselves rather than involve others. They can be stubborn, uncommunicative, and too serious.

Even trying to understand other people by their zodiac sign is better than making no effort at all to explain and accommodate their behavior. If you know what makes people tick, you can determine how to live or work with them rather than writing them off as assholes, bastards, or dumb shits.

Points to Ponder

- Some of the alternatives to vulgar names are more offensive, mocking physical deficiencies or ethnic origins.

- If you vilify others behind their backs, you risk harming your own reputation more than theirs.
- If you need to warn others about someone, use words that are more descriptive than meaningless swear words.
- Don't be hateful or jealous of anyone; everyone has problems.
- Find and focus on the strengths and good qualities of everyone you know and meet.
- Train yourself to be amused and entertained by the habits and behavior of others.
- If you know what makes people behave as they do, you will be more understanding and capable of dealing with them.

TAJADA SCARBROUGH, 53, SOCIAL WORKER

Swearing for me depends on the day and the environment. It's selective. When I'm angry, I want people to understand exactly what I'm going to say. So when I need to tell someone to back off, I do not swear because it could detract from my meaning. If I am in a very formal setting, or at work, or around my grandkids, or at parties, I do not swear. It's only when I make a mistake doing something that you might hear me saying "Shshshshshit."

I'm not your stereotypical black woman. I do not have a horde of children, receive a welfare check, or have children on drugs or in jail. I do not enjoy loud music, and I don't like or appreciate most rap. I like the opera and classical ballet as well as jazz. But I am the typical black woman. Family is uppermost on my list. I expect always to be treated like a lady, and I demand respect. I can be a real witch, but because I demand respect, I also give it. So I make a concerted effort not to swear.

I had to stop doing casework because I couldn't close up the folder at night and leave it behind. I got too involved. A lot of women feel they're not important enough to take care of themselves and they become victims. I had this one case where a woman had five hundred stitches on her upper body after her man threw her through a plate glass window. And afterwards she's still saying, "But I love him so much, and he loves me. He was drunk, he didn't mean it." These are the women who are usually pulling all of the weight in the household. They always go back to these same men and keep on taking care of them, paying their bills, and being abused. That kind of thing made me climb the walls.

But as far as the language goes, the economic factor has a lot to do with swearing. If people have less, they seem to need to say more. Swearing is a way of thinking they're leveling the playing field. It definitely is a reflection of lower self-esteem and a need to be seen and heard. It changes the way people see you and how you see yourself, so your quality of life is affected.

When I was in high school, we said things like, "Groovin'." Today they might say, "Bitchin'." But generally I was too busy carrying a full load to have time for swearing. I was working, and in school, and I had to be home to help take care of brothers and sisters. I took music and dance and precision drill classes on top of that. Forget about using swear words to flirt with guys. I wasn't even interested in dudes back then. I just didn't have time. And in college and graduate school I was just as busy. Somebody had to pay my tuition and I was it.

My mother would slap me upside the head if I ever used a swear word around her. I remember one time—and I don't know to this day how she heard me—she told me I couldn't go somewhere I wanted to go and I said under my breath something like, "that damn mother of mine." She was standing at the sink with the water running, washing greens, and talking to my Nanny, and I was halfway up the stairs with a wall between us and she heard me through all of that. She chased after me and popped me one. I got slapped in the mouth. No, I still don't swear or smoke or drink in front of my mother. Maybe a beer once in a while, but that's it.

Today swearing is just a part of everyday language. It's every other word for kids now. It makes them feel adult. My son can have a foul mouth. That's a guy thing, I guess. It's so natural for young people today. Just a part of their language. There's no taboo. With my grandkids now, I don't know what kind of peer thing goes on. So it's hard to control the influence.

I think a lot of the colloquial expressions have been lost because people swear instead. I don't even remember any myself. I just remember my dad saying "Dang" or "Heck" or "I'll beat the stuffin' out of you" or "I'll pinch you on your tail" if I ever did something wrong. And my mother used to say, "Come here, chocolate child," which isn't the same as swearing, just one of those expressions she'd say with a smile, which said she loved me. "Come here, chocolate child." My mother didn't need to swear. She's got eyes. She's got eyes that say it all.

TEN
Finding Alternative Words

BEFORE VENTURING INTO THIS chapter in search of the simple solution—clean words that nevertheless have a gratifying kick to them—review and promise yourself to practice these recommendations presented in previous chapters:

1. *Don't allow yourself to get into the state of mind that causes you to curse.*
2. *Think positively: avoid negative thinking, complaining, and name-calling.*
3. *Work at reducing your casual cursing; it is unnecessary and easier to control than causal cursing.*
4. *Don't use cuss words when you can make a point without them.*
5. *When you need alternative words, try the standard euphemisms or simple words that are part of your everyday vocabulary.*

You might be highly motivated to master the emotions and to conquer the moods that make you swear, but, admittedly, breaking the habit and transforming your temperament is no easy task. It takes effort and time. But you will be pleased as you see yourself—and hear yourself—making progress.

Meanwhile, as you struggle to become a paragon of propriety and emotional maturity, you will undoubtedly have many moments when some blundering fool, an incident of injustice, or a malfunctioning piece of machinery will tempt you to spew forth a blue streak. You will be wishing you had a mental stockpile of optional words at your command. Training yourself to use substitute words isn't as easy as putting clean sheets on the bed, but it's more expedient than altering your patterns of behavior.

The trick is finding alternatives and getting in the habit of using them. Initially, you will want to have a key word to substitute for each of your favorite and most frequently used foul words. It's sort of like eating frozen vanilla yogurt instead of chocolate swirl ice cream with butterscotch topping. It's not much fun at first, but you feel better about yourself. You will gradually find additional words with more zip and flavor to break the monotony.

Words that are mild or even funny are desirable because they take the edge off, reduce tension, and prevent you from exposing an emotion that you might regret later. In the process of collecting options, you will not only expand your working vocabulary and sound less abrasive, you will discover that using smart, clever, and humorous words and phrases makes the source of your annoyances much easier to deal with and makes you more pleasant—or at least more tolerable—to be with.

Almost every day you read or hear words, terms, and expressions that would be good substitutes for swear words or foul expressions. You hear them, then forget about them. You see them in print, but keep on reading. And, even more likely, it doesn't occur to you that certain words you hear are excellent candidates for cuss word substitutes. Beginning today, start making a conscious effort to record words or phrases that will serve your purpose or, for some reason, simply sound good to you.

- Create your own thesaurus (list of synonyms).

Some of the useful and appealing terms you discover will be easy to recall, but you should jot them down on pieces of paper, napkins, or your forearm if you have to, transferring them later to a database that you can refer to from time to time. There are a dozen ways to keep records. Storing them on a personal computer provides flexibility as your lists grow. If you don't have access to a computer, lined paper kept in a three-ring binder is a good option.

To keep it simple, you only need four sections: Exclamations, Adjectives, Verbs, and Names. Write in alternative words and phrases as you find them. If your list expands for any of the four categories, you can easily add pages for that category.

If you want to be more precise, keep a separate page for each swear word that falls under each category. This will be somewhat confusing, since words like *fuck* fit under all four categories, and the alternative words for some vulgar terms will be the same for other bad words. The only advantage to keeping records this way is to find alternatives that sound similar (*Gosh darn* for *God damn*) or have the same number of syllables as the swear words (*buttercutter* for *motherfucker*).

- Start with this book.

The pages of this book include alternative words and phrases for swear words, some that are simple, funny, intelligent, or standard euphemisms. Many of them will generate a reaction or get the listener's attention more readily than a common cuss word. Assemble the substitute words from these pages to start your own collection.

You should also take a few minutes to think of the alternative words you already know and use from time to time. Sit with a few friends and see what they come up with.

- Include phrases.

Don't restrict yourself to single words. The inventive way some people assemble words can be impressive and entertaining. You will probably hear a few powerful phrases that you would love to use someday to get attention or make a point. Go ahead, displaying borrowed brilliance as if it were your own.

If you find expressions or phrases that appeal to you but they don't fill in for foul words, write them down anyway. Reserve a few pages in your homemade lexicon for these gems. You will develop an appreciation for the language that will inspire you to speak more intelligently and help you avoid trashy talk.

- Read more often.

If you know people who are articulate and rarely swear, they are probably voracious readers or were at a time when they had more time. The more exposure you have to well-written books, magazines, and newspapers, the more likely you are to absorb simple but powerful words and know how to put them together smoothly and intelligently. Printed words provide a visual reinforcement that strengthens your vocabulary.

- Don't expect it to be easy.

Solitary nouns and adjectives that are excellent substitutes for curse words don't always jump out at you, and phrases are even harder to identify as alternatives. Be forewarned that searching for strong but socially acceptable words is harder than playing Scrabble, and learning how to deftly drop them into your dialogue is a craft. If you can locate and remember at least one suitable substitute a week, you are doing okay. Try it out at the first opportunity.

Replacing your casual cuss words will get easier and even be fun at times, but coming up with options for causal cursing will be more challenging. A purposeful search will certainly uncover some suitable substitutes, but the process will convince you that using different words isn't the best solution for washing away angry language. You must change your tone, be tolerant, brighten your outlook, and lower the intensity of your ire.

If you think foul words are absolutely necessary to be forceful, count to ten and think again. Nonswearers, for the most part, simply look people in the eye, make straightforward statements, and wait to see if their intention was clearly understood. They will admit that a stern expression or a raised voice is often necessary, but swearing isn't.

Keep in mind that, throughout most of your life, you have been in situations where you knew it was not proper to swear, and you didn't, even if you were angry. It can be done. This chapter makes it even easier to express yourself with words that are effective but not offensive, clean but not mean.

Our magazine is geared toward career-minded young men. Many of our readers use bad language, but our general policy is to exclude it from our pages. We review articles and interviews and will leave in curse words only if they are germane to the story or necessary to understand the topic. Occasionally, we will leave in curse words from celebrities if we feel it provides insight into their personalities. If it doesn't fit, we consider it superfluous and inappropriate.

—Michael Callahan, managing editor, *P.O.V.* magazine, in an interview for this book

PHRASES ARE FUN

Finding and employing potent phrases could be considered an advanced lesson in language enhancement. Often, you won't realize that a statement you hear could serve as a superb replacement for profanity. That's why it's wise to make a note of any word or expression that appeals to you, either because it's more descriptive than other words, or you simply like the sound of it. Include it somewhere in your personal thesaurus, and later you might find a way to apply it.

For example, here are a few terms from the first few chapters of a book called *Comfort Me with Apples,* written by humorist Peter DeVries. Beneath them is what could be considered a common cusser's boring way of saying essentially the same thing:

His remarks were a "deluge of words and a drizzle of thought."
(He talked too long and it was all bullshit.)

It was a "dazzling display of dexterity."
(You should have seen that goddamn catch!)

The passageway was "choked with encumbrances."
(All kinds of shit was in the way.)

His conclusion was a "brilliant feat of unravelment."
(I don't know how the fuck he figured it out.)

If you stumbled across these sentences, would you consider them alternatives to the pathetic sentences in parentheses? Probably not, but borrowing them and other clever phrases will dress up your speech and prevent you from consciously cursing. They might not sound like you, or might strike you as pompous, but if you say them jokingly or with exaggerated arrogance, your friends will be amused as well as impressed.

One of the sad realities of the ordinary, worn-out comments shown in parentheses is that their ease of use discourages the development of clever colloquial expressions that were once common in different regions of the country and among ethnic groups. For example:

Boring and confrontational: Shut the fuck up or I'll kick your ass.

Option: Quit that rootin' and tootin' before I break loose with some cuttin' and shootin'.

Source: Overheard on the street, spoken by an African-American.

Comment: The message is clear, but the humor of the rhyming words indicates that the threats are not real.

Boring: Eat shit and die.

Option: I hope you sustain an injury that's not covered by workman's compensation.

Source: *Messages from My Father,* a book by Calvin Trillin.

Comment: It's a wordy and bizarre thought, too goofy to be taken seriously.

Boring: I wouldn't trust that lying son of a bitch.

Option: That man is lower than a rattlesnake's belly in a wagon wheel rut.

Source: Line from an old cowboy movie.

Comment: Clever, but long, unusual statements that are from a period in history will have limited applications. Also, if they create a reaction, they can't be used more than once among the same people.

This last example should inspire you to create your own expressions. Metaphors, similes, and exaggerations work well, but thinking of them is an art. Learn the formula, and see if you can develop a more contemporary version: A *rattlesnake* is more sinister than *snake,* the word *belly* is funnier than *stomach,* and *wagon wheel rut* is alliterative.

Finally, statements have the most effect if they appear to be original, conceived on the spot. Any terms you borrow you should always use as if they are your own. Don't say, "That happened to Frasier once, and he said . . ." Just use the line, and if someone recognizes it, you can always admit you didn't originate it, but you will get the laugh first.

Where to Look and How to Listen

Many resources exist, some of which you encounter in the course of a day, and some of which you have to search out. Keep your eyes and ears open and be alert for the following:

- Exclamations to replace the nasty ones you use now
- Descriptive adjectives
- Witty similes and metaphors that soften insults and complaints
- Derogatory names that identify specific flaws or behavior
- Words that sound like swear words but are not
- Sayings and remarks that make you laugh
- Words that have a ring to them that you like

Vocabulary-Building Books

Reading these books is a smart thing to do under any circumstances. For your immediate purposes, however, you should focus on nouns, verbs, and adjectives that are negative or derogatory. Many of them you will rarely hear anyone say, and you are unlikely to use them yourself, but look closely for single words within the definitions that are considered synonyms. These are the simple words you are more likely to use as swearing substitutes, not the more exalted words.

If you already have an expansive vocabulary, you can skim the list of words for ones that could serve as substitutes for crude terms. In the process, you will be reminded of some excellent words you are familiar with but seldom use.

Following are a few randomly selected words from a vocabulary book, grouped under the profanity they could represent. The words in parentheses were options given in the definitions.

Instead of calling someone a *bastard,* explain that he is

> contentious (quarrelsome)
> despicable (vile)
> dour (stubborn)
> malicious (hateful)
> pugnacious (combative)

The statement wasn't *bullshit,* it was

> ambiguous (unclear)
>
> hyperbole (exaggeration)
>
> fallacious (unsound, ridiculous)
>
> fraudulent (deceitful)
>
> implausible (unlikely)

The task wasn't *fucking impossible,* it was

> arduous (strenuous)
>
> formidable (difficult)
>
> insuperable (insurmountable)
>
> onerous (burdensome)
>
> interminable (endless)

The situation wasn't a *God damn mess,* it was a

> calamity (disaster)
>
> cataclysm (upheaval)
>
> debacle (collapse)
>
> fiasco (failure)
>
> quagmire (predicament)

Directories of Synonyms

A *synonym,* in addition to being as difficult to say as *cinnamon,* is a word having the same or nearly the same meaning as another word. The best-known resource for synonyms is *Roget's Thesaurus,* which is as difficult to say as *pterodactylus.* There are other fine sources, such as *The Synonym Finder* compiled by J. I. Rodale (Warner Books). These books are designed to do exactly what you want to do: find alternative words. Unfortunately, what you are looking for isn't exactly at your fingertips. For example, *Roget's SuperThesaurus* includes *asshole* but not *anus,* and *tit* but not *shit. The Synonym Finder,* which boasts that it has more than a million words, contains hardly any vulgarities. You would think that the publishers of both books, obviously convinced that certain vulgar words should not be used, would list them to help you find alternatives for avoiding them. For the scummy words, you need a dictionary of slang.

The Synonym Finder has more options, but with both books, you need to skip around to find what you need. *Roget's SuperThesaurus* doesn't list *fuck,* but it does include the word *screw* with three major definitions: to twist, to cheat, and to have sexual intercourse. Under the sexual intercourse definition of screw there are seven terms, all verbs with an asterisk to indicate they are slang, with the exception of *copulate.* There is no word given as an alternative to the use of the word as an exclamation, nor as an adjective.

The best option offered for cheat is *swindle.* Look up that word and you learn that, instead of saying you got *screwed* or *fucked,* you can say you were *burned, hustled, gypped, duped, fleeced, bamboozled,* or *bilked.* These are all good words.

Screw up is listed in *Roget's,* which is a milder form of *fuck up.* Among the eleven choices are some standards, such as *mess up* and *goof up,* and a couple that are fun because they aren't worn out: *bungle* and *botch.*

Since you won't find the adjective *fucking* in either book, you can look up *lousy,* which has thirteen choices in *Roget's* and twenty-four choices in *The Synonym Finder.* Among the most useful are *atrocious, rotten, disgusting, terrible, contemptible, despicable, wretched, miserable,* and *sleazy.* If you look up *atrocious* in both books, you will find dozens of other words that aren't listed under *lousy,* including *abominable, appalling, horrible, horrendous, outrageous, dreadful, hideous, heinous, cursed, hellish, unspeakable, ungodly, insipid,* and *mawkish.*

So a bit of work is required, and each word has its own special meaning, but stick with it. Finding words you like and using them appropriately is a more intelligent decision than giving up and resorting to the F'ing adjective.

Dictionaries of Slang

A variety of slang guides are available, including one called *Forbidden American English* by Richard A. Spears (Passport Books), which claims it is "formulated in such a way as to provide guidance to persons, especially nonnative speakers, who are not familiar with the meanings of these expressions, and who wish to avoid the social consequences of offending people with this kind of vocabulary."

Among the best directories of slang is *Wicked Words,* authored by Hugh Rawson and published by Crown Publishers. It has so much history and interesting narrative that you can almost read it like a nonfiction book rather than a reference book. The best way to use it, however, is to scan the key words to find some that the author considers wicked but that are actually far less offensive than notorious cuss words. For example, under D you will find *dolt* (a stupid fellow), *doxy* (a loose woman), *dud* (a loser), *duffer* (an incompetent person), and *dung* (excrement). *Hogwash, hokum,* and *drivel* have their own listings and are excellent alternatives for *bullshit.* All three are defined as *nonsense*—another logical alternative—and refer you to *bunk,* yet another usable option.

If you go straight to a vulgar term, you will find some options that are equally vulgar, but a few that are not. The entry for *ass* is seven pages long. It doesn't mention many of the alternatives for the anatomical *ass* (*butt, rear end, bum, seat*) but focuses on various terms with this word and the definitions you can use in their place. Among them are the following:

> badass = tough or malicious person
>
> bare-ass = naked
>
> burn [one's] ass = to anger
>
> candy-ass = weakling, sissy
>
> get your ass in gear = get moving
>
> haul ass = move quickly, hurry up
>
> a kick in the ass = a setback, disappointment, defeat
>
> pain in the ass = nuisance

Newspapers, Magazines, and Novels

When you are relaxed and reading at home, always have a pen or pencil handy to circle words and phrases you like. The daily newspaper is one medium that still outlaws profanity, and you will find the more colorful and intelligent writing in the editorials.

News magazines are cleaner than the magazines aimed at young adults, but don't neglect the hip publications. They have many cleverly written articles that aren't completely laced with raunchy words.

Books by John Grisham, one of the best-selling authors ever, rarely have any swear words and never any graphic sex scenes. This in itself is interesting, proving that books with tense drama and action can entertain without resorting to base interests. But, as with magazines, don't limit yourself. Start with the authors you know and like.

When you first start monitoring your reading material, your search for words will interrupt the flow of your reading. Eventually, good words will jump out at you. Circle them quickly, finish reading, then go over the article or book and review what you marked. Try to store the circled words in your memory bank, then add them to your thesaurus.

Television and Videos

Conflict is one of the standard ingredients in any televison drama or situation comedy. Well-written shows are loaded with banter and teasing and exclamations of shock, surprise, and anger. Cop shows have a lot of tough, angry talk, and they often use single words rather than clever expressions. In thirty minutes, you can pick up more fodder for your folder than you can in a week of conversations with friends and coworkers.

NYPD Blue was the first network television show to use vulgar words, but it was created by writer Steven Bochco, who also wrote the equally popular and cuss-free *Hill Street Blues* in the 1970s. *Chicago Hope* is written by David E. Kelley, who also writes *Ally McBeal.* All are considered excellent shows. Bochco's work proves that high-tension dramas can be equally well presented with or without profanity. One of Kelley's programs entertains viewers with life-and-death stories, and one amuses viewers with frequent sexual innuendo. All offer different examples of how we communicate, and you can decide if any of the language can improve your own.

One way to find alternatives to swear words on television and rented movies is to purchase TV Guardian, a foul language filter that you can connect to your TV and VCR. TV Guardian is marketed by Principle

Solutions, Inc., to parents who don't want their kids exposed to the profanity found on TV programs and videos. It decodes and monitors the hidden closed-caption text that was designed for the hearing impaired, and automatically mutes the sound when it detects an offensive word or phrase. A substitute word or term flashes on the screen, immediately alerting you that a violating word was used and providing a different one that does the job.

"Unlike the V-chip that blocks out entire programs, TV Guardian allows families to watch decent shows without hearing offending words," explains Rick Bray, creator of the device. "It's capable of catching about 150 words, but only 15 or so bad words are used repeatedly. When curse words are used as exclamations, TV Guardian mutes the sound and doesn't bother to flash substitutes. They usually aren't necessary to the story."

TV Guardian doesn't work on unscripted programs, such as live sporting events or talk shows. It also does not catch the clever expressions and innuendos that could be substitutes for swearing, but it's an excellent way to find alternatives words in scripted shows without concentrating so hard that you can't enjoy what you are watching.

Another technique when watching TV is to put down that remote control and, instead, hold a small dictaphone or the mike to a tape recorder. Repeating lines into a recorder is swifter and less distracting than writing them down. Listen to the tape afterward, evaluating what you recorded and adding only the best words and phrases to your thesaurus.

This technique is even more effective when you are watching a rented video because you can pause or stop the tape while you record, or rewind and replay lines that you liked but didn't catch entirely. The drawback, of course, is that you are going to annoy the bejeezus out of anyone watching the show with you. Even talking into a mike without stopping the show might spoil the program for your family members or friends. Obviously, this isn't a problem if you don't have a family or any friends, but that could indicate a deeper and sadder problem. Your best bet is to encourage your viewing partners to join in to help you and to mend their own mouth manners. Extra ears might hear a few good words and comments that you miss.

The challenge for everyone is to avoid getting so involved in the show that you fail to detect and record what you are listening for. Second, you will find that phrases are more common than singular words, and that they are specific to the context in which they are used. Record what grabs you anyway. Later, you can filter out the ones that you are not likely to use, and determine which ones you might be able to modify to work for you.

You can do the same thing by taking a small dictaphone to the movie theater, but be careful whom you sit next to. It's better to make mental notes than to act like a mental case. Ask the person who came with you to do the same, then review them and write them down when the movie is over. If that doesn't work, and the dialogue in the movie was exceptionally eloquent, wait for the video to be available.

We have become so accustomed to the swearing in movies that you could walk out of the theater after watching certain films and not be able to recall if it contained bad language or not. Fortunately, Hollywood still knows how to produce a few romantic comedies and action adventure movies without gratuitous cussing, and it's almost amazing to discover how they do it. You might be surprised to learn that there is no swearing in James Bond movies, despite the action, violence, and sexual plays on words. Most movies with Harrison Ford or produced by Woody Allen (with the exception of *Deconstructing Harry*) are among the others that tend to be profanity free. Renting some of these flicks is faster than waiting for the next one to arrive at the theaters.

Rented movies have several advantages. You can pick a few that you have seen before, which means you will be less distracted by a plot you already know. You can anticipate scenes that you recall involve conflict or humor, and be prepared to listen closely for the diatribes or exchange of clever put-downs.

Modern-day movies sometimes appear on network TV after their runs in the theater and in the video market. If you spot one in the TV programming guide that you know includes profanity, other words will be dubbed in to make it more acceptable for family viewing. If you are savvy about swearing and a good lip reader, you will know what Mel Gibson is really saying in *Lethal Weapon* when he refers to the bad guys as "funsters"and yells "no way!" and "that's terrific."

Movies made prior to 1965—found on the American Movie Classics (AMC) cable channel and shown periodically on other stations—have very few swear words, but the characters were politer and more civil to each other back then. Watching old movies and imagining how current-day remakes would be spiced up will reveal that the way we treat each other has deteriorated. The good news is that many of the choice words the characters used to grumble and quarrel are tame by today's standards, making them suitable alternatives.

What Other People Say

Every now and then, you hear an amusing remark from a friend, a family member, or a fellow worker that is worth remembering and repeating when the occasion arises.

"We were sitting down to dinner when my son came in and left the door wide open on a cold day, so I yelled at him to go back and shut it," recalls Bill, a father of four. "My 5-year-old daughter, who apparently was repeating something she had overheard, said, 'Yeah, shut the door, you mother father son of a biscuit.' We all laughed, and my wife and I started saying 'son of a biscuit' when either of us was mildly irritated. It's now an automatic replacement for much of our cursing."

Jim recalls a funny remark he heard more than thirty years ago: "I was in a very nice hotel restaurant in Detroit with two friends when we spotted the hostess ushering a hefty young man to table. He was wearing overalls and long underwear, as if he had just finished plowing a cornfield. I was staring at him and was about to say something trite like, 'Look at the fucking hillbilly,' when one of my friends said, 'That boy's gonna be mighty disappointed when he finds out they don't serve grits here.' I thought that was a very clever comment, especially compared to the unnecessary insult I almost made. He wasn't exactly being nice, either, but his sarcasm was funny and said without malice or prejudice."

If you know someone who is witty and has a good disposition and outlook toward life, be extra alert when you are with him or her. Afterward, try to recall if he or she said anything amusing that you would have voiced as an insult or complaint. Add it to your collection of cursing alternatives.

Stand-up Comedians

These folks weren't given much credit in an earlier chapter, but not all of them are tasteless perverts relying on sex and vulgarity for easy humor. In a typical routine, most comedians relate some embarrassing experience or complain about something, yet they do it with humor. This is an admirable talent, and even the comedians whose jokes fall flat should be given credit for trying. If we all had the ability to see the humor in our problems and could generate laughs when we gripe, any cussing that might accompany our complaints might be excusable.

Tune in to Comedy Central or HBO during stand-up comedy nights, and listen closely to determine how they do it, excluding the profanity. Make a note of whatever makes you laugh out loud. Once again, you will discover single words are not the trick, but keen observations, witty analogies, exaggeration, and other techniques are. However, if a comedian is complaining and you don't even smirk because he sounds like a whiner, imagine how people respond when you're seriously upset about something.

MAKE UP "CURSE" WORDS

Most of the common exclamations we hear that are not swear words come close to sounding like the real thing, such as *gosh darn, geez, cripes, phooey, son of a gun,* and *mother lover.*

Some people use real words just because they like the sound:

> That's a bunch of Bolshevik.
>
> I don't give a wick.
>
> I don't give a pumpernickel.
>
> You gargoyle!
>
> You Fudrucker!
>
> Now isn't that a sticky wicket.

Comedian W. C. Fields created expletives out of terms and names he found in newspapers, such as *citrus crisis* and *Great Godfrey Daniels.* Former tennis pro Billy Jean King used to say *peanut butter* when she was mad, and Oprah Winfrey claims she yells *shazam!* Don Rickles calls people names like *hockey puck* and *lug nut.*

Some nonsensical expressions and names started nowhere, caught on, and have been around for years, such as *fuddy-duddy, flibbertigibbet, flimflam, fiddle faddle, dweeb, dingbat, cockamamie, nickerfutz,* and *boondoggle.* Two goofy terms that originated from TV commercials in recent years are *ratsafrat, pack a loomis,* and *Great Oogoly Boogoly.*

Try your hand at making up your own expletive or oddball name for people you don't like. Who knows, you might start something. Most swear words have been around for a long time, and we have run out of body parts, bodily functions, and devious sexual acts to use as insults. Someone needs to invent some new words that can't be considered vulgar or seriously rude.

TRY FOREIGN WORDS

Yiddish words like *schmuck* and *putz* have become mainstream words. They sound funny, and many non-Jewish people aren't sure of the meaning but assume they are dirty, so they are sort of half-innocent, devilish words to use.

The French word *derriere* was once frequently used as a polite term for *buttocks,* but it has faded into obscurity as *ass* and *butt* moved into common parlance. By the way, the term "Pardon my French," an apology for using profanity, originated in the nineteenth century as part of a long British tradition of blaming everything evil on the French.

If you study a foreign language, don't look for swear words. Instead, use words that sound like swear words to your fellow Americans unfamiliar with the language. Randy, a public relations consultant, has been doing this for years. "For an exclamation, I like to say *mama ou popaski,* which is Russian for 'mother is at grandmother's,'" says Randy. When he is frustrated or angry with someone, he mutters to himself in gruff

German, *Sie haben keine Tassen im Schrank,* because it sounds like he is angry. The literal translation: you don't have any cups in your cupboard.

When you use foreign words, you risk annoying people who are convinced you are swearing and resent the fact that you are hiding it. "And what is *that* supposed to mean?" they demand. When you provide a translation that is not profane or meaningful, they don't know what to say, which is good.

Points to Ponder

- Alternative words work at times, but you should continue to try to think positively and learn to control the emotions that make you swear.
- Keep a list of suitable substitutes and add to it whenever you come across words and phrases that make the point and are intelligent or funny.
- If you find yourself using the same alternative word repeatedly, don't worry. It will never become as stale as the ancient cuss words everyone else uses.
- As you become more aware of other words and better ways of expressing yourself, you and the people you spend time with will find it rewarding to hear you speak more intelligently.

BRENNA MCDONOUGH, 40 SOMETHING, ACTRESS AND AUTHOR

Even though I consider myself a nonswearer, I probably swear at least once a day. Usually over a physical hurt, like stubbing a toe, or if the kids aren't moving fast enough, situations like that. If I have a disappointment earlier in the day and I let it build up, a swear word might burst out. But I try not to let it build up.

I grew up in a household that considered "shut up" to be swearing. Religion was a factor I'm sure. My parents tried to control it, so I rarely heard them talk that way. I probably heard a couple of "go to hells" muttered during some morass, but that was about it.

Swearing took off for me during my twenties. It was just new-found independence. That sense of freedom. I was working evenings as a waitress in a bar in Chicago at that time. I swore for the same reason I smoked then: to fit in. That bar crowd wasn't quite as provincial as what I'd known growing up. I wanted to be one of them, like a neighborhood kid, not someone from the suburbs where I was raised. Although I did gravitate toward the people who shared the same background, we were all trying to outgrow our upbringing in a short period of time. I just wanted to be one of the people at that bar scene. At the law firm where I worked during the day it was, of course, a different atmosphere.

When I was a little older and I lived in New York City, I found the shock value of swearing to be terrific, because I didn't look the part. The mouth didn't match the costume. People would think, "Oh, she looks so nice and she talks like that. She must be faster and looser than she appears." So I would do it to get attention. The words really tripped off my tongue. My mother, now, she tried it and she is a lousy swearer. She just couldn't pull it off. She's an actress, too, but she couldn't do it.

I avoid swearing around children, people I don't know, any scholastic situation, and when I'm teaching my acting classes. Most situations, really. But I had one job last year where I had to swear on camera, and it really felt great. The characters I've always played are straight, warm, energetic, sincere, credible—not radical. So in this film I was portraying, for a change, what a radical person would do. It was a training film for the Communications Workers of America union. I portrayed a union spokesperson being interviewed. I had to say, "You son of a bitch." They stopped the audio at that point—you could read my lips—and bleeped out the language. The character I played was being interviewed by the media and as soon as I said that phrase they froze the frame and a narrator said, "This is not the way you want your interview to go. It sends a negative image of the union." So the message was: don't swear, it makes the union members look bad. But for me it was a chance to play a different type of character.

When I'm with friends and I want to get a point across or sound hipper or cooler, or even a bit dangerous, I will swear a little. I don't want people to think I was born in a suit and pumps. I have to really lose my temper to swear uncontrollably but that doesn't happen very often. I avoid getting angry. I don't let things build up. If I do, I have a tendency to go off into my own corner instead. I might start crying. I might eat, or get on the phone and bitch. When my kids get angry and jealous, one thing I don't say is, "Don't feel that way." I generally say, "That would make me angry, too. Why don't you come in for a while and play on the computer? Or go see what so-and-so is doing over at her house."

I might be out with a crowd of people at a film site and I'll say, "Jesus Christ, it's cold out," but just for a laugh. My profession is pretty stressful, in its unpredictability. The audition is always the toughest. I have trained myself to look at anxiety as excitement, though. I'm happy in my profession and that makes me less inclined to swear. The technical people with whom I work swear more. I don't mean to disparage them, it's just that they don't need to present an image. They don't have to pick and choose their words as carefully as an actor would. If you get into the habit of swearing, it gets into everything. And we're so unconscious about it.

I don't know if not swearing has helped me professionally because I try not to take my temperature there too often, but I think swearing is a poor choice for me. I'm sure I've added to my vocabulary by avoiding it. Ever since I started thinking more about this swearing business, I've noticed something. I've been observing myself, without getting too self-absorbed, if that's possible for an actress, and I do think it's raised my consciousness.

I'm highly offended if I'm out with my husband and I hear men swearing around me. In today's social climate, I would not say "please don't swear around me." I would prefer that my husband speak up for me, if possible. And with my children I'm very protective. We forget how delicate kids are. Their vocabulary is so limited. Every word that comes their way is precious. Swear words don't have value. A word like preposterous has a number value. Shit has no value, at least a very low one. Sometimes my kids say, "I want to tell you a story but there's a curse word in it." So they just say the first letter of the word when they tell the story.

In the media swearing is sometimes appropriate. If you took a David Mamet play and removed the profanity it wouldn't be the same. But I don't like it on TV. What's crept into the vocabulary a lot is "It sucks." It's a very sexual term, in my opinion, and our kids are sexualized too soon as it is. During that Clinton business, because I live in the Washington area, the national and local news together were a constant barrage of that story. With all those sexual terms, I had to do some explaining to my kids. I do want them to know that I know the terms, that I'm not a dinosaur. But it was very uncomfortable for my older child.

One day I parked too closely to a car next to me in some parking lot. Someone had written "Asshole" in lipstick all across my windshield. Such an aggressive and cowardly thing to do. And I felt hurt. I felt diminished. I was so glad I was alone . . . that my children weren't there to see it. Written like that it had more impact. That visual image was forced on me.

I don't like terms like crap. I think that's a pitiful substitute. And Gosh darn sounds like I just got off the Good Ship Lollipop with Shirley Temple. What is it about saying a word like shit that satisfies? Is it the plosive experience, the physical release? I'd like to think I'm intelligent enough to think of something else to say. Anything to get me out of the habit. Cruddy, I hate that word. I wouldn't use it as a substitute. It sounds like the stuff behind your ears. I can't even think of anything my family would say. Just expressions like "fine and dandy" or my father would say, "You're as welcome as the flowers in May." I don't know what would work as a substitute for swearing. I'll have to think about that.

What annoys me the most? Well, I can be unnecessarily self-righteous at times, and on bad days I can find fault with all people. "Why can't he get gas tomorrow? Why is she wearing that dress? Why did he turn that way?" On those days I really should not go out. I try to live and let live. But on days when I'm disappointed or I feel I'm always on a deadline or there's a job I didn't get or an idea I didn't formulate it's more of a challenge. I should stay home and take it out on the bagworms. I'll go out in the morning in my nightgown and flick them off my roses with my fingers. And I'll say, "God damn it! Get off my roses. And I mean now!" But I would like to think I could find other words to say to them.

ELEVEN
Exercises for Exorcising Offensive Language

CHURCH LADY, THE PIOUS but perverse talk-show host created by Dana Carvey on *Saturday Night Live* in the 1980s, was continually chastising her guests for allowing Satan to lead them astray. Years earlier, comedian Flip Wilson performed a routine as a wacky woman who excused her behavior by shouting, "The devil made me do it!"

At one time in history, violently disturbed people who were truly believed to be possessed by the devil were put through an exorcism, the ritual of expelling evil spirits from the body. The word is based on Greek terms meaning " to make one swear, or to administer an oath to." Only the holiest of holy men had the power and the right connections in Heaven to pull off the miraculous stunt of liberating tormented sinners from Satan's insidious stranglehold. This practice faded as spiritual leaders concluded that Satan decided to use his time wisely by only possessing humans bent on destroying entire civilizations, such as Iraq's Saddam Hussein, Yugoslavia's Slobodan Milosevic, and South Park's Eric Cartman.

Many religious people, however, have not abandoned the notion that our use of dirty words is the devil's work. Alfonzo King Surrett, Jr., an evangelist and author of a book on understanding the destructive effects of bad language, believes that Satan originated profanity and that he and his legions of demons do, in fact, invade our bodies to spread their mischief in the physical and material world. In *What Did You Really Say?* (Ebed Publications), Surrett writes: "When we use profanity and curse, we are willingly allowing the spirit of Satan to use our tongue; and we, in essence, become his representatives."

Men and women with strong religious convictions are among the people who have no trouble keeping profanity out of their vocabulary. Some of them don't object to vulgarity, but would never use any form of blasphemy, including "Oh, God," or "For Christ's sake." Whatever motivates them, even if they are selective about what expressions are sinful, their effort is commendable. Religion doesn't have the broad social influence it once did, but the basic principles on how to lead your life and treat others are sound advice.

You might not buy into Alfonzo Surrett's suggestion that we "accept Jesus Christ into our hearts . . . so that our divided tongue will be set on fire from Heaven, and we will speak with new words which the Holy Spirit will utter through us." But he is on target in saying, "If we change the way we think, we will change what we say. If we change what we say, we will change what we do. And if we change what we do, we will change the world."

That last statement might be overly optimistic, but it's conceivable that we can at least change the smaller, individual worlds that we make for ourselves.

The book you are reading intentionally excludes advice on cuss control from religious leaders and doesn't offer solutions such as prayer to resist the compulsion to curse, not because they don't work, but to focus on a secular rationale for cleaning up your language and to offer practical techniques that should make sense to any reasonable man or woman, God-fearing or not. If your religion or being born again enhances your life, improves your disposition, and diminishes your cussing, go for it. Ignore whatever cynicism or skepticism might come your way.

The fact is, spiritual enlightenment might be the easiest cure for the common curse. You will be more motivated to bite your tongue to avoid offending God than to avoid offending the guy you want to cuss out for cutting in line at McDonald's and placing orders for his entire construction crew. If religion fails you or doesn't fit your mind-set, your best incentive is a personal commitment to improve your outlook on life and the perception people have of you.

SUGGESTED PROCEDURES

1. Your first step is to make an honest assessment of why you swear.

Is it lazy language and the usual array of daily aggravations and challenges? If so, read on. If you have deeper, underlying problems that gnaw on you constantly, such as a bad marriage, a misdirected career, serious health problems, or psychopathic tendencies and a passionate hatred for all people living and dead, you might have to resolve these issues before you can achieve any measurable decline in your cussing. If you are chronically in a bad mood and don't know why you are such a foul-mouthed sourpuss, investigate some of the therapies described in the last chapter of this book.

2. Begin with the easy stuff.

Earlier chapters noted that eliminating casual or recreational cussing is a good starting point since it is easier to do. Just drop the bad words, or use the words you selected as your alternatives in civil emergencies. Eventually, you will use those simple, politer words as instinctively as you currently use cuss words.

3. For swearing prompted by emotions, practice with the annoyances that don't involve interaction with other people.

You can't blame or involve anyone else when you cut yourself shaving, you misplaced your wallet, you have to clean up a mess you made, you need to do your laundry, the scale says you gained five pounds, or you are too tired to do the work you brought home. Don't let these things get you down. View minor tasks as challenges you can resolve quickly for a sense of accomplishment, and strengthen your resolve to reach your longer-term goals. You will replace some of your personal stress with achievement, and your early successes will be rehearsal for the bigger problems.

4. Move on to the swearing that causes you problems.

You will want to advance quickly to your more emotional swearing that is harming your relationships at home, getting you in trouble at work, or preventing you from making friends. This is the category of swearing that has consequences.

5. Tailor the following suggestions to fit your personal needs.

The exercises listed here address some common situations that incite swearing. Everyone's life is different, so you should think about the times when you do the most swearing. You might need to modify these suggestions, or come up with your own. Just remember that any effort will bring a rewarding improvement for you and for anyone in your life who would enjoy a more congenial and gracious you.

THINK IN CLEAN LANGUAGE

If you swear frequently, you probably swear mentally when you are mulling over a problem. Although you don't want to feel so restricted you can't even curse in your own private thoughts, thinking bad words only encourages your impulse to say them. When you "hear" yourself think a bad word, ask yourself what word you could have used instead. Say it out loud to condition yourself to use it every time the cuss word starts to surface.

THINK POSITIVELY

What a no-brainer this one is. A positive attitude is the not-so-secret solution offered by every self-help program ever developed, just packaged differently. In the case of swearing that reflects a negative attitude, thinking positively is as logical as getting up after you have fallen down. After you swear, ask yourself if you were expressing a negative thought. Find the positive side of your topic, and say, "Of course, it isn't all bad," or "It would be a great place if it weren't for that one aspect," or something to that effect. You are not going to feel upbeat about everything, but try to see the good in as many people, places, and things as you can.

STOP SWEARING AT YOURSELF

You sometimes curse quietly to yourself, but also around your family or fellow employees when you make a mistake, break something, realize you are late, forgot to call someone, can't understand the directions for the VCR, whatever. When you feel tempted to swear, say instead, "I can take care of it." You will not only nurture a positive attitude about yourself but also project an admirable quality to your family or the people you work with—the ability to take action or recover quickly. They expect you to be competent and confident, so don't draw attention to your blunders with a defeatist, self-deprecating invective.

TAPE FAMILY PHOTOS TO THE CAUSE OF YOUR CURSING

What object makes you swear? Your computer? Your car? Your telephone? Tape on it somewhere a picture of your children, your mother, the pope, or someone else you would never swear in front of. If it works at first but fails later, try a new picture. A photo of you with that person is effective because it reminds you of a relationship you don't want to destroy.

IMAGINE GRANDMA OR THE KIDS ARE LISTENING

You can't be sticking photos of Grandma or your kids everywhere you feel the urge to curse, so use your imagination. Visualize them standing next to you, or in the chair against the wall, or standing between you and the person you are swearing with or at. Imagine what they would think if they heard your language or the way you are shouting, badmouthing someone, or talking dirty. If you tell your kids not to swear, you wouldn't want them to know you are a hypocrite. And if Grandma heard you, she surely would never make you another batch of chocolate chip cookies.

RELATE A PROBLEM WITHOUT SWEARING

When you have a bad experience, do you tell someone about it? It is natural to seek sympathy when you feel you were mistreated or someone was shockingly inconsiderate. Try to report the incident without swearing.

One approach is to let the situation pass, see the humor in it, and relate the story almost as if it happened to someone else. The person you are talking to would rather hear a funny story than a complaint. Venting might make you feel better, but what else does it get you? Do you really want people to think you were a victim or, even worse, unable to handle the situation? If you feel you can't tell the story without swearing, don't tell the story.

WRITE IT DOWN

If you can't resist talking about a bad experience and using profanity to express your anger or annoyance, try putting the same story in writing, using the cuss words. A day or so later, when you are less annoyed, read what you wrote. How did you sound? Make edits to the story, cleaning up the language and softening the tone. You will realize it's possible to convey your feelings without profanity.

PIPE DOWN AND LISTEN UP

If you are in a conversation and hear yourself swearing too frequently or unnecessarily, switch to being a listener instead of a talker. More than likely, you are making negative comments or observations. Follow the old rule that if you don't have anything nice to say, don't say anything. Even if you are using the words casually, pause long enough to remind yourself to keep it clean.

STOP COMPLAINING

Before you start griping and whining about something, remind yourself of an important reality: *no one wants to hear it!* Why would they? If you don't enjoy being with someone who always complains, gets angry, and is foul-mouthed as well, don't be like that yourself. Make certain you avoid complaining about matters that you and the people you are with have no control over. A brief comment about the bad weather or a stifling crowd is okay to establish a bond of sympathy, but don't let yourself or the other person take it too far.

If you must address an issue, look for and openly express the humor that can be found in most problems. You might have friends who are skillful at this. Pay attention to how they do it. While you are at it, let them know you admire their ability to see the foolishness and comedy in otherwise annoying behavior.

For seemingly insurmountable problems, try to offer a solution. Others will admire your common sense, wisdom, leadership, and calm approach to the problem.

ELIMINATE AGGRAVATIONS FOR SOMEONE ELSE

In most families, each member hopes someone else will replace the burned-out lightbulb, clean up the dog's mess, replace the empty roll of toilet paper, change the baby's diapers, or do the dishes. Neighbors wait for someone else to move the broken glass, dead branch, or dead animal out of the street. At work, who's going to reload paper into the copy machine, make the coffee and clean the cups, or fix the fax machine? These are all small details that you can do willingly to prevent someone else from being aggravated and swearing. Don't expect thanks from anyone, just do it and feel good about it.

LISTEN TO OTHERS SWEAR

Review the list at the end of chapter 5 called "Twenty-Five Reasons to Stop Swearing." With a heightened sensitivity to bad language, you will discover you don't like hearing it from anyone, even when it comes from buddies or relatives who have been using it for years. Don't pass judgment on them like a reformed smoker would frown upon the coughing crowd huddled outside the door of an office building. Just remind yourself that you don't want to use those words anymore.

THINK OF WHAT THEY COULD HAVE SAID

Whether you swear for fun or out of frustration, you rarely realize how bad you sound. The tone behind coarse words is much more obvious to you when someone else is saying them, particularly if you don't share the same mood or sentiments. Take a moment to think of what another person could have said to be more effective. Suppose someone says "I hate those fucking Dallas Cowboys" in front of people who like the team. What could he have said to make his point but avoid offending the Cowboy fans? Since you can't always catch yourself sounding bitter or offensive and change your temperament, practice with remarks made by others.

The best way to work on your own speech is to reflect on a conversation after you had it. That night or the next morning it occurs to you that you were confrontational or rude. Think of how you could have phrased your statements. Over time, you will think, speak, and act differently.

DON'T SWEAR WHEN YOU KNOW YOU CAN

If you are with friends or coworkers who swear or aren't bothered by your swearing, try to hold back anyway. They probably won't even notice. Over time, they might sense something is different about you and will probably like the change without realizing that your laundered language and improved disposition is what makes you easier to be with.

TELL YOUR FRIENDS YOU'RE TRYING NOT TO SWEAR

If no one knows that you are trying not to swear, you are giving yourself the leeway to revert to your wicked ways without guilt or embarrassment. Let your friends know you have made a personal decision to cut back on your cursing. They might tease you when you tell them, but secretly they will respect you for it.

The purpose in telling friends is to put pressure on yourself since self-discipline is tough. Your friends will also taunt you when you slip, but expect and welcome their reminders. Laugh with them and report that you haven't been completely purified yet. If the task or the teasing gets to be too much, cuss them out and say you're taking time off for bad behavior.

Make certain they understand you are not asking them to stop swearing or behave differently in front of you. They might tone down anyway, since your efforts will make them more aware of the coarseness of their own cursing.

HAVE SOMEONE RECORD YOU

This can be tricky, but it can be done if you alert people to watch for an opportunity. You might work in an office where some people have handheld Dictaphones. If one of them hears you talking to another employee and you're cussing casually or in anger, he can join you or stand nearby with the Dictaphone turned on and concealed in his shirt pocket. Or say you call a friend who picks up the phone after the answering machine has been activated, and she leaves it on while you converse. After a few minutes, she can ask if you realized how bad your language was, then play it back for you.

FORM A SUPPORT GROUP

After announcing your plan or later convincing your friends that your effort to engage in discourse without being coarse is making a difference in your life, some of them might want to give it a try. Get together with them on a regular schedule, once a month or more, for dinner, cards, or other activity. Spend some of the time sharing ideas and experiences involving swearing, then socialize as you normally would. If someone swears, stop them and discuss what they could have said instead. Keep it fun, not formal. Make a game out of it or place bets, with the loser paying for the dinner or drinks.

START FRESH WITH ADDITIONAL FRIENDS

If you swear intensely and so do most of your friends, you are going to have a tough time stopping in an environment that places no restrictions on you or expects you to talk tough. Expand your social life by joining a group involved in something that interests you—a camera club, bowling league, book club, sailing club, community organization, art league, charity group—anything where you will meet new people unaware of your jarring jargon and unlikely to use it themselves.

MAKE FRIENDS WITH A CLERIC

You are not going to cuss when you spend time with the religious leaders of your church or temple. Invite your parish priest to a picnic, play bridge with the bishop, go running with the rabbi, invite the parson over for a repast, mingle with the ministers, summon the nuns for Sunday brunch, go golfing with some of God's delegates.

Making friends with members of the clergy can be rewarding in many ways, even if you are not religious or even involved with a church or temple. Spiritual leaders have perspectives on life that are worth hearing informally rather than from a pulpit. They add to the variety of people you associate with, broadening your experiences.

Many religious leaders, particularly those without families, don't enjoy being left out or separated from society's mainstream. They will appreciate a friendly gesture and can learn from the realities of your life as well as you can learn from them.

WHEN CONFLICT APPROACHES, PLAN AHEAD

Sometimes you know you are going to engage in an emotional or heated confrontation that will ignite the flames beneath your furnace of foul language. You discovered that a colleague at work is trying to sabotage the project you've proposed, and you have a meeting with her. On the way home, you have to stop at the service station to find out why your car now sounds and feels worse after you paid $300 for a tune-up. The argument you had with your wife last night was never resolved and will continue as soon as you get home.

In each case, you have time to determine what you will say and how you will say it. In similar situations in the past, you envisioned yourself taking the upper hand, demanding an explanation, insisting on better treatment, and, most important, winning. You can take a different approach while seeking the same outcome. If you lose control and start shouting and swearing, both your anger and your language will make the other person more defensive and resentful. Tell yourself to be firm but to remain calm and rational.

Anticipate your colleague's objections to your plan, be prepared to answer them, and consider compromising to win her support.

It is possible that the auto mechanic made an honest mistake. Wait for him to say there is no additional charge to fix it before you demand free service.

What's it going to take to end the argument with your wife? If the two of you have a different take on the situation, tell her you understand how she feels but calmly convince her you have legitimate reasons for a different perspective. Suggest you both forget it and move on.

CONSIDER INTERRUPTIONS TO BE OPPORTUNITIES

Unless you are a forest ranger in Alaska and live alone and have no phone, interruptions are part of your life. At work, you might be concentrating on a task you are eager to complete. At home, you could be paying the bills or mowing the lawn, or simply enjoying a TV show or a good book. When the interruption comes from someone who wants you to do something, your tendency might be to swear out loud or to yourself. Either way, your body language reveals that you don't appreciate being disturbed.

Change your attitude by being grateful that you are needed. Estimate how long it will take for you to help out. If you don't have time, say when you will be able to do it. If it requires only a few minutes, get it done and consider it an accomplishment as well as a good deed. The person you helped will be grateful, especially if you didn't grumble and swear about it. A thank-you might not come or will sound mechanical, but if your associate or family member is not accustomed to your cheerful assistance, your willingness won't go unnoticed.

PRACTICE BEING PATIENT

We hate waiting. As busy people in a fast-paced society, we have no patience with anything that wastes our time. Do three things.

First, determine whether you have no choice: you are stuck in traffic, the waitress is busy, the line is moving as fast as possible, or the person in front of you has a complicated problem that unavoidably will take a while. If you can't leave or get in another line or pursue some other option, getting restless won't help.

Second, ask yourself if it really matters. Are you really in a hurry, or can you spare a few minutes? Often, you don't have to be somewhere else right away. If you do, call to say you will be late. If you can't get to a phone, accept your fate and explain the delay later.

Third, use the waiting time to do some of the thinking you claim you never have time for. If you are in your car, you also have the option of listening to talk radio, the news, soft music, or a book on tape. If you are standing in a line, start a conversation with someone, but talk about something pleasant, not the fact that you are both angry about the wait. If the other person is distraught, challenge yourself to get him or her to relax.

Helpful hint: If you're going someplace where you anticipate lines, crowds, and traffic, leave in time to get there early.

DRIVE LIKE AN ANGEL

And now, prepare yourself for the ultimate test. Even people who rarely swear can become sour-mouthed monsters behind the wheel. The fury begins when you can't find your keys and ends when you finally find a parking space.

For some reason, it is always other people who are aggressive, thoughtless, and reckless drivers, not you. Swearing at fools from inside a closed and tightly sealed car is almost fun and seems harmless when we are alone at the wheel, but it is not healthy venting. When you get angry, your driving gets crazy. You work yourself into a frenzy that often stays with you long after you've exited your car.

Pledge that you are going to be the Good Samaritan who brings civility and courtesy to the roadways. Keep in mind that bad drivers don't know it's you in the car, it's just your car that's in their way. So put aside your ego and paranoia, and try being humble:

- If someone is trying to pass you, let him. It's better than being tailgated. Assume that the anxious person has a good reason to be in a hurry, like a case of diarrhea.
- If someone wants to squeeze into your lane, wave her in. Maybe the driver needs to get off at the next exit, or truly is in a hurry. If not, you will only fall behind another twenty yards or so, not enough to make you late.
- The car in front of you is going ten miles per hour below the speed limit. If the driver looks like a 1,000-year-old man, give him credit for being brave enough to still be driving. Imagine he is your grandfather, and be thankful you don't have to take him everywhere.
- Try to be patient with the stupid things drivers do: cut in front of you, fail to use their turn signal, accelerate too slowly when the light turned green, stop at an intersection when they don't know which way to turn, not bothering to look in the rearview mirror to see if they are holding up traffic. Remind yourself that, at one time or another, you have done the same stupid things. Don't assume dumb drivers are doing it on purpose. If they are, stay away from them to avoid being part of their eventual accident. Careless people end up carless.
- Never think to yourself: Someone needs to teach this guy a lesson.

Points to Ponder

- You can stop swearing if you practice self-control, but that could require being a superior being. Specific exercises for common cussing occasions will get you on track.
- It is easier to reduce casual swearing that is not provoked by an emotion.
- Identify the causes of your worst swearing, whether it is your work, your teenagers, your neighbors, commuting. Develop your own exercises for controlling your internal combustion and cleansing your verbal emissions.
- Practice without expecting a quick cure. Feel good every time you know you prevent yourself from spitting out a foul word.

DEBBIE GILL, 40 SOMETHING, OFFICE ADMINISTRATOR

I swear about four times a day, especially when I'm angry. That's a very important part of getting angry. For me it's an expression of how I feel. Swear words come in very handy for that. It's either laziness, or the inability, or the lack of desire to articulate exactly what I'm feeling. I don't want to give a person any more info than that.

I don't swear around children, or older people, or around people I respect. I don't want them to judge me for my language. But at work, I swear. Absolutely. It's the only way to get my point across. Makes them pay attention. They are much more apt to listen to what I say if I precede it with a swear word.

My parents didn't swear. Well, my mother used the word shit *once in a while, only on the golf course, and she didn't really say the word. All you heard was "sh sh sh sh . . ." I think I started swearing in my early twenties. I'm not sure why it suddenly became okay. Drugs maybe. George Carlin had that comedy routine about the seven words you can't say on TV. Maybe that had something to do with it.*

I got in trouble once in high school for swearing. I went to a Catholic school for girls. I was setting up some audiovisual equipment and didn't know the mike was on. I kept saying, "Damn, damn, damn," not knowing it was blaring all over the school. One of the nuns came running out after me. But it was a misunderstanding. I had this friend whose last name sounded somewhat like "damn," so of course we nicknamed her that. She was helping me set up the equipment, and I was just calling her over, "Damn, Damn, hey Damny."

Swearing is overused today. As a constant, it's an ignorant person's way of talking. Once in a while it adds emphasis, but used too often, it detracts. I remember when I was a kid, before I had the swear words at my disposal, I used to have this expression that would get people's attention. I'd say, "You insignificant piece of supercility, born from vulgarity, thrown into a flood of ignorance; how dare you make such diabolical insinuations. My statement is copious, I wish you would scrapulate." I can't remember why I made this up. I believe I was in the eighth grade at the time—just getting into the dictionary, undoubtedly.

One time in Kansas City, this woman who had the personality of a gnat was interviewing me for a job, and the interview had dragged on for an hour. She asked me yet another bloody behavioral question, "If you were in a partners' meeting and being ignored, how would you get their attention?" I was so annoyed, I just told her the truth: "I would raise my voice an octave and use the word fuck *in a sentence." Needless to say, I didn't get the job.*

But I did really embarrass myself once, about ten or twelve years ago when I was playing tennis much more competitively than I do now. I made a mistake on the court and I yelled loud enough for everyone to hear, "Fuck!" I felt so badly about it I took myself out of the game for three months. It made me realize I was losing my perspective, to get so upset about a game. What did I think, I was going to play Wimbledon?

TWELVE

The Hard Part: Controlling Anger

THERE ARE TWO OCCASIONS when a cutting cuss word can explode from your mouth before you even know you said it. One is when you feel sudden and sharp pain—a stubbed toe, a smashed finger, a banged shin. The other is when you see or hear something that infuriates you. Of all the causal reasons for swearing, pain and anger can ignite vocal volcanos unlike mere irritations, aggravations, disappointments, unpleasant surprises, shock, frustration, impatience, or any other emotion. But the similarity of pain and anger stops right about there.

For one thing, profane outbursts caused by pain are more forgivable. This doesn't give you a license to swear with every ache and owwie, but even if it did, you wouldn't use it very often. You experience pain far less often than anger, unless you are a nearsighted carpenter, a shoeless football player, or a kindergarten teacher with twenty kids who simultaneously attack you with wooden building blocks to get your attention.

Nevertheless, a sudden jolt like cracking your head on the open door of a kitchen cabinet can knock the cussing right out of you. It's more of a physical reaction than a rational and intentional response. If you think you offended someone, you can apologize after the soreness has subsided. Besides, anyone who saw what happened is more likely to be sympathetic rather than upset with your horrid language.

The situation changes, though, if you incorporate anger into your agony and scream, "God damn it! Why do you always leave the @#!%ing cabinet doors open?!"

If the person you are yelling at isn't to blame, the sympathy evaporates with your accusation. If it was his or her fault, a plea for forgiveness is not going to have the same degree of guilt and sincerity behind it, if any.

"I'm sorry! Are you okay? I didn't do it on purpose. And I don't *always* leave them open. Besides, how could you not see that the door was open? It's not my fault you're a klutz. You always blame me for everything. And you don't have to swear at me. You don't love me anymore. I hope you die!"

When you experience and express serious pain, your friends or family wish they could do something to make it go away. When you express serious anger, they wish they could do something to make *you* go away. Rather than running for a first aid kit, they would rather just run.

If you are screaming about something they did or failed to do, you might get your way, but that doesn't mean you have won their long-term cooperation and devotion. They might give in to avoid the tension of further argument. If you are carrying on about a situation, not blaming anyone in particular, the people who have to listen to you spill your bile will prefer to spend their time with someone less cantankerous. The only mutual benefit is that you and the others, for different reasons, will feel better when you stop.

We all get angry at times—at the actions of other people mostly, but also at our own blunders, aggravating situations, and things like product packaging that requires a blowtorch to open. But it seems we are becoming more aggressive and angry, and controlling our ire is getting more difficult for us to do. In a national survey conducted in the spring of 1999 by Scripps Howard News Service, 88 percent of the respondents believed that people are more likely to express anger these days than they used to. The key word here is *express*. We might be just as angry as ever, but we are less hesitant to let people know about it, and less shy about using offensive words.

IT'S THE OTHER GUY'S FAULT

Strangely, only 26 percent of the individuals who believe people are angrier these days said they personally feel more angry than they used to. So who are all the grouchy people out there going ballistic? You can ask around, but you must be careful before you accuse someone of having a bad temper. They might blow up at you.

Whenever an antisocial behavior spreads in our society, most of us believe the increase comes from others, not us. In recent years, several surveys on public behavior have shown that about 90 percent of Americans believe incivility has spiraled upward, but only a fraction of the people surveyed said they were contributing to the increase. Could it be that the survey takers always manage to overlook the perpetrators of our misdemeanors? Or are we failing to make an objective assessment of our own conduct?

Fortunately, a growing number of people are disturbed about their own short fuse and are trying to do something about it. The Scripps Howard News Service notes that there was a dramatic increase during the 1990s in the number of books, tapes, seminars, Internet programs, and classes specializing in anger management. In addition, some of the best-selling books during the decade focused on finding happiness and contentment, and the books on understanding the people responsible for much of our fury—members of the opposite sex—usually sell well.

A single chapter in a book about swearing can't review the volumes of advice available from qualified professionals. This book can help calm you down so that you don't swear (so much), but it can't solve chronic anger that drives you to beat your children or spouse, become an alcoholic, get divorced, go to jail, or have a heart attack. You can assess your own level of madness, and find the resources to help you lighten up. This chapter offers some insights and suggestions for overcoming the anger that all of us have now and then.

There are three important points to keep in mind:

1. *If modern-day life makes us angrier than in previous years, the need for civility is greater.*

Crowded cities, demanding jobs, and the anonymity of our neighbors are making us irritable, suspicious, hostile, and withdrawn. We all appreciate it when others are polite, considerate, helpful, and friendly toward us, so we should make an effort to be the same way, doing our part to contribute to a more cooperative community. We might even reduce the chances that someone would just as soon kill us.

2. Swearing intensifies anger and adds to its incivility.

Regardless of what sets you off, adding profanity to your bark hastens your transformation from a civilized human into a crazed mongrel. Your metamorphosis will be short-lived, but it will be a memorable moment for the people who spend part of their life with you, even if it's only during the morning commute.

3. You only get mad because you allow yourself to.

It is hard to believe you are responsible for your own anger, but ask yourself: Why do some people laugh at the same things that infuriate you? Rarely does anyone intentionally want to make you mad. Rather, you allow yourself to get mad because of your expectations and values, the behavior you expect of others, your demands, your pride, your ego, and your attitude.

DOES IT FEEL GOOD TO SOUND BAD?

Anger is a natural and common emotion, and mental health experts believe expressing our anger is a healthy and beneficial method of communicating because of the following:

1. *It allows us to get things off our chest, to be honest, to air our grievances and ultimately find solutions.*
2. *It can be a defense mechanism, giving us the power to protect ourselves against people trying to cheat us or physically harm us.*
3. *It pumps adrenaline into our system and gives us the energy to prove to our critics that we can accomplish what they said was beyond our capabilities.*
4. *Confronting people directly prevents us from committing devious acts against them out of revenge or because of a simple misunderstanding.*
5. *By addressing rather than repressing our feelings, we can prevent or reduce our chances of becoming grouchy, depressed, cynical, and difficult.*

These points make sense, and you can use them to justify your free expression of anger. But anger is a complex emotion. If you give it free rein, it can turn you into a borderline brute and barbarian. According to a 1999 study conducted by the American Psychological Association, acting out anger increases a person's hostility. The study showed that people who hit punching bags or other objects to relieve their anger actually escalate it and become more aggressive. Also, the study concluded that people who hear or read that venting anger is healthy consider this the excuse they need to let off steam.

Many psychologists will stand firm on their belief that a good way to start Monday morning is with a primal scream, but before working yourself into a frenzy with the assumption that releasing anger is good for your health and welfare, analyze why you are angry:

- Are your grievances legitimate and warranted?
- Are you certain someone is trying to cheat you, or are you misjudging them?
- Is someone taking advantage of you, or are they just asking for a favor that will help you build a rewarding relationship?
- Does your anger give you the energy and motivation to do something you really shouldn't do?
- Do you openly express what is bothering you but continue to be grouchy, depressed, cynical, and difficult?

You might find yourself getting irate for the wrong reasons. If you consider yourself mature, reasonable, and fair, it is hard to justify these typical motives:

1. *You figure you can get your way if you make a big stink.*
2. *You want to prove that no one can take advantage of you or push you around.*
3. *When something goes wrong, you assume someone did it intentionally.*
4. *Swearing and talking tough makes people fear and respect you.*
5. *You have to demand your rights.*

There is nothing wrong with being assertive and watching out for your own interests, but as a philosophy toward life, these statements reflect paranoia and a selfish lack of consideration for the legitimate interests of the other side. You will not contribute to your health and welfare if you are suspicious of everyone, turn every little disagreement into a confrontation, and believe your pursuits take precedence over everyone else's. You might end up being the winner, but not in your relationships. Over the long haul, your relationships are more important than a self-satisfying victory.

Furthermore, you are not going to win every battle. If you think the world is trying to undermine your every move and you become obsessed with having your way, you torment yourself. In the movie *Network* from the 1970s, a newscaster on the brink of a breakdown screamed repeatedly, "I'm mad as hell, and I'm not going to take it anymore!" He announced he was going to be blowing his own brains out on the evening news. Some solution.

Then there are those little jabs like jealousy, possessiveness, resentment, vengeance, and prejudice. You know these feelings are not right, and if you can overcome them, you can control much of your anger.

An important step is to realize why anger is harmful to you and your relationships, just as you have learned that swearing has a similar negative impact. When your anger is directed at another person, keep these thoughts in mind:

1. *Anger incites anger, and no one wins. Just as you impulsively fly off the handle, your victim instinctively goes on the defensive, denying allegations and counterattacking. Resolution only comes after you both settle down and consider the facts unencumbered by heated emotion.*

2. *If you are the type to throw a fit, anyone who isn't involved but witnesses your fury will feel ill at ease with you.*

3. *Anger makes you say things you later regret, including some unsavory name-calling. You bring up old wounds, you exaggerate, or you say too much. Extreme case: you accuse your wife of cheating on you and, out of spite, you confess to your own affair. Worst case: you say it in front of the kids.*

4. *What you say can be forgiven, but never forgotten.*
5. *Intense anger can lead to physical violence.*

CUSSING WHEN YOU ARE OUT OF CONTROL

Swear words don't always accompany screaming and shouting, but if those words are part of your vocabulary, keeping them caged during the heat of your wrath won't be any easier than keeping your face from turning red. Your bad language intensifies an already tense situation, making it a thoroughly unpleasant experience for anyone who has to endure your tantrum.

The greatest drawback to turning a tirade into an even muddier mess with profanity is that it further distracts listeners from your message. They are already distracted by your anger and the fear that you might become violent. Even if they have previously heard you use vulgar language, curse words become more explosive when they are part of the fireworks.

Josephine, a line foreman in an assembly plant, was reprimanded by the plant manager for not informing him that her production would be down for the month. "I know I should have told him I was experiencing problems with the labeling machine," she admits. "I deserved to be yelled at, but not insulted. His language was completely uncalled for. I was so stunned that I couldn't pay attention to what he was telling me to do to fix the situation. I had to go back and ask him, which was like returning to the lion's den to have a second arm chewed off."

Expressing outrage at work is not uncommon, and it certainly happens in the home, but voicing anger in public is considered improper behavior because it exposes innocent bystanders to hostility. An employer is unlikely to loudly berate an employee as they are walking down the street to a meeting. Mothers try not to cuss at their children in stores for shrieking and demanding the hottest new toy, and annoyed shoppers restrain themselves from taking a swipe at the kids and telling their moms they are raising impudent primates.

Some people take advantage of this social convention, anticipating a better chance of survival if they take their spouse to dinner at a nice restaurant to break the news that they invited their sister and her kids to spend a week, quit their job, or lied about everything for the last three years.

Unbridled anger in public places is uncivilized, but lacing it with profanity ratchets up its ranking in the list of acts of incivility. Arguments with loud swearing increase the possibility that someone will press charges for disorderly conduct or disturbing the peace.

A 54-year-old man was arrested in the prosperous community of Highland Park, Illinois, when foul words weren't the only thing he was flinging. He was walking his dog when a delivery truck pulled up to the stop sign. He accused the driver of speeding on a residential street, but the driver said he had been going twenty-two miles per hour, below the speed limit of twenty-five. The dog walker threatened him, hollering profanity. The driver, noticing that two girls were coming down the sidewalk and a woman crossing guard was on the corner, told the man not to swear. This further enraged the man, who was obviously a respectable citizen, not only because he took it upon himself to admonish speeders but also because he complied with the city ordinance of cleaning up after pets. He threw his bag of dog feces at the driver, striking him on the arm and soiling the dashboard of his truck.

Your anger is probably ignited by issues far more serious than a perceived speeding violation, but serious issues have more profound consequences. And maybe you have flung objects at someone that were more fragrant than feces but, unfortunately, painfully more firm. The fact is, things get ugly when you get angry. Language is one of them, and its impact should not be underrated.

You Can Be Angry, But Not Pissed Off

Some people consider it necessary to shout, swear, and thrash about to get attention and persuade others to take their gripes seriously. To eliminate any doubt, they announce at a volume several decibels above a hockey fan's cry for the opposing team's blood, "I am really pissed off!" If they want to be certain they receive everyone's undivided attention, they will go a step further, bellowing with the help of the infamous word that still wields some power, "I am so *fuck*ing pissed off!"

Most young people and some adults don't realize that *pissed off,* in addition to its harsh sound, is a vulgar term. It is related to the word *piss,* a noun and verb related to urine that dates back to the thirteenth century. The derivation for anger is believed to have originated during World War II. At the Battle of the Bulge, a map was prepared for General Dwight Eisenhower that indicated the enemy positions and their anticipated lines of attack. Felix, a Scottish terrier owned by his driver, Lieutenant Kay Summersby, urinated on the map and made it indecipherable. The enemy was literally pissed off, and so was General Eisenhower.

Can you recall anyone announcing they were pissed off to launch their missiles of complaints and demands? Do you remember your reaction? Did you immediately stop what you were doing, look concerned, and say, "Oh my gosh! What's wrong? Sit down and tell me what's bothering you. How can I help?"

Or did you just stare at the person and say to yourself, Oh brother, what is it this time? I'm not in the mood for this. I better stiffen up in case I need to defend myself.

If the second response is more accurate, that's the way people will respond to you if you use this tired attempt to be assertive. There's a more effective approach. If you are confronting the person who made you mad, don't do it in front of others, be firm but not loud, look straight at the person and say, "I'm very upset about something and I need to talk to you."

Although this sounds ominous, he or she will sense the matter is serious and that you want to discuss it in a mature manner, not like a screaming maniac from Mars or Manhattan. In others words, the person will be cautiously receptive and hopeful that the issue can be resolved without the loss of teeth or hair.

Maybe the cause of your consternation has nothing to do with the person or people you are addressing, but you want to talk about it. Again, be calm but firm, and say, "I am really upset." If this doesn't grab anyone's interest, follow it up with, "I need your advice on what to do." People love to give advice. Once they realize they are not the object of your ire and will get a chance to talk rather than just listen to you moan, you have a sympathetic ear.

The word *upset* solicits more compassion than *pissed off*. It is gentler than the words *mad* or *angry*, but even those words will get more sympathy than *pissed off*. Another effective word is *disappointed*, but its meaning is more specific.

To raise the caliber of your vocabulary, don't use the term *pissed off*, not even to describe someone else's mood. You have plenty of other options. They all have their own levels of passion, but to simplify the language purification process, pick one of the words as your regular substitute. An alternative word recommended for most occasions: *furious*. If you want to keep it informal, use one of the similar-sounding euphemisms, *ticked off* or *teed off*. Other choices include:

mad	angry
aggravated	annoyed
miffed	enraged
outraged	frustrated
fuming	infuriated
inflamed	incensed
irate	riled
ruffled	seething
livid	steamed
piqued	perturbed

WAYS TO AVOID ANGER

Whatever methods or techniques you decide to use to control your anger and reduce your swearing, make it your three-point goal to reduce your self-inflicted stress, be perceived as a rational person in charge of his or her emotions, and make the world around you more serene.

1. Get the facts before you get mad.

When something goes wrong, don't blow up until you investigate thoroughly. Don't draw conclusions, make assumptions, or think the worst.

Maybe your teenager only did minor damage to the car, and it really wasn't her fault. Maybe that secondhand information about your boyfriend isn't true. Find out if the boss really wants the whole project redone, or just modified. Taking the time to get to the truth also allows you to get control of yourself before you say something you will regret or have to apologize for.

2. If what you heard is true, decide if anger is the right reaction.

If your daughter was drinking when she totaled the car, your anger might scare her into never doing it again. But did you tell her you are glad she didn't get hurt? Your boyfriend did kiss another girl, but will he want to salvage his relationship with you if you threaten to castrate him? You thought you did a good job on that project, but now that you have the boss's perspective, can you make it better? Disasters do happen, but look at each occurrence to determine if it really qualifies as a disaster.

3. Ask yourself if anger helps or makes matters worse.

You go to a restaurant and sit in a chair where someone spilled a glass of water. You are mad as well as uncomfortable, but making a fuss or steaming about it all through the meal will ruin the night for everyone else. Accept the manager's apology graciously, and maybe you will get a free dinner or dessert. Demanding one might get you a salad with mysterious things hidden in it.

The airline loses your luggage. Will they find it faster if you scream and cuss? The guy at the lost baggage department isn't the guy who lost it, he is the guy trying to help you. Be the one person that day he doesn't hate.

A colleague at work criticizes your work during a meeting, humiliating you. You want to strangle her. But is this someone you have to get along with? How mad can you afford to be? It might be better to let her know you did not appreciate it, and she should realize that everyone feels she did not act professionally. If you bad-mouth her to others, you become equally unprofessional. Tell her she should discuss her objections with you before telling the world.

An obnoxious driver who thinks you are driving too slowly cuts around you and gives you the finger. You say to yourself: Where's a heat-seeking missile when I need one? But he doesn't know who you are, you don't know who he is, and the only chance of you seeing him again is if he wraps his car around a light pole up the highway. Pick your battles wisely and safely.

4. If you must argue, remain calm.

Controlling yourself when someone else is yelling and swearing is a major challenge, but you will win the psychological battle every time. Anger can keep you from thinking clearly, and sometimes spurs you to exaggerate in hopes of strengthening your case. Let the other person lose credibility and appear out of control, which will certainly be the case in contrast to your regulated manner. Try not to be goaded into screaming back. If others are present, they will side with you if you appear to be a victim, your points sound reasonable, and you stick to your convictions. Instead of trying to impress them and your opponent with how tough you can be, show them how mature and sensible you are.

Your objective shouldn't be just to win, but to have a discussion, not an argument. If you are calm, the other person might realize that his or her hysteria looks foolish and will tone down.

5. Let the other person "win."

We hate to be wrong, and we hate to be challenged when we feel strongly about something. But viewpoints differ, and rarely is any issue a clear-cut case. When someone gets you steamed over an issue that really doesn't matter and can't be proven—such as who was the greatest football player of all time, and what percentage of the population is gay—just say, "You might be right." You can eliminate dozens of ridiculous squabbles this way.

A man who plays golf every Saturday morning takes heat from his wife for not mowing the lawn instead. He is too tired when he gets home from golf and does it on Sunday morning when she wants the two of them to go to church. Weary of the weekly battle, he announces that he will mow the front on Thursday night and the back on Friday night. It's a drag, but he wishes he had proposed this peaceful solution years earlier.

Even if you think someone feels too strongly about a reoccurring situation, accept their concern and find a way to accommodate or compromise.

FORGET ANGER, AND GO FOR THE LAUGHS

You can get bogged down struggling to control your anger. A different or supplemental approach is to find the humor in annoying situations while they are happening. When you do something clumsy and others laugh, laugh with them rather than be incensed. You would laugh if it happened to them, right?

Venting angry might be good for your health, but so is laughter. The American Association for Therapeutic Humor believes laughing boosts the immune system and sends pleasure-inducing beta endorphins to the brain. Laughter increases gamma-interferon, a disease-fighting protein, as well as B-cells, which produce antibodies that also destroy disease. Studies have shown that laughter lowers blood pressure, while the stress hormones of hostile people attack the heart and suppress the immune system.

As an added benefit, Dr. Edward Dunkelblau of the association says, "Medicinal humor is inexpensive and has no negative side effects."

Train yourself to recognize the absurdity of mistakes and embarrassing situations, and get yourself and everyone else not to take them too seriously.

"I have gone on dates with men who were cruel and thoughtless," reports Maris, a woman who really knows how to find the humor in horror. "I have several single girlfriends, and we love to talk about our disastrous nights. My favorite nightmare date was with a guy who didn't drive but claimed he hated taking taxis because their daredevil driving made him vomit. He took me to a restaurant on the other side of town by bus—three of them, in the dead of winter. It took almost an hour each way, and he kept making snide remarks about various people who got on board.

"I was starving when we got to the restaurant. He ordered egg rolls and pot stickers right away, but without asking me what I wanted. When the waitress came to ask for our dinner orders, he said, 'That's all. I'll take the check.' The bill was eight dollars and nine cents. He used a Visa card, but instead of signing the bill, he had a rubber stamp that was a paw print. The restaurant wouldn't accept it, but he made a scene, claiming it was unsafe to use his signature. Finally, I had to pay, because his only cash was the exact amount for the bus fare home.

"Throughout the night, most of what he said about his life and his job were obviously lies because he contradicted himself. I purposely asked him questions that would trip up his story. The whole night, I kept making mental notes about his most outrageous statements and laughing to myself, thinking about how hysterical my friends were going to be when I could tell them about it."

Don't Worry, Be Happy

If you have trouble chuckling at the oddballs and oddities in life, you might be a surly or unhappy person. The problem could be your relationships, not your job, your lack of wealth, or your sinus condition. Studies on happiness reveal that our associations with other people are on top of the list of things that make us happy—romance, family, friends, and the groups we join. The University of Chicago's National Opinion Research Center found that people with five or more close friends are 50 percent more likely to say they are very happy than people with fewer friends. And despite all the jokes you hear about marital discontent, 40 percent of the married people in the center's survey said they were very happy, compared with 26 percent of the unmarried people.

Ed Diener, a psychologist at the University of Illinois, estimates that 50 percent of happiness is genetic. Combined with the kind of life you are born into, that doesn't leave you much to work with. Maybe researchers will someday discover a joy gene that can be implanted to alter our testy genes and mean genes, but until then, we have to work at making our own happiness.

Attitude is the trick. Adjusting your attitude will brighten your life and diminish the anger and grouchiness that prompts much of your swearing. A positive attitude requires you to know what is important in life, such as making close friends with the Joneses instead of trying to keep up with them. Happy people tend to be loving, forgiving, nonjudgmental, and trusting, as well as energetic and decisive. In reviewing the literature on happiness, psychologist Diener identified four basic traits of happy people:

1. *They have high self-esteem.*
2. *They have control of their lives. (This doesn't mean they are self-employed or independently wealthy, but that they aren't in prison, nursing homes, or living under repressive governments.)*
3. *They are optimistic.*
4. *They are extroverted.*

The Dalai Lama, the spiritual leader of Tibet and author of *The Art of Happiness* (Riverhead Books), believes the purpose of life is to seek happiness, and you can achieve it by training yourself to be more compassionate and understanding of other people, including those who make you angry.

"We must develop good human qualities—warmth, kindness, compassion," he states. "Then our life becomes meaningful and more peaceful, happier. If you approach others with the thought of compassion, that will automatically reduce fear and allow an openness with other people. It creates a positive, friendly atmosphere."

In the simplest terms, accept the fact that people are different, and that they all have problems of their own. Stop focusing on your own needs, and try to connect with everyone. The Dalai Lama acknowledges that this requires effort and empathy: "Despite the fact that the process of relating to others might involve hardships, quarrels and cursing, we have to try to maintain an attitude of friendship and warmth in order to lead a way of life in which there is enough interaction with other people to enjoy life."

When someone makes you mad, you have to separate the person from his or her actions, rejecting the action but not the person. If you know why they behave or think the way they do—because of their upbringing or priorities in life—you will have more patience and tolerance.

"Patience and tolerance seem to have a flavor of weakness, of passivity," the Dalai Lama observes. "One should not see them as a sign of giving in, but rather as a sign of strength. They involve active restraint, which comes from a strong, self-disciplined mind."

Points to Ponder

* Modern pressures have made people angrier and less civil, so we must try harder to restore civility and maintain social order.
* Venting anger to release pressure has merit, but only if you have a legitimate reason to be angry.
* Freely expressing your anger opens opportunities for you to say things that you will later regret.
* In arguments, yelling and swearing hide the points both of you are making behind emotions; no one wins.
* The way in which you announce that you are angry determines how much anyone is going to care.
* Our attitude makes us mad, not people and situations. Learn to laugh at many of the things that anger you, or try not to take them too seriously.
* Friendships make you happy and less likely to be angry. Treat everyone with compassion, and your manner will create friends, not enemies.

KEN, 50, HABERDASHER

Sometimes I swear, but other times I only think it. Swearing can be used to emphasize, but I don't think it should be done to offend. I usually have the weather vanes up and know what will fly, so it's rare that I offend someone. But I'm sure that I have at one time or another. I suppose there's a fine line between swearing and vulgarity, but in either case, it's a poor choice of language.

I don't hear much swearing at the clothing store where I work. I know that from time to time I will say, behind closed doors of course, "Oh that person is full of shit" if some customer has been unreasonable. But my coworkers haven't taken me aside with the statement, "Could you be less expressive in the back room, because it offends me." Of course, asshole gets expressed in the back room quite often. And I do use it myself, I confess. I find it the most appropriate noun in certain declarative sentences. We are talking salespeople. There can just be those tendencies to swear. Thus you hear that unmentionable word sometimes among the ranks.

As for customers, most of them are quite civilized. I do have one client who was on the phone and simply frothing at the mouth. He's wacko. We were just strategizing how to dump him. His perspective, shall we say, is a little off. But I don't want to dwell on that subject too long because I think it's related to my current outbreak of gout.

When I'm really angry, I will swear under my breath. For example, there are some things in the morning, during the public transit scenario, that inspire me to inaudibly mutter mildly offensive epithets, which, if overhead, could endanger my life, I suppose. Where I hear swearing most often is on the streets. You know, those crack cocaine soliloquies one hears littered with obscenities. For them it's probably an attempt to seize power. They amp things up, to attract attention. As far as the other people on the street who swear, you hear a lot of white trash—or whatever trash—indulging their racist attitudes. I have one friend, in fact, who will occasionally make racist comments. I will always bust her for it. To me it's as bad as swearing, or worse. I find it very offensive.

I don't watch television, so I miss whatever swearing goes on there. Television I find in general to be an obscenity. In films, some of the language is a little shocking for me. I recently stayed at a friend's house who has cable. I went through the motions of spinning through the channels, and I found the swearing to be outrageous. My not having a TV has bugged my friends for some reason so they give me their old sets. At one time I had a closet full of them. I kept a little black and white. They're quite chic now, you know. People put them in their kitchens.

When I was young I went through a brief phase of swearing. I had a friend who used to push the envelope in her home, so I tried it in my house. My parents made it clear it didn't play in Peoria. My father would say occasionally, "Get the hell out of here." But my parents were pretty refined, so not swearing could have been a class thing. They had both come from fairly strict religious backgrounds. My mother's mother was an immigrant from Austria. There were occasions when she would say something in German when I knew she was expressing, shall we say discreetly, some very powerful emotions. I got the impression she was not speaking general-menu German. And she would occasionally say, "Go to the devil." Especially since Jews don't believe in hell, it was powerful to imply there was one.

I'm sure that as children my brothers and I all at various times got the taste of Ivory soap. If you resisted, it got stuck in your teeth and it would be on there for quite a long time. The taste had a tendency to linger. Brushing your teeth might have helped but that took effort and, depending upon what drama was ensuing, you might not have had the wherewithal to manage it.

When I was in college, I believe I swore. Wasn't it part of that sixties scene to say things unmentionable or shocking? I don't like the way this sounds, but I suppose it could have been more commonly heard as you went down the socioeconomic scale. People with less education might have less of an ability to express themselves so they resort to the tried and true. I studied forensics and journalism so that probably accounts for my broader vocabulary. I was team captain of a sit-in in an administrative office. But I did my rabble-rousing for civil rights or against the war with panache. I wasn't crude about it.

I suppose we ascribe certain power to swear words because they are verboten. The forbidden character supercharges the words, gives them their cachet. But I don't like it. It comes off generally offensive. I'd like to try to eliminate it. It is tempting to try to give the word jerk the same power and satisfaction as asshole. You might have to add an adjective, or some extra inflection, and say, "You inSUFFerable jerk."

Public swearing is symptomatic of deterioration. Especially when someone is screaming at someone else. It's symptomatic of how transient society is. When you don't know your neighbors and there is no community censor, you don't need to conform or moderate yourself. I believe that accounts for a lot of the deterioration in this country.

I get most frustrated when there are long lines in places where there is staff who could be helping. Especially when there are people sporting title-bearing badges walking around doing nothing. In those instances I will complain, but with a solution in mind. To expedite matters, I will ask someone to please open another register. And then there is that jurisdictional stuff at work. The managers will usually decide if there's to be a face-to-face between the combatants or a private resolution. I prefer the private method. I try to avoid this sort of confrontation, but if I need to, I will move into uncomfortable terrain and grab the bull by the horns. I usually handle those situations fairly smoothly.

I think my avoidance of unseemly language does help me professionally. The general perception is that I am more of a gentleman. But when I'm alone at home, I do say things to myself that I am too embarrassed to repeat. And then, as I mentioned, there are those urban transit moments. If we all were to swear in French, I'm sure we would sound much more refined.

THIRTEEN
Therapies to Help You

SO THERE YOU HAVE IT. Swearing isn't a big crime or a capital sin, but if you control your emotions and focus on being more civil, you will be able to mind your mouth manners or at least reduce your use of verbal vomit. You will achieve greater peace of mind, be a more pleasant person, and sound more intelligent. At a minimum, your language will not offend anyone or jeopardize your relationships. You might make a fool of yourself in other ways, but not by swearing.

You have learned that using alternative words is only one approach to breaking the cussing habit. Casual swearing is simply lazy language, an effort to be informal or humorous, and you can't be faulted for that if the circumstances allow it or call for it. For causal swearing, a more significant solution is to change your attitude about the people and situations that annoy you. That's the hard part, but it can be done. You won't succeed every time, and sometimes it will feel great to blow off steam with the help of some reprehensible words, but any progress will be good for you, your family, your friends, and society. Work at it, and you will be rewarded with more self-esteem and a greater sense of contentment.

Many of the problems that make you curse are not going to go away. They might even get worse. You have to deal with them, you have to cope. You can try saying, "I won't let those things bother me anymore," but you will also need to call on the exercises and mental reminders offered throughout these pages.

If they are not enough, you should give serious consideration to the various relaxation and stress reduction techniques that have improved the quality of life for thousands of people. You don't have to be told that exercise and a healthy diet are good for the brain as well as the body. Unfortunately, if you simply don't have the time or the motivation to care for the carcass you drag around all day, the guilt is probably adding to your stress. Do little things! Forget joining an expensive health club that you will rarely go to. Don't buy the latest instrument of torture hawked on infomercials by lumpy guys who look like a stack of doorknobs in Saran Wrap, and by fat-free babes who are somehow busty but bottomless. If you want to relieve tension, take the stairs instead of the elevator every morning, go for a walk at lunchtime, listen to soft music instead of rock as you drive home, stretch or do stomach crunches while watching TV.

What you feed your body can have more impact than the way you crunch it, stretch it, or flex it. We all know that fruits and vegetables are good for us, but did you know some of them can impact your moods? There are nutrition experts who are convinced that the mineral manganese as well as the blue in blueberries soothes the nerves, and both apple cider vinegar and lemon juice in water can cure you of mild depression. If you care to take the time to dry out watermelon rind in the sun, then boil it in water and drink it as tea, you can reduce tension. Cucumber and celery salad with dill helps calm the mind, and a handful of strawberries can cure a hangover.

Go ahead, laugh, but keep two things in mind: (1) a host of bizarre remedies have had positive results on generations of people, and (2) many of the traditional treatments you may have tried for a sound mind and body failed to work, exhausted you, cost you money, and still left you ornery and miserable.

The Eastern practices that we once mocked, from acupuncture to yoga, are earning greater acceptance within the Western medical community, as well as by common citizens bright enough to realize that droves of diapered Indians didn't stand on their heads and hordes of Chinese didn't become human pincushions in hopes of getting their own tent at the carnival. There is something to these mind-mending and body-bending exercises and remedies. We need to stop looking for the easy solution: a pill to pop.

Actually, in homeopathic medicine, there is a pill that can help you control your swearing! Anacardium soothes the mind of people who are chronically crabby, sometimes violent, bent on wickedness, and prone to uncontrollable bursts of profanity. Unfortunately, it is difficult to find.

A widely regarded philosophy is that whatever you firmly believe works will work. Conversely, if you are skeptical, it won't work for you. For example, many Japanese believe oolong tea dissolves and washes away fat. If you happen to like oolong tea, you will convince yourself that it will slim you down. And maybe it will, if you start drinking it in place of high-calorie soft drinks or sugar-saturated coffee.

If you consider these little tricks equivalent to sorcery, ask yourself if there is some ritual you do that relaxes you. Filing your nails? Rubbing a stone or a lucky charm? Doing crossword puzzles? Nick, a messenger service dispatcher who says he is a nervous wreck most of the day, calms down by making coffee. Not drinking it, just making it! He finds the smell of freshly brewed coffee very soothing and relaxing.

"I'm certain it is psychological," he says. "When I was a child, my grandmother lived with us. She was a very calm and loving person. I remember her on cold winter days, sitting comfortably in her chair, wrapped in a shawl and sipping coffee, with a little smile on her face. She looked so cozy and content."

Psychology works. If you run around the block once, you only work off the number of calories found in about four M&Ms, but you feel better. If you reach for a banana instead of a piece of pie, you will be proud of yourself. So run a little farther next time, eat fruit every day, or do anything that you know is physically or mentally good for you, and you just might feel like saying something nice to somebody instead of swearing. You need to find *something,* whether it is small routines or daily obsessions, to offset the forces working against your psyche and prompting occasional outbursts of profanity.

Fortunately, we are richer than ever before in resources that help tame our anxiety, depression, and stress. If you can find your way through the information overload, somewhere there is an article or book or video or Web site or clinic to answer all your questions about neurolinguistic programming, Feldenkrais body/mind integration, shiatsu acupressure, transcendental meditation, feng shui, and any other life-enhancing system you might have heard about.

Whether you favor the conventional approach to what ails you, the exotic Eastern route, or Grandma's chicken soup and common sense, there are several options that, with a little investigating, should suit your temperament, fit your schedule, and conquer your cynicism.

TRY SOMETHING DIFFERENT BUT TESTED

Chinese medicine and Indian Ayurvedic medicine were around long before the Western medicine that we know so well. Then as now, both the Chinese and Indian techniques consider all aspects of a person's body and lifestyle—the holistic approach of recognizing the interdependence of diet, nutrition, herbs, acupressure points, massage, meditation, and breathing exercises. They also consider body type, emotional levels, and daily routines. We, on the other hand, as firm believers in the scientific and practical approach to problems, began to discredit the Chinese and Indian theories about the time our country was created. If something was diseased, we cut it out or chopped it off. If it was only damaged, we threw on some ointment and patched it up. For internal ailments, we learned to take pills. All bodies were treated the same.

In recent decades, we have slowly recognized the advantages of certain Eastern medical practices, but particularly the emphasis on preventive medicine. We also have recognized that a troubled mind needs to be treated before it goes over the edge. We need to keep our spirits healthy as well as our bodies. Something as simple as a bad attitude can eventually take its toll on you, just as others literally get sick of hearing your negativity.

When you are upset or under too much pressure, you will be argumentative, confrontational, irrational, difficult to deal with, and shamefully foulmouthed. If you can pinpoint what makes you so miserable, such as a demanding job or terrible marriage, you will have to do more than relax with a cup of tea or mutter a mantra while perched on your roof. Absent a huge personal problem, there is one thing you can do to control your emotions that is free, fast, and almost effortless: breathe.

Breathing is the basis of many relaxation techniques, such as meditation and yoga, but proper breathing is also stressed in exercise programs. Even the way you sit and the way you stand can impair proper breathing and keep you from thinking clearly. How often have you taken a deep breath when you were overwhelmed by the number of tasks you faced or you felt frightened or exasperated? It is a natural reaction, but something that you should do consciously, from the diaphragm, slowly and deeply, several times a day, preferably out in the fresh air instead of in a stall in the company bathroom. You need a fresh supply of oxygen to refresh your brain and your blood.

If you want to go further, look into these techniques that you can do alone in the comfort of your home. Whether you practice one or more of them with dedication or only occasionally, they will enhance your overall well-being.

MEDITATION

Next to breathing, this is the easiest thing you can do. You don't even need special shoes. All that is required is some quiet time, and you can insist on it from your family. By taking twenty minutes or so to clear your mind, you can cure yourself of psychosomatic illnesses and improve your concentration, memory, creativity, and mental alertness. Essentially, you put yourself in a relaxed position and setting and concentrate on the rhythm of your breathing, cleansing your mind of clutter.

YOGA

If jogging and other strenuous exercise is not your cup of tea, sitting on a bed of nails and holding your body in the shape of a pretzel might work for you. Actually, you don't have to be a contortionist, and you can sit on pillows if you wish. There are postures called asanas for the nonnimble that require no strain or pain. Yoga is the union of physical, mental, and spiritual health for tranquility, and you can engage in complex or simple exercises.

AROMATHERAPY

If you are particularly skeptical of this one, ask yourself why you sniff shampoo and soap before you buy it. The fragrance will relax you, not just make you smell pretty. Essential oil extracts from flowers as well as plants and trees stimulate the release of hormones and neurochemicals to alleviate fatigue, irritability, anxiety, depression, and other physical and emotional ailments. Essential oils are also found in candles to fill the air and can actually penetrate the skin through massage.

POSITIVE VISUALIZATION

Imagine good things happening to you and they will, with the exception of winning the lottery. Try something with better odds than ten million to one. If you have constant conflict with someone in your family or at work, picture the two of you getting along, talking in a normal tone of voice, and not swearing at each other. This isn't make-believe, but a method of getting you to act differently, to be more calm and cordial, so that the other person mirrors your manner. We emit energy like a magnet and attract whatever people or events we think about.

MASSAGE

Massaging your own body is about as much fun as having sex by yourself, but if you know what you are doing, you can accomplish more than temporary pleasure. Eastern cultures discovered that energy flows through our body along pathways called meridians. Pressure applied to the meridians releases blocked energy and restores balance to our bodies, our minds, and our emotions. This theory is the basis of massage, acupuncture, acupressure, and reflexology (a foot massage that's not for the ticklish). You can apply pressure to a point between your thumb and forefinger that will ease the pain of a toothache, and points on the bottom of your feet that will help release toxins from your internal organs.

Conclusion

This book might have given you more information than you expected, but if halting your swearing was as easy as brushing your teeth, you wouldn't have read this book in the first place. Maybe you didn't find a quick solution to your cursing, and maybe you didn't expect the cure would require so much practice, but overcoming that quick-fix mentality of our Western culture will provide you with the patience you require to change any habit.

One thing is certain. When you swear, you will be more aware of it than you were before you read this book. When you hear someone else swear, it might not sound as harmless as it once did. Your awareness has been heightened, and you have been given sensible incentives to improve your language and contribute to a more civil society. If you can lower your reading on the swear-o-meter, you will be proud of yourself. *Darn* proud!

INDEX

ABOUT THE AUTHOR

James V. O'Connor is the president of his own public relations firm, O'Connor Communications, Inc., and the founder of the Cuss Control Academy. He lives in the Chicago area.